David   Peter.

ADVANCE PRAISE

"*Beyond Default* offers readers a much-needed wake-up call, as well as a safety net, for an improved future. The book presents a pragmatic and empirically informed view of strategy. It contrasts with traditional approaches of navigating the VUCA (volatile, uncertain, complex and ambiguous) world to create a 'secure' future that may only steer organisations to a default position that is no more than their demise. This timely book shows, through the practical insights drawn from many years of consulting practice, how to avert this default future and create a more promising and viable one through collective leadership. It is a much-needed guide for all those concerned with strategic action."

Professor Elena P. Antonacopoulou, GNOSIS, University of Liverpool Management School

"This is the first real management book I have read in a long time. It is thoughtful, carefully researched and well written. Trafford and Boggis explore why some enterprises succeed over time, while others fail – and take on the harsh reality that most mergers, acquisitions and transformational efforts fail to achieve their goals. But the book goes well beyond analysis to present the powerful concepts of facing a *default future* and developing a *strategic intent*, as ways of powerfully operationalizing strategy. A serious read will force a management team to answer the profound question "what will be the future if we choose to do nothing?", and then develop and operationalize a real strategy to change the enterprise's trajectory."

Jim Champy, co-author of *Reengineering the Corporation: A Manifesto for Business Revolution*

"Every book I ever read on strategic management, good and bad, always seemed to me to be lacking one vital chapter describing the role of 'LUCK'. Understandably, this book is no exception! However, it really excels in the depth and breadth of examination, and in its explanation of failures and successes. It also explains how the need for 'happen chance' might be minimized; and how the odds can be more favourably stacked in our favour. This is a thought-provoking book and far more than a tabulation of case histories: it digs deep to explain the cause and effect in a way that is easily understood. It would be wrong of me to steal the authors' thunder, but I'm sure they won't mind me highlighting that right from chapter 1 they get to work dismantling markets and management myths, and all that proves to be false – or at least unwise and very risky. These span mergers and acquisitions, management buyouts, strategic reorganizations, and the wholesale replacement of CEOs and boards. This is done against the backdrop of 'the default future' of companies surviving by doing the same thing in the same old way, oblivious to the tsunami of change heading their way at speed.

"The authors encourage you the reader – manager or leader – to contemplate the status quo and where it will take your organization, and what your default future might be! They do this against a back-drop of numerous cases studies and examples. To my mind, the content and style of this book conjures more than a lifeboat of ideas and examples; they provide a lifeline of consideration into the future. With all this in mind this book comes to you with my strongest recommendation. Do enjoy the read – I did!"

Dr Peter Cochrane OBE, Consultant,
Entrepreneur and Senior Manager

"Business strategy is a strange and perhaps elusive concept. Theories and frameworks can be based on industrial economics, organizational behaviour, military science, biological analogies and what might loosely be called 'general management'. Strategy practice is just as varied and often puzzling. For example, what does a strategy actually look like? Can we easily distinguish a good one from a less good one? Who owns, develops and implements strategy? Why can we apparently find successful organizations that seem not to have a formal or agreed strategy? Is strategy what an organization actually does or indeed what it rationalizes *ex post*? And so on.

"A claim that can be made today is that we are living in a period of great change and uncertainty. Whether it is technological change, new geopolitical contexts, self-questioning about the purpose of business, demographic time bombs, environmental challenges or other concerns, stability cannot be assumed.

"Trafford and Boggis present their construct of a 'default strategy', the place an organization will end up if no action is taken other than that currently planned. This may be an acceptable or attractive destination, but if not then decisions and actions have to be made to alter course. Given the instability of our context today, I would venture that organizations cannot afford to rest on a default strategy, whether wittingly or unwittingly. At least, a forensic analysis of the default strategy is required.

"The authors, experienced consultants and mentors, develop a praxis of exploring a default strategy and charting a viable trajectory and destination. This praxis is well argued and clearly presented, with a vital recognition of organizational realities."

Michael Earl, Emeritus Professor of Information Management, University of Oxford

"History shows clearly that most companies don't genuinely understand where they are heading – what would happen if you simply stepped back and took your hands off the steering wheel. Yet altering this course – with its powerful combination of internal momentum and changing external environment – is what 'strategy' is all about. This thought-provoking book throws an interesting new light on the topic."

Sir George Cox

"Many business books claim to change the reader's perspective and offer a new way of looking at strategic management. However, few live up to their claim. Trafford and Boggis' book offers a wonderful and welcome exception. Their view that all organizations are on a default trajectory, and that strategy fundamentally is about making the organization change direction, is both original and insightful. The authors clearly have a wealth of experience on the topic, but I thought the book was, laudably, much broader than that, in the sense that it transcends their personal experience to include examples and lessons from many other companies and events. It makes *Beyond Default* a delightfully accessible, thoughtful and practical book."

Freek Vermeulen, Associate Professor of Strategy and Entrepreneurship, London Business School

"*Beyond Default* challenges the view that organizations are powerless to respond to the accelerating pace of disruption in their industries. The book provides a clear roadmap to navigate through the change necessary in order to achieve a future state that is far superior to the 'default' option. The book is packed full of current examples of success and failure, and includes practical tips for executives to shape positive and productive organizational responses to radical market change. Unlike many books focused on strategy, *Beyond Default* explores both organizational and individual level factors to build a holistic approach to change management in today's volatile and unpredictable business environment."

Michael Wade, Professor of Innovation and Strategy, IMD

Published by
LID Publishing Limited
The Record Hall, Studio 204,
16-16a Baldwins Gardens,
London EC1N 7RJ, United Kingdom

31 West 34th Street, 8th Floor, Suite 8004,
New York, NY 10001, U.S.

info@lidpublishing.com
www.lidpublishing.com

A member of:

www.businesspublishersroundtable.com

© David Trafford & Peter Boggis, 2017
© LID Publishing Limited, 2017

Printed by CPI Group (UK) Ltd, Croydon CR0 4YY
ISBN: 978-1-911498-44-5

Cover and page design: Caroline Li

DAVID TRAFFORD & PETER BOGGIS

BEYOND DEFAULT

SETTING YOUR ORGANIZATION ON A
TRAJECTORY TO AN IMPROVED FUTURE

LiD

LONDON MONTERREY
MADRID SHANGHAI
MEXICO CITY BOGOTA
NEW YORK BUENOS AIRES
BARCELONA SAN FRANCISCO

Dedicated to Pam Trafford and Margaret Boggis, whose encouragement and support over the years have enabled us to pursue careers where we had the opportunity to learn from so many interesting people, organizations and situations – the resulting insights and experiences of which form the foundation of this book.

CONTENTS

FOREWORD

Over the last few decades strategy has been in and out of fashion – for many businesses that followed the trends, mainly out. During the early 1990s, strategy was replaced by 'reengineering' – a term invented by the late Michael Hammer that turned out to mean rationalization of business processes and cost cutting. During the mid and late 1990s, strategy was replaced by a get-rich-quick mentality that 'the internet changes everything' (which is true) into the hope that 'all things done on the internet will prove lucrative' (which was rubbish). There were egregious excesses and spectacular market capitalizations based on absurd or non-existent business models.

Once the dotcoms crashed in 2000, strategy was replaced by 'execution', inspired by Larry Bossidy and Ram Charan's 2002 book of the same title. To be fair, good execution is important, but as an overarching approach to competitiveness this was a bogus view. It led followers to think that all they had to do was execute well to survive, and no doubt many executed bad strategies well, on their way to oblivion.

Then the crash of 2008 relegated strategy to the background once again as companies everywhere cut costs to survive the worst recession since the Great Depression.

A number of factors are conspiring today to end these dog days of strategy and move it front and centre again. But the new rules for competing require fresh thinking. Business fundamentals indeed; fundamentalism, no. Which is why *Beyond Default* is important.

'The times are a changing.' I don't ever remember a time when so many tenets of business orthodoxy were being challenged. A new paradigm in technology is emerging as we enter the Fourth Industrial Revolution. The geopolitical order is being turned on its head by anger, populism and demagoguery. A new generation of digital natives has entered the marketplace, workforce and society, and they are different to anything we've seen. And changes to our climate threaten civilization itself.

It was Peter Drucker who observed that in stable times you need good management, and in uncertain times you need good leaders.

Similarly, in relatively stable markets you need good execution on whatever your competitive advantage is, such as differentiated products, low cost or superior customer relationships. Historically, these have been the ways to compete. There have been important contributors to the whole area of business strategy, and it's generally recognized that two of the most important are Harvard Business School Professor

Michael Porter and the former Dean of the Rotman School of Management, Roger Martin.

In *Beyond Default: Setting Your Organization on a Trajectory to an Improved Future*, David Trafford and Peter Boggis detail how the successful corporation must go beyond execution and tinkering to make strategic decisions to ensure growth of shareholder value. The book lays out the steps necessary for a company to make informed choices on what is required to change the company's trajectory to one that leads to greater competitiveness. An organization's trajectory of strategic reality is determined by forces both within (endogenous) and outside (exogenous) the company. Only by understanding the impact of these forces can a company make informed choices on the best trajectory. A strategy's purpose is to change that organization's trajectory. To do this, strategies should be operationalized by 'pulling from the future' rather than 'pushing from the present'.

The authors identify a number of exogenous factors that need to be considered: population dynamics of growth, demographics, urbanization and international migration, globalization and international trade, energy usage and availability, climate change, and the internet.

I agree with all of these, but let me comment on one in particular: the internet.

In the past 20 years, we have seen spectacular successes with start-ups seizing the opportunities afforded by the internet. But each of these success stories is also a story of massive failure by existing companies. Huge corporations didn't realize the opportunities that were within their grasp.

Why didn't Rupert Murdoch create *The Huffington Post*? Why didn't AT&T launch Twitter? Yellow Pages could have built Facebook. Microsoft had the resources to come up with Google's business model. Why didn't NBC invent YouTube or Snapchat? Sony should have pre-empted Apple with iTunes. Craigslist would have been a perfect venture for the *New York Times* or any regional newspaper. As *Beyond Default* makes clear, most existing organizations are willing to accept the status quo and thus are doomed to be eclipsed.

My son Alex and I are convinced that the internet is currently entering its second era. The first era was the internet of information. The second is the internet of value. This will enable unprecedented opportunities. Blockchain technology will bring profound changes, and few business leaders understand the potential that is waiting to be seized.

Just as there were at the beginning of the first internet era, there are great unprecedented possibilities for creating economic value, customer value, shareholder value, and community value.

After 2008 companies hunkered down and tried to find ways to survive. But that has passed, and we are seeing many new business strategies emerge. Facebook's impact continues to expand as it uses data fracking to extract value from the information stored on its servers. The company is constantly experimenting and entering new markets. Digital conglomerates such as Google and Amazon are continuously pioneering new services. In Asia there is Alibaba, which is eating up whole parts of the economy. Alibaba has massive data resources that allow it to enter new markets.

Even some of the most recent internet bright lights might soon fade into darkness. Companies like Uber and Airbnb are now threatened by new blockchain business models. Most of what these companies do can be replaced by smart contracts or autonomous agents.

This is not a time for tinkering. Strategy is coming to the fore once again, and *Beyond Default* provides the tools to take strategy to the next level.

I get asked to comment on business books every day and I take a pass on nearly all of them. It's tough to come up with an original thesis, let alone one that is probably correct and actually useful. This book has achieved that: read it and prosper.

Don Tapscott

INTRODUCTION

Have you ever wondered where your organization is headed? Have you ever asked yourself why some companies are more successful than others? Have you ever reflected on why once-great companies like Pan American World Airways (Pan Am), Lehman Brothers, Woolworths Group, Blockbuster, General Foods and Marconi no longer exist? Why companies like Xerox, Blackberry, Kodak, Royal Bank of Scotland and Yahoo are a shadow of their former selves, and others like Rolls-Royce, Hewlett-Packard, Anglo American, Standard Chartered Bank and Tesco are struggling to regain their once dominant position? And yet others, for example IBM, Apple, GE, Amazon, Walt Disney, BBVA, Jaguar Land Rover and Lenovo, continue to go from strength to strength.

We've asked these questions many times over the past three decades. Initially, when we were younger and, yes, less experienced, we thought it was simply due to the calibre of the organization's leadership and the strategies they pursued. Then, for a period of time, we thought it was because successful organizations applied the latest management thinking, whether it was TQM (Total Quality Management), Business Reengineering, LEAN, Employee Engagement or Core Competencies. But, experience has shown that it's not as simple as that. While such initiatives can undoubtedly bring some benefit, they rarely deliver the 'silver bullet' that their advocates promised. Equally, while the calibre of leadership is important, along with the strategies they pursue, they in themselves were not the answer to our questions. Eventually we came to the conclusion that there must be something more fundamental at play – something that ultimately determines the destiny of an organization. But what is it? And, can it be controlled in a way that increases the chances of success?

We don't claim to have the complete answer, but we have, over the years, gained a number of insights and developed a point of view on this important question. This idea was born from the realization that leaders have less control over the destiny of their businesses than they think they have or would like to have. While these individuals are perceived to be very powerful, in reality their strategies and policies rarely change the course of their organization to the extent they had hoped.

The reason for this is that the context within which they operate is more powerful than the strategies (and supporting resources) they deploy. All too often leaders focus on the future they would like to have, rather than the one they are likely to get: a future that is determined by a set of factors, some of which are completely outside their control.

Those factors that are, in theory, within their control are generally so powerful and embedded within their organization that their influence is often ignored or underestimated. Strategies that are not cognizant of the context within which they are being executed have very little chance of success.

The organizations we are referring to are well established and have been successful in the past, but are now struggling to find renewed success in the ever-changing environment within which they operate. Without necessarily knowing it, they rely on strategies that have served them well in the past. They often have very skilled, experienced and dedicated people who have benefited from the successes of the past, and who very much hope that these successes will continue into the future.

While our perspective does not directly relate to start-ups or newer organizations that are enjoying early growth, one day they too will become 'established' and morph into the type of organization our point of view relates to.

Our view has been formed through experiences as practising consultants and trusted advisors, rather than as academics – though one of us did spend six years as a Research Fellow and Senior Lecturer at a leading UK postgraduate university. While practitioners at heart, we also consider ourselves to be students of management and organizational leadership. Over the years we have read hundreds of books and thousands of articles on strategy, leadership and organizational change, and our conclusion is that there are as many answers to our question as there are academics, management gurus, consultants and leaders. If indeed the answer to our question 'why are some organizations more successful than others?' lies in the published body of knowledge, we have not yet found it.

Our resultant hypothesis is that all organizations, whether they are commercial or not-for-profit, are on a trajectory towards what we call their *default future* – where they will end up if they do nothing beyond their currently planned course of action. If the default future is an acceptable future state, then no further action is needed – just enjoy the journey. If, however, this is deemed unacceptable, then decisions need to be made and actions taken to change the trajectory to an improved future. In many respects, there's nothing new in this thinking – it's always been the role and accountability of leaders to steer their organizations to a better future. What's different is accepting that organizations are on a given trajectory for a reason. Only by understanding and addressing these factors can leaders stand any chance of successfully changing their organization's *default future*.

This thinking has led us to believe that the purpose of strategy is simply to change an organization's trajectory to one that will take it to an improved future.

In essence, we have developed a new approach to the practice of assessing, developing and executing strategy. It is an approach that begins by identifying and assessing the factors that define the current trajectory and the default future it will bring. Only then can alternatives be explored and informed choices made about which trajectory to pursue.

We begin by making the case for a different approach to assessing, developing and executing strategy. In chapter 1 we look at evidence indicating that over the past three decades the success rate of organizations changing their trajectory to an improved future has not significantly improved. We argue that most companies continue to confuse ambition and targets with strategy, and we present evidence to indicate that most mergers and acquisitions (M&As) destroy rather than create value, and that the majority of transformation programmes fail to deliver their target outcomes. This evidence makes a compelling case for a different approach to assessing, developing and executing strategy.

In chapter 2 we explore this notion further by arguing that it's the accountability of leaders to confront their organization's default future. Furthermore, it's equally important that they understand the exogenous (external) and endogenous (internal) navigating forces that determine the current trajectory – what we call the *trajectory of strategic reality*. Only by understanding the nature and influence of these navigating forces can informed choices be made to change the organization's direction.

In chapter 3 we focus on one of these endogenous navigating forces – the capabilities that an organization has built up over time. Acting like strong muscles, these organizational capabilities can serve as powerful anchors, keeping an organization on its current trajectory of strategic reality.

In chapters 4 and 5 we explore how exogenous forces ultimately shape strategic opportunities and present this as an organization's *trajectory of strategic opportunity*.

In chapter 6 we introduce the notion of an organization's *trajectory of strategic intent*. This is informed by strategic opportunities and takes into account what is practically possible by assessing the forces that determine the current reality.

In the last three chapters we offer some approaches for changing an organization's trajectory of current reality to bring it in line with the trajectory of strategic intent. In chapter 7 we explore how to make strategic intent more meaningful to others, and in chapter 8 how 'pulling from the future' is more effective than 'pushing from the present'. We conclude with chapter 9, in which we argue that successfully changing an organization's trajectory begins with exercising collective – as opposed to individual – leadership.

This book will not tell you what your strategy should be, nor will it aim to present a multi-step methodology for developing a strategy. Its purpose is to share insights that explain why developing and executing strategy is such a challenge. We certainly wouldn't presume that we know enough about your organization, or the context within which it operates, to know what you need to do to put it on a trajectory to a better future. However, we do believe that we know what questions to ask and what conditions need to be put in place for an organization to have any chance of successfully changing its trajectory.

We must thank the many CEOs and executives with whom we have worked over the years. We value the opportunities they presented to us and their trust and confidence in our ability to help them succeed. We are also indebted to our colleagues, past and present, whose input, constructive challenges and candid feedback helped shape our thinking. As we argue in chapter 4, the most powerful form of learning is experiential, and we are grateful for the learning experiences we have had over the past 30 years and the insights they have brought us.

Finally, we know that some of the content of this book will be familiar to you – for which we make no apology – and that some of it will be new. What is different is the way we have brought it all together, so that it is both relevant to the challenges today's organizations face, and of practical value to today's leaders. Our goal is simply to share our thinking in the hope that it will inspire and help those who are passionate about changing their organization's future for the better.

CHAPTER 1

HOW SUCCESSFUL ARE ORGANIZATIONS AT CHANGING THEIR FUTURES?

"I saw great businesses become but the ghost of a name because someone thought they could be managed just as they were always managed."

Henry Ford (1863–1947)
Industrialist, founder of Ford Motor Co.

The fundamental premise of this book is that all organizations have a default future – as do individuals, families, communities and societies. It's the place they will end up if no action is taken, other than that which is currently planned. If the default future is judged to be an attractive destination, then there is no need to take any action; you'll arrive there soon enough. However, if that default future looks less than desirable, decisive action must be taken to steer the organization to an altogether different future.

Unlike other books on strategy and change management, this one isn't going to define what a 'better future' means for your organization – that's for you to decide. A better future is totally contextual and depends upon a number of factors, including whether you're a private or publicly quoted company, a not-for-profit organization or government agency, an established organization or one that is relatively young. Regardless of your context, we know that getting to a better future involves changing the trajectory you're currently on.

This is the essence of strategy: making choices about an organization's direction. Regardless of what these choices are, their intent is to make the organization more successful than it might have been had it continued along its current path. This may sound easy, but how successful are organizations at really changing their trajectory? The generally held view is: not very. It's often said that only about 5% of large-scale transformation programmes are successful, and that more than 80% of M&As actually destroy shareholder value rather than increase it. In his best-selling book *Good Strategy/Bad Strategy*,[1] Richard Rumelt argues that the gap between legitimate strategy and the jumble of things people label as 'strategy' has grown over the years. Furthermore, strategy is not the same as ambition, leadership, vision, planning or understanding the logic of competition.

The fact is that corporate history is littered with examples of organizations that were unable to change their destiny. These include once-venerated names like General Foods (1990), Pan American World Airways (1991), Arthur Andersen (2002), Rover (2005), Marconi Corporation (2006), Lehman Brothers (2008), Woolworth Group (2009), Borders Group book stores (2011) and British Home Stores (2016).

In this chapter we look at evidence that tells us how successful organizations are, or are not, at changing their futures. We'll look at the evidence from a number of perspectives – including the churn of companies in the Fortune 500, Standard & Poor's (S&P) 500 and the FTSE 100; the length of tenure of CEOs; the success rate of major transformation programmes; and the extent to which M&As create, or destroy, value. We also look at what academics and other observers think about the quality of today's corporate strategies.

THE CHANGING FORTUNES OF COMPANIES OVER TIME

It's axiomatic that for organizations to succeed, they need to change. For organizations that have been successful in the past this can be particularly difficult, as changing what made them successful may be something they don't recognize they need to do, or are not prepared to do. It could be argued that the most successful organizations are never satisfied with the status quo and are continually mapping out new potential trajectories – even if they don't fully understand the default future that their current trajectory is carrying them towards.

But how successful are organizations at doing this? How can we measure success and what insights might this bring? One way is to track a company's perceived worth, in terms of its stock market value, over time. Another is to track the churn of companies in lists like the Fortune 500, S&P 500 and FTSE 100 over time.

When Mark J. Perry of the American Enterprise Institute[2] looked at this in 2014 he found that 88% of the Fortune 500 companies in 1955 (the year the list was first compiled) no longer existed in 2014. Furthermore, there were only 61 companies that appeared on both years' lists, meaning that only 12% of the Fortune 500 companies in 1955 were still contenders 59 years later. To put this another way, almost 88% of the companies that made it into the index in 1955 have gone bankrupt, been acquired, merged, or still exist but have fallen from the Fortune 500.

Companies that were in the Fortune 500 in 1955, but not in 2014, included American Motors, Brown Shoe, Studebaker, Collins Radio, Detroit Steel, Zenith Electronics and National Sugar Refining. Companies that made the list in both 1955 and 2014 included Boeing, Campbell Soup, General Motors, Kellogg, Procter & Gamble, Deere, IBM and Whirlpool. And companies that appeared there in 2014, but not in 1955, included Facebook, eBay, Home Depot, Microsoft, Office Depot and Target.

Further analysis by the Ewing Marion Kauffman Foundation,[3] a US-based organization that promotes entrepreneurship, shows that the annual churn of companies leaving the list has risen over time, from an average of 25 in the 1950s to nearly 40 in more recent years. The analysis also showed that the number of companies remaining in the index after a period of time reduced more quickly depending upon the decade in which they entered the list. For example, the list of companies that entered in 1955 declined far more slowly than those that entered in 1975.

Furthermore, the life expectancy of a firm in the Fortune 500 was around 75 years some 50 years ago; today it's less than 15 years and declining steadily.[2] Some of the best-known corporations that are no longer with us include Compaq, WorldCom, Eastern Airlines, Enron, Woolworth Group, Pan Am, Arthur Andersen, General Foods, TWA and DeLorean Motor Co.

Research by Professor Richard Foster of Yale University[4] showed that the average lifespan of an S&P 500 member in the 1920s was 67 years. Today that has fallen to a mere 15 years. He predicts that in the future it will take only eight years for three-quarters of the S&P 500 to be populated by firms we haven't even heard of yet.

When looking at the UK, an analysis in 2014 by Greg Mohan[5] of investment firm Rathbones showed that of the original FTSE 100 companies in 1984, only 30 were still present in the index and only 19 had been continually listed over the 30 years. These included BP, Marks & Spencer, GKN, Tate & Lyle, Imperial Tobacco and Rolls-Royce.

While analysis of the Fortune 500, S&P 500 and FTSE 100 is not without its caveats – for example, service companies were not included in the Fortune 500 until 1984, there are repeat entries and exits of many companies, and the concentration of churn is towards the bottom of the lists – it does provide evidence that a sizeable proportion of large companies failed to sustain their perceived value over time. It's therefore reasonable to conclude that, in all probability, there is no guarantee that once a company makes it into the Fortune 500, S&P 500 or FTSE 100 it will stay there.

There are many reasons why a company might fall out of these lists; our assumption is that they did not do this out of choice. Even those that were acquired probably would have preferred to have remained independent. Our point is that if your measure of success is to become and remain a Fortune 500, S&P 500 or FTSE 100 company, the chances are that over time you are likely to fail.

On the other side of the equation, there are companies that didn't exist ten years ago and are now multi-billion-dollar organizations. These include Airbnb, Uber, Tinder, Snapchat, Transferwise, Instagram, Fitbit,

Twitter, Spotify, Dropbox, WhatsApp, Quora, Tumblr, Viber, Kickstarter, Hulu, Pinterest and BuzzFeed. All of these, and many others, were created by the digital revolution.

THE SUCCESS OF MERGERS AND ACQUISITIONS

One of the most common strategic options for changing trajectory is to either acquire or merge with another organization. It's not only an obvious choice, but a very popular option. According to Wilmer Cutler Pickering Hale and Dorr LLP, in their *WilmerHale 2015 M&A Report*,[6] global M&A deal volume was 31,427 in 2014, up 17% from 2013. Global M&A deal value also surged 57% during that period, from $1.87 trillion to $2.94 trillion. In their 2016 *M&A Index*,[7] Deloitte expected this figure to reach more than $4 trillion in 2015.

Examples of recent big deals include Facebook's acquisition of WhatsApp for $22 billion in 2014; Dow Chemical and DuPont's planned $130 billion merger announced in December 2015; and ChemChina's acquisition of the Swiss company Syngenta for $45 billion, announced in February 2016 and China's largest foreign takeover to date. It's worth noting that some mergers may be blocked by regulators for various reasons. Recent examples are the planned merger of Office Depot and Staples, blocked in May 2016; the proposed merger of oilfield services companies Halliburton and Baker Hughes, blocked in April 2016; Pfizer's planned $160 billion takeover of Allergan, blocked in April 2016; and Three's £10.25 billion takeover bid for mobile phone operator O2, blocked in May 2016.

As we've noted, there is also a generally held belief that most M&As are not successful as they actually destroy, rather than create, value. This view is supported by Clayton M. Christensen, Richard Alton, Curtis Rising and Andrew Waldeck in their *Harvard Business Review* article "The New M&A Playbook",[8] where they claim that somewhere between 70% and 90% of M&A deals actually destroy value. A survey of almost 90 M&A professionals conducted by McKinsey & Company in 2010[9] showed that even with the new approaches to M&A on-boarding and integration that have emerged over the past 10–20 years, the failure rate is still between 66% and 75%.

Some of the most cited examples of M&As that destroyed value include the $164 billion deal in 2000 between AOL and Time Warner. In less than two years, the deal started to unravel when the merged group reported a loss of $99 billion and a $45 billion write-down. The total value of the stock subsequently went from $226 billion to about $20 billion. In October 2011, Hewlett-Packard (HP) acquired 87.3% of the shares of UK-based Autonomy for $10.3 billion, valuing the company at $11.7 billion overall. Within a year HP had written off $8.8 billion of Autonomy's value. In 2015 Microsoft wrote off 96% of the value of the handset business it had acquired from Nokia the previous year for $7.9 billion. In 2011 News Corporation sold Myspace for $35 million after acquiring it six years earlier for $580 million. In 2005 eBay acquired Skype for $2.6 billion and sold it four years later for just $1.9 billion. And in 2014 Google got just $2.9 billion for Motorola Mobility, for which it paid $12.5 billion in 2012.

According to Professor Michael Porter, as cited in A *Comprehensive Guide to Mergers & Acquisitions: Managing the Critical Success Factors Across Every Stage of the M&A Process*, by Yaakov Weber, et al,[10] one of the best ways of measuring M&A success is to look at the percentage of organizations that subsequently divorced five or more years after the deal was done. In the sample, the percentage of organizations that subsequently divorced was above 50%. Porter's assertion was that an organization would only divest an acquisition in this period if it were not able to realize the expected benefits. This was certainly the case with Daimler eight years after it acquired Chrysler for $36 billion in 1998. While the share price rose immediately after the merger was announced, some two years later the stock value had declined by 50%. In 2007, the two organizations divorced and in 2014 Fiat purchased the remaining 41% of Chrysler's shares to form Fiat Chrysler Automobiles, the world's seventh-largest automaker.

But not all divorces are the result of failure to deliver synergy benefits. In 2015 eBay spun off PayPal for $49 billion,[11] after acquiring it in 2002 for $1.2 billion. After the divestment eBay was valued at about $30 billion. According to Dr Tom Kirchmaier of the London School of Economics, "parent companies tend to do worse than their spin-offs".[12] PayPal has since gone on to make a series of acquisitions designed to position itself as the payment platform of choice for a wider range of customers.

In some cases, organizations get so large and complex as a result of multiple acquisitions that their only option is to 'pull themselves apart' again. The most obvious example is probably HP, which is fondly recognized as Silicon Valley's first start-up. Founded in 1939 in a garage in Palo

Alto by Bill Hewlett and Dave Packard, it grew rapidly, both organically and through acquisitions. After 1958 it made well over 100 major acquisitions, the most notable being Compaq in 2002, Snapfish photo sharing in 2005, Electronic Data Systems in 2008, Palm Inc. in 2010 and Autonomy in 2011. However, in 2015 HP decided that it would fare better if it split into two separate companies – HP Inc., focusing on printers and computers, and HP Enterprise, focusing on information-technology services.

In May 2016, HP Enterprise announced it would spin off and merge its struggling IT services business with Computer Sciences Corporation (CSC), allowing the combined organizations to focus on cloud services and other fast-growing units. Shares in CSC – which in 2015 spun off its US public sector business – jumped 19.5%.

Some divestments are intentional and part of a deliberate strategy to change trajectory. One example is General Electric (GE), which in recent years has actively sought buyers for some of its businesses. In 2015 it completed the sale of major parts of GE Capital, and in January 2016 it announced that it was selling its domestic appliance business to China's Haier Group Corporation for $5.4 billion. These deals are central to Chief Executive Officer (CEO) Jeff Immelt's strategy of making GE a digital industrial company,[13] where its Predix Industrial Internet platform will help customers run GE's – and third-party – machines more efficiently. Another example is IBM, which sold its PC, laptop and low-end server businesses to China's Lenovo.

Another organization that aggressively divested businesses in an attempt to get back onto a trajectory that it knows well, and one that has been successful for it in the past, is the UK supermarket retailer Tesco. Following a decade of international expansion and diversification under the leadership of Terry Leahy, it sold its US Fresh & Easy business in 2013 at a reported loss of $1.2 billion. It later merged its business in China with China Resource Enterprise for a 20% stake. In 2015 it sold its South Korean Homeplus business for £4.2 billion, and in 2016 it sold half its stake in Lazada, a South East Asian online retailer, to China's Alibaba for about £90 million. Also in 2016, Tesco sold its 95% stake in Turkish grocery business Kipa to local rival Migros, and divested itself of the Giraffe restaurant chain and the garden centre chain Dobbies.

So, if the probability is that such a strategic move will fail, why is there so much M&A activity? Like many other consulting and accounting firms, Deloitte produces an annual M&A activity report.[14] One of the things it captures in the survey is the rationale for pursuing a merger or acquisition in terms of its strategic importance. It lists the following rationales:

- Pursue cost synergies or scale efficiencies
- Expand customer base in existing geographic markets
- Enter new geographic markets
- Diversify products/services
- Obtain bargain-basement assets
- Acquire talent
- Acquire technology.

In 2014, the most important of these categories was 'expand customer base in existing geographic markets', followed by 'pursue cost synergies or scale efficiencies'.

The only sustainable and defensible rationale for either acquiring a company or merging with it is to improve the default future of the acquiring company, by taking it on a trajectory that differs from the one it's currently following. But in some cases, the rationale has more to do with satisfying the ego of the CEO. It could be argued that this was the case with Fred Goodwin, then CEO of the Royal Bank of Scotland, who paid €71 billion for part ownership of Dutch bank ABN Amro in 2007, just as the financial crisis was worsening. Arguably, other examples include HP's Léo Apotheker, who pursued the $10.3 billion acquisition of UK-based Autonomy, and Peter Marks of the UK Co-operative Group, who pursued the acquisition of rival Safeway, merged its financial services business with Britannia Building Society, and failed to acquire 4.6 million customers and 632 branches from Lloyds Banking Group.

In the case of the merged or acquired company, the only defensible rationale is that they could not change their trajectory independently and their best option was to be acquired. Examples here include Jaguar Cars, which as an independent company following the breakup of British Leyland recognized that it needed to be part of a larger automotive group. In 1990 it was acquired by Ford.

THE SUCCESS OF TRANSFORMATION PROGRAMMES

Another popular way of changing an organization's trajectory is to set up some form of transformation or change programme. A 2011 study by Willis Towers Watson[15] of 604 organizations from various industry sectors and regions around the world showed that the majority had experienced significant change over the last two years, and had typically gone through at least one of four common organizational changes. Those surveyed had reorganized, implemented a new performance management system, changed corporate focus or direction, or downsized. A 2008 IBM report, *Making Change Work*,[16] showed that the percentage of CEOs expecting substantial change climbed from 65% in 2006 to 83% in 2008. However, those reporting that they had successfully managed change in the past rose just four percentage points, up from 57% in 2006 to 61% in 2008. More significantly, the disparity between those expecting change and feeling able to manage it – the 'Change Gap' – nearly tripled between 2006 and 2008.

All evidence suggests that change is the new norm.

As with M&As, the generally held belief is that organizations are not good at delivering significant change and that the majority of transformation initiatives fail to achieve their intended outcomes. A failure rate of 70% is often cited. But the picture is more complex, as the success (or failure) rate is dependent upon a number of factors. These include whether the change is incremental or transformational; the industry sector in question; whether the change is within a commercial enterprise, not-for-profit organization or government agency; and the extent to which the change is dependent upon IT. While it's not always possible to identify these distinctions in the available research, the evidence overall indicates that the success rate is poor and by all accounts has not noticeably improved since John P. Kotter wrote his seminal *Harvard Business Review* article "Leading Change: Why Transformation Efforts Fail"[17] in 1995.

In 2014 the Association for Project Management[18] surveyed 862 project professionals across a range of industries. While the survey's objective was to identify the factors that determine project success, it also captured participants' views on the success of their projects. The criteria included delivering to:

- Time
- Budget
- Specification and an appropriate standard of quality
- Funders' satisfaction
- Key stakeholders' satisfaction
- Overall success.

Across these criteria, 22–36% of the projects were considered wholly successful, 29–50% very successful and 6–17% unsuccessful. This suggests a better success rate than the frequently cited 30%. Whether the outcome was influenced by the fact that the figures were provided by project professionals – as opposed to key stakeholders of the projects – is open to question.

IBM's global *Making Change Work*[16] report also concluded that most projects fall short of their objectives. The study involved some 1,500 project leaders from 15 nations, across 21 industries, who expressed the view that project success was hard to come by. While the results showed that 41% of their projects were considered successful in meeting project objectives within planned time, budget and quality constraints, nearly 60% failed to fully meet their objectives and 44% missed at least one goal – time, budget or quality. Furthermore, a full 15% of projects either missed all goals or were stopped by management.

The UK National Audit Office briefing[19] to HM Select Committee for Public Accounts contained some startling insights into the size of the UK government's project portfolio and the level of confidence in individual projects' prospects for success. As at June 2015, the whole-life cost of the 149 major projects in the portfolio was £511 billion. Of these, 34% were considered by the Major Projects Authority to be in doubt of successful delivery or entirely unachievable unless corrective action was taken.

When it comes to change today, it's inevitable that IT is involved in some way. Whether it involves reconfiguring systems following a reorganization, replatforming the IT landscape to replace legacy technology, or creating a mobile user experience using the latest digital technology, IT has an increasingly critical role to play. But IT projects are notoriously difficult to bring in on time and to budget, as was illustrated in a 2012 joint research project[20] between McKinsey & Company and the BT Centre for Major Programme Management at the University of Oxford. The research, which looked at 5,400 large IT projects with budgets exceeding $15 million, found that 45% went over budget and 7% over time, while delivering 56% less value than predicted. In fact, the study found that after comparing budgets, schedules and predicted performance benefits with the actual costs and results, the projects had a combined cost overrun of $66 billion – more than the gross domestic product (GDP) of Luxembourg.

These findings are supported by The Standish Group,[21] which since 1994 has published its annual survey on the state of the software development industry. The 2015 report covered some 50,000 projects from around the world, ranging from tiny enhancements to massive new system implementations. It's interesting to note that from 2011 to 2015 the percentage of projects deemed successful remained steady at 29%, the number rated as 'challenged' increased slightly from 49% to 52%, and those that failed dropped slightly, from 22% to 19%. Or, to put it another way, based upon this research the likelihood is that 1 in 5 of your software development projects will fail.

In 2011, Geneca, a US software development company, surveyed[22] 600 US IT executives and practitioners on why teams struggle to meet the business expectations for their projects. Alarmingly, they found that 75% of respondents admitted that their projects were either usually or always "doomed to fail from the start".

There are many reasons why projects fail to deliver their intended outcomes. One 2013 study[23] by Strategy& (formally Booz & Company) surveyed more than 2,200 executives, managers and employees on the major obstacles to transformation success. It found that 65% of respondents had experienced some form of change fatigue; 48% felt that their organizations did not have the necessary capabilities to ensure that change is sustained; 44% said they didn't understand the change they were asked to make; and 38% didn't feel the need for change in the first place.

TENURE OF CEOS AND OTHER SENIOR EXECUTIVES

Changing CEOs, perhaps the ultimate manoeuvre to change an organization's trajectory, is considered by many the option of last resort. After all, if the Board and shareholders were happy with the direction the CEO was taking their organization in, they would not replace them. On the contrary, they would do everything they could to retain them. Equally, if they'd lost confidence – either in the direction the CEO wanted to take the organization, or in their ability to successfully execute their strategy – the Board might see no alternative but to find a new leader who can renew their confidence. So, what do we know about the tenure of CEOs, and are organizations changing their CEOs more or less frequently in these increasingly competitive times?

In the mining industry, for example, three out of the five major mining groups have replaced their CEOs in the last few turbulent years – mainly due to what were seen as overly ambitious acquisitions that did not deliver the expected results. The deposed CEOs included Cynthia

Carroll of Anglo American (2012), Tom Albanese of Rio Tinto (2013) and Marius Kloppers of BHP Billiton (2013). In the technology sector, HP has seen a succession of CEOs come and go in the last few years, including Léo Apotheker, who was appointed in 2010 and left after only 11 months, following the acquisition of Autonomy; Mark Hurd, who left in 2010 following expenses irregularities; and Carly Fiorina, who left in 2005 after HP's share price fell by half during her tenure. The current CEO, Meg Whitman, who formerly ran eBay, was appointed one day after Léo Apotheker's departure and remains there as of this date.

An analysis by The Conference Board of CEOs[24] departing from S&P 500 companies showed that their tenure had declined from an average of 9.9 years in 2000 to 8.1 years in 2012. In 2013, CEO tenure was somewhat longer, at 9.7 years, but this was seen as an anomaly as retirements were delayed due to the global financial crisis. While this data may not be conclusive, it does suggest a downward trend in CEO tenure, probably driven by the increasing pressure on CEOs to navigate their organizations through an increasingly competitive global marketplace.

Another source of insight on CEO tenure is Strategy&'s *2015 CEO Success Study* report,[25] which tracked the turnover of CEOs in the world's 2,500 largest companies. The study showed that turnover rose globally, across all industry sectors, from 12.9% in 2000 to 16.6% in 2015, with the lowest departure rate, 9.8%, occurring in 2003. Interestingly, across the US and Canada the turnover decreased by 3.6%, but in Western Europe and other mature regions it increased 7.7% and 7.9% respectively. However, in the BRIC region (Brazil, Russia, India and China) it rose from 4.0% to 19.1%, and for other emerging regions from 1.8% to 16.7% – increases of 15.1% and 14.9% respectively. Across all regions, the sector that saw the biggest turnover increase was telecoms, which rose from 10.0% to 24.7%. Somewhat surprisingly, turnover in the IT sector dropped 3.4%, from 13.9% to 10.5%. The study also found that in recent years companies have been making a deliberate decision to bring in an outsider as their new CEO, presumably in an attempt to introduce fresh thinking. In the four-year period from 2012 to 2015 organizations chose outsiders in 22% of planned turnovers, up from 14% in the period 2004 to 2007, an increase of nearly 50%. Furthermore, the study found that an outsider CEO was more likely to be appointed – 30% compared with 22% – if the company was low-performing, and for three years running (2012–2015) outsider CEOs delivered higher median total shareholder returns than insiders.

Another role that feels the heat when an organization's current trajectory is not delivering the expected results is that of the Chief Financial Officer (CFO). Data from the 2015 *Crist|Kolder Volatility Report*,[26] by the Chicago-based recruitment firm, showed that CFO turnover had decreased from 17.3% in the year 2000 to 13.7% in 2014. The survey looked at the turnover of C-Suite executives from 672 American companies in the Fortune 500 and S&P 500. The study also showed that CEO turnover in this group dropped from 15.3% to 9.7% over the same period, which differs from the Strategy& data, though this study only covered US companies, whereas the Strategy& study was global.

As previously mentioned, IT plays an increasingly key role in changing an organization's trajectory, and the Chief Information Officer (CIO) is critical in both defining and delivering this transition. So, how comfortable are CIOs in their current role and how likely are they to move on – either by choice or by being replaced? Every year, the global recruitment firm Harvey Nash conducts a survey[27] of CIOs that captures the views and mood of technology leaders worldwide. Its 2015 survey reflected input from 3,691 technology leaders from more than 30 countries, with a combined IT spend of more than $200 billion. The survey found that 29% had worked for their current organization for a period of two to five years, and 22% from five to ten years. Of these, three in ten had changed roles in the past two years, and six in ten in the past five years. Interestingly, while most felt fulfilled in their current role, 48% expected to move on in the next two years, and 79% within the next five years. Of these, 22% were actively seeking and applying for new positions, 38% were open to taking a call from headhunters, and a further 30% were keeping an eye on the market. Only 11% were not considering moving.

Finally, KPMG's 2014 *Guide to Directors' Remuneration*[28] reported that 'during the last 12 months, more than half of the FTSE 100 had a change in executive director and almost a quarter had a change in CEO – the highest levels in the last five years'.

What we can't see from this data is the correlation between the movement of CEOs, CFOs and CIOs and their reasons for leaving. It is not clear whether the moves were due to them failing to keep their organization in the Fortune 500, S&P 500 or FTSE 100, not achieving the benefits of a merger or acquisition, not delivering the intended outcomes of a transformation programme, or something else entirely. However, it seems reasonable to assume that the greater the failure rate of these initiatives, the greater the churn of C-Suite executives. It's also likely that if the initiatives were successful the churn rate would be lower.

HOW GOOD ARE ORGANIZATIONS AT DEVELOPING STRATEGY?

In order to successfully change an organization's trajectory – to one that leads to a better future – two key capabilities are required: first, the ability to make the right decisions on what trajectory to take, and second, the ability to actually travel the chosen trajectory. The former is strategy development and the latter strategy execution. But how good are organizations at developing and executing strategy? To what extent do they have the necessary capabilities in place? And is the essence of what makes a good strategy really understood?

In reality all organizations have a strategy; it may not be explicitly defined, but its leaders' daily decisions and actions are a reflection of that strategy. The question is how effective the strategy is in changing the organization's trajectory.

While there is plenty of material available on what makes a good strategy – in terms of approaches and killer strategic frameworks – little research is available on the extent to which organizations actually have one in place. Nor is there any research that we're aware of on how effective organizations are at developing and executing strategy, other than the above-referenced work on M&As and transformational change success rates. However, there is plenty of material on organizations that got their strategy wrong, including Starbucks,[29] whose decision to increase prices and open 9,000 new stores from 2002 to 2007 resulted in a substantial fall in profits and the departure of its CEO. There was also Swissair's[30] strategy to grow through the acquisition of poor-quality airlines across Europe, which resulted in the grounding of its fleet in 2001.

All too often, organizations that are seen as successful are deemed to be good at strategy, and conversely it is believed those that are not successful must be bad at strategy. But what about organizations like Enron, WorldCom, Royal Bank of Scotland, Tesco, Lloyds Banking Group, Rio Tinto, HP and many others that in the past have not only featured on the front page of business journals, but have also been the subject of multiple case studies on how they got their strategy right? In fact *Fortune* Magazine named Enron the 'Most Innovative Company in America' for six years in a row, from 1996 to 2001. Its growth was indeed spectacular; Enron became America's seventh-largest company in just 15 years.

When the flawed foundation on which the company was based imploded in 2001, it not only resulted in the corporation's bankruptcy, but also in several executives being found guilty of fraud and the demise of Arthur Andersen, a global accountancy firm. WorldCom was another company that it seemed could do nothing wrong. From 1995 to 2000 it purchased more than 60 other telecom firms, including MCI for $37 billion in 1997. By 2001, it owned one third of all data cables in the US and was handling 50% of all American internet traffic and 50% of all emails worldwide. In 2002 it filed for bankruptcy, making it the largest business failure in US history, dwarfing that of Enron. Its apparent success was later found to be based on fraudulent practices, resulting in the CEO and CFO being jailed.

For a brief period before the financial crash of 2008, the Royal Bank of Scotland was the world's largest bank. Not only did it own Citizens Financial Group in the US, it also held a 10% stake in the Bank of China. The events of late 2008 led it to seek support from the UK government, which reluctantly injected £45 billion of taxpayers' money into the failing institution. In February 2007, its shares were worth more than £60, but by January 2009 they had plummeted to just above £1. Following a lengthy inquiry, it was concluded that there was insufficient evidence of criminal behaviour to bring charges against the bank or any of its directors.

For a period of time, these organizations were considered hugely successful, with many academics and commentators holding them up as masters of strategy. However, if the purpose of strategy is to achieve sustainable success, they clearly failed in many ways.

Freek Vermeulen of the London Business School believes that the majority of organizations don't actually have a genuine strategy.[31] On the basis of observing "a heck of a lot of companies" and "listening to strategy directors and CEOs present their strategies", he believes this figure to be at least nine out of ten. What's more, he believes that "most companies and their top executives do not have a good rationale for doing the things they are doing and cannot explain coherently how their actions will lead to superior performance". Furthermore, he believes that most of what pass for strategies are not genuine strategies because they:

- Are not making real choices
- Are stuck in the status quo
- Have no relationship to value creation
- Are mistaking objectives for strategy
- Are kept secret.

His views certainly concur with our own experience and that of Richard Rumelt,[1] who as previously mentioned has seen the gap between good strategy and the jumble of things people characterize as strategy grow over the years. He believes that good strategy is the exception, not the rule, and that while most leaders say they have a strategy, they actually do not. They may have some semblance of a strategy, but it's often what Rumelt calls a bad strategy – one that "skips over pesky details such as problems, ignores the power of choice and focus, and tries to accommodate a multitude of conflicting demands and interests". He says most bad strategies "contain a mishmash of pop culture, motivational slogans and business buzz-speak that short-circuits real inventiveness".

Another trap that many leaders fall into when developing strategy is to seek comfort from planning. "If good strategy is about confronting a future we can only guess at, deciding where to focus and making decisions that explicitly cut off possibilities and options, the risk of getting it wrong can be both scary and a potential career wrecker", says Roger L. Martin in his 2014 *Harvard Business Review* article "The Big Lie of Strategic Planning".[32] As a result, he believes that most executives 'protect' themselves – and their companies – by falling into the following three comfort traps:

1. **Strategic planning**: where the word 'strategy' is paired with the word 'plan', as in the process of 'strategic planning'. This subtle slide from strategy to planning occurs because planning is a thoroughly doable and comfortable exercise.
2. **Cost-based thinking**: where the focus of planning leads seamlessly to decision-making that's too heavily weighted towards cost considerations. Costs are comfortable because they can be planned for with relative precision.
3. **Self-referential strategy frameworks**: where the strategy, or plan, is based upon either a popular strategic framework or one that's personally preferred by the CEO. Comfort here comes from knowing the framework, regardless of whether it's relevant to the organization in question.

Martin believes that considerable time and resources are spent preparing comprehensive plans for how the companies will invest in existing and new assets and capabilities in order to achieve a target. By the end of this process, everyone feels comforted by the effort that has been put in, and a lot less scared. Martin believes this is "a terrible way to make strategy, as fear and discomfort are an essential part of strategy making".

In his book *The Trouble with Strategy*,[33] Kim Warren takes his critique of strategy a stage further by saying that it has "become the subject of journalism, not professionalism". He argues that most strategies are amateurish and unacceptable, as their outcome frequently leads to "destroyed wealth, disappointed customers, impoverished investors and employees losing their careers". He believes that the state of strategic management is so poor that it cannot truly be called a profession when compared with other professions such as engineering, medicine, finance and law. He makes his case by comparing what you see in these other professions with what currently exists in strategic management. In summary, he believes a field of endeavour can only call itself a profession when its practitioners:

- Speak with a common, defined language
- Have a shared understanding of how things work (i.e., what causes what)
- Build new ideas on what is already known, rather than making it up as they go along
- Apply standard procedures that have been developed over many decades and are built upon solid foundations of understanding
- Put safety first, with regard to the continued health of the organization, as opposed to adopting a cavalier attitude with an eye towards achieving immediate glory
- Train, mentor and develop other people in their profession
- Are governed by a professional body that establishes and upholds professional standards, including awarding recognized certification of its members.

Warren's view is that the current body of practice in strategic management falls short on all of these criteria. Furthermore, he warns that we should not assume that a requisite degree of professionalism exists in the strategy consultancy firms or is taught in management schools.

FINALLY, OUR PERSPECTIVE
Over the last 30 years we have been involved in many change initiatives, including M&As, enterprise horizontal integration, IT replatforming and digital transformation. We've also helped organizations develop strategies, deliver large and complex change programmes, and establish

conditions for the success of transformational change. Additionally, we've quality-assured major investments and 'forensically analysed' change programmes that had gone terribly wrong. We've also seen management fads come and go, from the early days of gaining competitive advantage from IT, through business reengineering, time-based strategies and employee engagement, up to today's focus on 'being digital'. Irrespective of the organization, industry, region or culture, we have seen patterns emerge that have not fundamentally changed over time. As Mark Twain once said, "History does not repeat itself, but it rhymes." The five most common patterns that we have repeatedly seen are:

1. The term 'strategy' is overused and frequently misused, to the extent that it has lost any meaning in most organizations and some CEOs have banned its use entirely. As we will discuss in chapter 6, a strategy is only a strategy if the choices are difficult, if not impossible, to undo. The rest is planning, which can be changed – albeit at a cost. Furthermore, the quality of these choices will determine whether, in Rumelt's[1] words, it's a 'good strategy' or a 'bad strategy'.

2. When developing strategy, organizations tend to adopt either a conservative or a radical approach. The conservative approach is predicated on the view that what has made us successful in the past will continue to make us successful in the future – we just need to 'turn up the volume'. The radical approach is based on blue-sky thinking, where everything is possible. This usually results in such far-out ideas and proposals that they are never accepted – even if some of them have potential. Only rarely are the conservative and radical approaches fused to produce something of sustainable value.

3. Some strategies are just too complex – or too incoherent – to understand. We find that these strategies tend to come from an individual rather than a team. This could be the CEO or head of a function, like marketing or IT. As these so-called strategies are explained to us, we've found ourselves repeatedly asking, "How by doing this will you achieve the following outcomes?" Over the years, we have found that this simple question reveals the flaws of the strategy and often triggers a difficult but constructive rethink.

4. When a strategic approach is agreed upon and approved, the focus turns to execution, which inevitably involves some form of change initiative (which best practice mandates) led by an executive

sponsor. What we've found is that most executive sponsors don't volunteer, they are assigned by the CEO (often as part of their professional development plan), especially when the change is cross-functional. What we see is that the majority of these sponsors have neither the experience nor the bandwidth to carry it out. As a result the pace of the change initiative is dictated by their availability and not what the initiative requires to be successful.

5. If the change is to be delivered through a formal programme (which in many cases is necessary) the programme leader often comes from outside. Why? We find that most managers within the organization are reluctant to take on the role for two reasons: first, they may feel that they don't have the experience for such a high-profile initiative; second, and perhaps more significantly, they don't want to put their career at risk. As a result, the organization looks to fill the role from outside, either from the consultancy firms or the contractor market. While an outsider may bring experience in change and programme management, they don't know the culture of the organization they are charged with changing. As a result they often leave before the job is done.

THE CHAPTER IN SUMMARY

The evidence we found certainly supports the generally held view that changing an organization's trajectory carries significant risk of failure. Furthermore, there is no evidence that the success rate is noticeably improving. Obviously there are some examples of organizations that get it right, but fewer are capable of continually changing their trajectory as their context changes. Equally, there are few strategy professionals and executives who really understand what strategy is and know what it takes to deliver sustained change. And they're not only few and far between, but often undervalued when compared with their peers in more traditional executive roles.

FIVE QUESTIONS FOR REFLECTION

1. Does your organization know what its current trajectory is – and the default future it will bring?

2. Does your organization have a strategy for changing its current trajectory? If so, how would you describe it to someone for the first time?

3. What is your organization's success rate in M&As? Have they increased or destroyed value?

4. What is your success rate with change initiatives? What proportion achieved all their objectives?

5. Does your organization have the capability to develop good strategy? If so, how would you describe the approach?

CHAPTER 2

UNDERSTANDING AND CONFRONTING THE DEFAULT FUTURE FOR WHICH YOU ARE ACCOUNTABLE

"*The great thing in this world is not so much where we are, but in which direction we are going.*"

Oliver Wendell Holmes, Sr. (1809–1894)
Chief Justice, US Supreme Court

On 13 December, 2012, Her Majesty Queen Elizabeth II visited the Bank of England in Threadneedle Street, London. After viewing the 63,000 gold bars stored in its basement vault, one of nine vaults spread across London, and signing a one-million-pound sterling banknote, she finally got an answer to the question she'd famously asked four years earlier during her visit to the London School of Economics: *"Why did nobody notice?"*[34]

The Queen was referring to the events of 2007 and 2008 that led to the credit crunch and the worst financial crisis since the Great Depression of the 1930s. Not satisfied with the answer economists had given four years earlier, her visit to the Bank of England was an ideal opportunity to raise the question again. In response, one of the Bank's officials likened the financial crisis to an earthquake – a rare event that's hard to predict. He went on to say that people thought markets "were efficient, and regulation wasn't necessary". He added that because "the economy was stable, there was this growing complacency. People didn't realize just how interconnected the system had become". The notoriously discreet Queen responded, "People had got a bit lax, had they?"

The official assured the Queen, who was accompanied by the Duke of Edinburgh, that Bank officers were there to prevent another similar catastrophe. That prompted the Duke's retort, "Is there another one coming?"

The Financial Services Authority (FSA) subsequently issued a statement acknowledging that regulatory safeguards before the 2008 financial crisis were flawed and had since been overhauled, and that the new Financial Services Bill awaiting Royal Assent would determine the powers held by a new set of regulators. On 1 April, 2013, the FSA was replaced by two regulatory bodies – the Prudential Regulatory Authority (PRA), which forms part of the Bank of England, and the Financial Conduct Authority (FCA), which covers companies' interactions with consumers. The Bank of England also gained direct supervision of the whole of the banking system through its powerful Financial Policy Committee, which provides guidance to the two new regulatory entities.

Whether the Queen was satisfied with the answer to her question or reassured by the FSA's statement we will never know, but her question "Why did nobody notice?" is surely one that will haunt bankers and politicians for many years to come.

If we look back at the early years of the new millennium it's easy to understand why nobody noticed – or indeed cared. The Year2K computer bug had not brought businesses and governments to their knees, as many had predicted it would, and the internet bubble's deflation, while unexpected, was more of a blip than a crash. We were all enjoying a period of unprecedented growth: the value of our homes continued to increase and global stock markets reached new heights that made us all feel that our pensions and futures were secure. Everything was going well; what we were experiencing became the new norm and we saw no reason why it could not continue indefinitely. Even our high level of borrowing didn't worry us. After all, the banks wouldn't continue to lend if they thought it wasn't safe, would they?

Yet we all knew it couldn't last. We knew that economies go through cycles and that bust always follows boom. Our hope was that there would be a soft landing and that things would return to normal soon after. Our mindset was one of 'let's enjoy it while it lasts and worry about tomorrow when it happens'. As Charles Prince, then Chief Executive of Citigroup, put it in an interview[35] with the *Financial Times* on 9 July, 2007 – just as the credit market was getting skittish – "As long as the music is playing, you've got to get up and dance, and we're still dancing."

We now know there wasn't a soft landing and that the crash of 2008 was the worst in living memory. And there was worse to come. Just as we got our heads around the impact of the credit crunch, we learned that many governments around the world – but particularly those in Europe – had also developed the habit of borrowing more than their economies could afford and were finding it difficult to meet their debt obligations. Ireland, Greece, Portugal, Italy and Spain were the most notable. As elected leadership across Europe changed, 'austerity' became a word new to many.

With the power of hindsight, it's relatively easy to look back and identify some of the factors that led to the events of 2008, including:

- The 1999 repeal of the Glass-Steagall Act in the US. Enacted in 1933, after the Great Depression, the legislation had prevented financial institutions from taking deposits and making loans while at the same time underwriting and selling securities
- The growth of unregulated complex financial derivatives – particularly collateralised debt obligations
- Government support for greater home ownership
- Eased lending criteria and the introduction of 100% mortgages
- The popularity of interest-only mortgages
- The relaxed approach to banking regulation, with governments allowing financial institutions to get 'too big to fail'.

So, why did nobody notice? And, if they did, why didn't they do anything to prevent it?

Actually, there were those who did notice and did try to do something about it. One such person was Gillian Tett, who was then assistant editor at the *Financial Times*. She was predicting an economic catastrophe some two years before the crash, but no one wanted to listen. Her doomsaying did not make her popular, and her cautions were either ignored or ridiculed. In an interview[36] with *The Guardian* newspaper on 31 October, 2008, she spoke of a trip to the 2007 World Economic Forum in Davos, where she was denounced on stage by one of the most powerful figures in the US government. He called an article of hers that predicted the problems at Northern Rock, a UK bank, "scaremongering".

Northern Rock did in fact get into trouble, and it was not the only bank to do so. Lehman Brothers – the fourth-largest investment bank in the US – declared bankruptcy on 15 September, 2008, making it the largest bankruptcy in US history. The Royal Bank of Scotland was rescued by the UK government, which injected £45 billion of taxpayers' money in return for an 84% stake, as was Lloyds Banking Group in return for a 41% stake that cost £20.5 billion. In Ireland, Anglo Irish Bank was nationalized and wound down in 2009; Allied Irish Bank was effectively nationalized; and Bank of Ireland received a €7 billion cash infusion from the government. In Iceland all three of the country's major commercial banks (Glitnir, Landsbanki and Kaupthing) collapsed, leading the Icelandic Stock Exchange to plunge by more than 90% and nearly bankrupting the country. Across Europe numerous banks – most notably ING, UBS, Dexia, Hypo and Bankia – sought support from their respective governments.

The fallout from the 2008 meltdown was profound. Millions of people lost their jobs and homes, thousands of businesses were destroyed and many investors lost everything. It created a recession and a period of austerity that many predicted would last more than a decade.

But this book is not about the financial crisis of 2008. It's about developing the ability to create a future we want, rather than one we end up with *by default*. The premise underlying this thinking is that all countries, organizations, businesses and even individuals have a *default future*. It's the place they will end up if no action is taken, other than that which is currently planned. It is where their current trajectory will take them, unless they take action to change course.

It's not about being able to *predict* the future, but about being able to *understand* why an organization is on a certain trajectory, and where this course is taking it. Only by understanding this can leaders make informed choices about what needs to be done to change their organization's trajectory to one that will lead to a better future.

Why is this important? As we discussed in chapter 1, most organizations are not all that good at change. Whether through mergers or acquisitions, transformational change initiatives or implementing 'breakthrough' strategies, corporate history is littered with organizations that failed to put themselves onto a trajectory to a better future. If the track record is as poor as the evidence indicates, it's important that we find ways of increasing the chances of success. This book is intended to help contribute to that thinking.

DEFAULT FUTURES ARE DEFINED IN TERMS OF OUTCOMES

A default future can be defined in many ways, provided it describes a future state in terms of outcomes. And one of the most effective ways of doing this is to imagine ourselves in that future and describe what we see, feel and hear.

Default future outcomes could be defined in terms of profitability, cash flow, competitive position, assets and liabilities, capabilities, geographic coverage, culture, ethical position, sustainability or customer loyalty – that's for you to decide. What a default future means is totally context-specific and depends upon a number of factors, including whether you're a private or publicly quoted company, a not-for-profit organization or government agency, an established organization or one that is relatively young. Regardless of the context, the purpose of defining the default future is so that it can be *confronted* and, if you're headed towards an undesirable destination, so that action can be taken to put the organization on a different trajectory.

HOW A CHANGE IN CONTEXT CAN CHANGE YOUR DEFAULT FUTURE

At its peak in 2004, Blockbuster – the video and DVD rental business – employed more than 60,000 people in some 9,000 stores around the globe. Six years later it filed for Chapter 11 bankruptcy protection and in 2013 it closed its remaining stores and ceased its DVD-by-mail rental service.

If, in 2004, the leadership of Blockbuster was asked what their default future would be, we're sure they would have said continued growth, not only in the US but worldwide. They certainly wouldn't have foreseen the demise of the company in six short years. So, what went wrong? Was it poor leadership or were there other factors that determined Blockbuster's destiny?

To answer these questions we first need to understand the reasons for Blockbuster's rapid success. The simple explanation is that someone – in this case David Cook, its founder, along with his ex-wife Sandy – had the right idea at the right time.

When Cook opened the first Blockbuster store in Dallas, Texas, on 19 October, 1985, there were a number of factors in his favour. First, from a technology standpoint, the VHS cassette had become the established standard, beating out the rival Betamax format. While many argued that Betamax offered better quality, its recording capability was limited to only one hour. Furthermore, Sony, which developed the Betamax format, would not allow pornographic content to be recorded on its tapes, while the JVC consortium, which developed VHS, had no such qualms. As a result, in 1987, ten years after its launch, the VHS format had seized 90% of the $5.25 billion market for video cassette recorders sold in the US.[37] In short order, the price of VHS video players dropped significantly, enabling every household in the US to own one. The home entertainment trend continued to evolve, with Philips, Sony, Toshiba and Panasonic inventing the DVD in 1995.

Second, in an effort to boost revenues – during a period when cinema audiences had been static for some years – the studios were willing to make their movies available for rental months before they would normally be available for purchase.

Third, advances in database technology allowed Blockbuster to manage its stock effectively and customize stores for particular neighbourhoods by loading them up with movies geared towards particular demographic profiles. Before launching Blockbuster, Cook had created and run Cook Data Services, a company that supplied computer software services to the Texas oil and gas industry. Shortly after the company went public in 1983, the Organization of Petroleum Exporting Countries (OPEC) cut crude oil prices and reduced output quotas to restrict the amount of oil on the over-supplied world market. This had a devastating impact on the industry, and on Cook's company. After selling what was left of the business to his managers, he turned his attention to creating Blockbuster and applying the computing application skills he'd learned in the oil industry to his new venture.

Finally, since the advent of television, people had become used to being entertained at home and they wanted more, particularly the opportunity to watch movies of their choosing, at a time that suited them.

Cook had a great idea, but more importantly there were a number of forces at play that defined the context in which Blockbuster operated, and thereby its trajectory. This context enabled, and drove, a phenomenal trajectory of growth, both organically and through acquisition. At its peak Blockbuster would open a new store every 17 hours. The company was a huge success, and was acquired by Viacom for $8.4 billion in 1994.

But, as Blockbuster found out, context can change quickly and the resulting trajectory can lead to a very different default future. In Blockbuster's case its context took an unexpected turn with the growth of broadband, the technology that enables high-speed access to the internet and, as a result, the ability to download films in a reasonably short time. From its inception in 1999/2000 the number of fixed broadband lines around the world grew to more than 654 million by 2013.[38] With the advent of broadband, movies could be downloaded to laptops and desktops for later viewing. Today, high-speed broadband allows movies to be streamed and watched in real time on a variety of devices, including tablets, smartphones, smart televisions and TVs with set-top boxes, through services such as Apple TV.

The emergence of broadband changed the context within which Blockbuster operated, and as its trajectory changed so did its default future. But why did Blockbuster fail to recognize this and respond accordingly? It did, and it tried, but it failed. The reason was that during its early, successful years, it developed a set of organizational capabilities that supported and drove its business model. To put it another way, it developed organizational capabilities needed to propel itself along what it thought at the time was a successful trajectory. These organizational capabilities included the ability to locate, open and run stores; establish franchise agreements; manage warehouses and ship video cassettes; and later deliver DVDs and video games. But the organizational capabilities needed to support an online video-streaming business were very different. Apple had them within its iTunes business, but Blockbuster did not.

DEFAULT FUTURES ARE NOT RESTRICTED TO ORGANIZATIONS

When parents see their child missing school or getting in with the wrong crowd, they think of what the future will hold if the child continues on this path. When a person is told they have a life-threatening illness, they immediately want to know what their chances of survival are and what quality of life they should expect. Thinking about our own default future is something we do every day; we create a mental model of what the future might be like and plan what we might be able to do to create an improved future. The mass migration of people that began in 2014, from the Middle East and North Africa to Europe, is a case in point. These migrants confronted their default future and concluded that they needed to take action that would lead them and their families to a safer, better future.

While 'default future' thinking is as valid for individuals as it is for organizations, and there are many parallels between the two, the focus of this book is on organizations.

CONFRONTING YOUR DEFAULT FUTURE

In October 2000, Anne Mulcahy was on an investor conference call when she candidly remarked[39] that "the company had an unsustainable business model". The company was Xerox Corporation and Anne Mulcahy had been promoted to president and chief operating officer (COO) the previous May. At that time, Xerox was in turmoil: the once mighty, 84-year-old company, famous for its Palo Alto Research Center, was haemorrhaging cash. After reaching its record-high share price of nearly $64 in May 1999, the stock languished at just $15. By March 2001, it had slumped to $7, a few dollars above the price at which it floated on the New York Stock Exchange in 1961. In the final quarter of 2000, the company posted a loss of $198 million.

Mulcahy was not new to Xerox – she had been with the company for her entire career, starting as a field sales representative in 1976. From 1992 to 1995 she was Vice President of Human Resources, and prior to becoming COO was president of General Markets Operations, which created and sold products for resellers, dealers and retail channels. She knew the business well, had enjoyed the good times and was now experiencing the most challenging period of her career. Her candid 'unsustainable business model' remark may have been ill-conceived – it certainly spooked the analyst community – but it demonstrated that she understood what the default future would be if drastic action was not taken to change the company's trajectory.

When Jeff Immelt took over as Chairman and CEO of GE in 2001, he probably thought that the company would continue on a path similar to that set out by his legendary predecessor, Jack Welch. During his first year alone he initiated $9 billion in acquisitions and in doing so further diversified the company by adding segments involved in wind power, security, cable-television channels, commercial and consumer finance, water filtration, and oil and gas services. But the new acquisitions failed to immediately contribute to the bottom line, and over the next 14 years under his leadership GE's share price slid 36%. Not surprisingly, many investors called for him to be replaced. In 2008, the company's financial services business, GE Capital, was badly hit by the financial crisis and needed $60 billion of guarantees from the US Federal Deposit Insurance Corporation. The challenge for Immelt was to decide what to do with one of the world's biggest diversified conglomerates – one that produced jet engines, electrical power plants, refrigerators, CT scanners and much more. It also owned America's seventh-largest bank. Immelt knew that if he did nothing, the default future of GE would be investors insisting that the company be broken up. He confronted this default future head-on, and in April 2015, on a regular early-morning conference call with Wall Street, stunned analysts by announcing that he was selling many of GE's biggest businesses.[40] His plan was to put GE on the road to becoming a coherent whole, built around industrial infrastructure businesses that included power generation, locomotives, jet engines, and oil and gas production equipment. It would all be underpinned by an industrial data-analytics/performance-management software platform that became known as Predix.

When the chairman of a mid-sized UK hospital recognized that yet more cost reduction was an unsustainable strategy, he knew that a different approach was required.[41] The hospital is a relatively small NHS Foundation Trust with an annual budget of around £110 million. However, it is a widely recognized centre of excellence for cardiac and thoracic care in the UK, and in 2012 was voted 'Provider of the Year' by the *Health Service Journal*. Over the years, it had excelled in its journey towards putting the patient at the centre of everything it does, and was recognized internationally as an exemplary provider of a positive patient experience. But like all NHS Foundation Trusts, it has to operate in a complex political, economic and regulatory framework that limits its freedom in many ways. The hospital operated in a context where, in October 2014, the chief executive of NHS England committed to meeting £22 billion of the expected £30 billion gap in its finances by 2020 through productivity gains of 2% or 3% a year. It was already well into its own cost-reduction programme and if it was to continue to deliver the same high-quality care, it needed to do so at a lower cost. The only way this could be achieved was through innovation and additional income derived from offering its services more broadly. The chairman had understood and confronted the default future for his hospital and decided to take action to change its trajectory.

Anne Mulcahy saw that if nothing was done, Xerox would need to file for Chapter 11 bankruptcy protection and ultimately be broken up. Jeff Immelt realized that the days of GE being a diversified conglomerate had passed and that its future was in digitizing in the industrial space. The chairman of the NHS Hospital Trust knew that if he took no action, his medical staff would struggle to provide the expected quality of care and patient experience.

In each of these cases, the leaders understood and confronted the likely default future of their organizations. They did this by taking time to reflect on where their current trajectory was taking them. They knew that the future they predicted may not be entirely accurate, but more importantly they knew that if they continued on the current course at the current speed their organization was headed towards an unacceptable place.

Understanding and confronting our default future is something we all do, almost all the time. It's a characteristic of the human condition that we worry about what the future might hold and what, if anything, we can do to improve it. The only difference is the role we play and the influence we have on changing the trajectory on which we or our organizations are travelling.

SOMETIMES THERE MAY BE NOTHING YOU CAN DO

In early 2007 we met with the CEO of a bank in the Eurozone whom we'd known for a number of years. He'd recently announced record profits and an all-time high share price. After congratulating him on his success we asked him how long he thought it could continue. Without hesitation, he replied, "It can't."

As events unfolded over the following months, the bank's position rapidly worsened. Reflecting on the conversation, it was obvious that the CEO knew exactly what the default future of his bank would be. Furthermore, he knew that he was powerless to do anything about it. The bank's trajectory had been set by the context within which it was operating, along with his past choices and actions and those of his predecessors, colleagues, fellow directors, shareholders and the industry's regulators. The bank subsequently went into state ownership, and is only now getting into a position where taxpayers have a chance of getting their money back.

NOT ALL DEFAULT FUTURES ARE UNACCEPTABLE

The examples above may give the impression that all default futures are unacceptable, but this is not the case. If a newlywed couple were asked to describe their default future, it would be reasonable for them to assume that they would spend many enjoyable years together and possibly start a family. In our research, we talked with a number of CEOs who described a very positive default future for their organizations. But as previously discussed, the context can quickly change and with it the default future. Blockbuster saw only continued growth until the rapid proliferation of broadband changed its context, and with it the company's default future.

A DEFAULT FUTURE CAN SEEM SO FAR AWAY AT TIMES

Sometimes the speed and direction of travel can be so slow and subtle that it's hardly noticeable, leading people to believe that nothing's really changing. This was effectively illustrated by Charles Handy in his book *The Age of Unreason*.[42]

Handy described this phenomenon as "the boiled frog syndrome". If you place a frog into a pot of boiling water, he said, it will of course frantically try to clamber out. Likewise, if you place a frog into a pot of freezing cold water, it will also try to jump out. But if you gently place a frog into a pot of 'frog-temperature' water it will make no attempt to escape.

If the water is then slowly heated the frog will initially perceive no danger and adjust its own internal temperature. As the temperature increases it will eventually reach a point where its body can no longer compensate and it will die. While there is some disagreement in the scientific community as to whether it would actually play out that way, we'll go along with it to illustrate that in our daily lives we're often too busy and don't always recognize the significance of small changes. It's the same when our children grow up – we don't notice how much they grow day by day until it's pointed out by others who don't often see them. It's the same in organizations: everyone is busy, the KPIs (key performance indicators) are looking good and morale is high, but incremental changes in context are not noticed until it's too late.

ESTABLISHING SHARED UNDERSTANDING

One can speculate about what the default future might hold, but it's another thing entirely to reach mutual understanding across a leadership team. A case in point is a UK beer company we worked with some years ago. For many years, everything had been going well for this company. Its brands were recognized globally and it operated in the 'virtuous circle' of profit growth driven by increasing market share among its core brands. Growth had been 4–5% above the declining on-trade market, and the take-home trade had been rejuvenated with fresh packaging and promotion. Along the way the company continued to surprise and delight with bold, creative advertising, creating the perception that it was a market leader with a truly 'cool' consumer goods brand.

Building on its success, it continued to invest in its future. The leadership team had been strengthened by the appointment of a director of transformation who oversaw a number of initiatives, including new production facilities (new breweries, kegging lines and stainless steel kegs); upgraded IT infrastructure; new beer-dispensing equipment; outsourcing of non-production functions; and increased training in the care and dispensing of its products to customers. These actions had a dramatic impact on its cost base, with headcount falling by almost 30% in two years. There was every indication that the actions the management team had taken would secure the success of the company for years to come.

But the finance director was not convinced. He had a gut feeling that the actions taken to date were necessary but not sufficient to secure the company's future in an increasingly difficult market. He understood the numbers, but more importantly he understood the business and the markets in which it operated. He also understood the forces driving the business and was able to articulate a future (the default future) that was different from what his colleagues saw. He was concerned that the actions they had taken to date were insufficient to steer the business away from what he saw as the likely (default) future. While the investments had undoubtedly delivered improvements, he felt that they had not addressed some of the more fundamental issues facing the business, including the functional silo mentality of staff and managers, poor process performance and a lack of focus on delivering a compelling customer experience. He was also concerned about how the organization delivered change, as past initiatives to improve processes and systems had only added to complexity and confusion. His overarching concern was how the beer market was changing and how the once-secure niche for the company's brands would be increasingly challenged by powerhouse global players.

His challenge was getting his colleagues to see things the way he did and for them to take appropriate collective action.

It was at this point that he sought our help. He wanted advice on how to get his colleagues to take time out to think about the default future. He was convinced that if they saw the future the way he did they would be able to plan a boldly appropriate course of action. And he acknowledged that if they saw things differently, it was probably because of him missing something. This would be okay provided they all had a shared view and took collective action.

He knew that delivering lots of analysis and presentations to his colleagues would not work. Neither did he think the leadership team would clearly see the inevitable default future if it was presented by consultants. He wanted to find a way of engaging them that would not rubbish what they had achieved to date and would enable them to retain ownership. He wanted his colleagues to be engaged, both intellectually and emotionally.

Our advice was to find a way of getting his colleagues to mentally model the default future. We proposed that he write an article set ten years in the future, where he would look back at what had happened over this period. In order to make it more credible, we suggested that the piece be mocked up to look like an edition of a reputable publication like *The Economist*, with a suitably eye-catching cover.

The finance director instantly liked the idea and set about writing the article. Once drafted, he shared it with his CEO and sought approval for it to be discussed at the next management offsite. Prior to the meeting, little information was given to colleagues, but as they checked into their hotel the evening before the session a copy of the article was waiting for them in their rooms. The impact was immediate and the serious work of defining an improved future for the business began over dinner.

What the article achieved was engagement and, with it, *collective* leadership. It painted a picture of a possible default future, and more importantly, laid out how and why it might happen. It did so in a way that management could understand, engage with and challenge. It triggered a level of enquiry and debate that no number of PowerPoint presentations and Excel spreadsheets could ever achieve.

The finance director succeeded where the *Financial Times'* Gillian Tett had unfortunately failed. While both had demonstrated individual leadership, the finance director was able to establish collective leadership through the simple technique of writing a 'default future' article. In Tett's defence, her challenge was much greater as she was trying to change the views of an entire industry!

The finance director was not out to prove that he was right and his colleagues were wrong. He simply wanted them to take time out and think about the likely future if they took no action, beyond what was currently planned. The article – read in an environment that was conducive to reflection – led to a deeper level of understanding and confidence that the default future he described was likely to happen. But we will never know, because the actions taken by the leadership team set them on a trajectory to an entirely different future.

Returning to the financial crisis of 2007/2008, why was Tett able to foresee a default future for a large swathe of the financial services industry and the millions of people who were impacted? What could she see that others were unable to see? One explanation is that her background is in social anthropology, in which she has a PhD from the University of Cambridge. "As an anthropologist you're trained to look at how societies or cultures operate holistically, so you look at how all the bits move together," she said in an October 2008 interview with *The Guardian*.[36] "And most people in the City don't do that. They are so specialised, so busy, that they just look at their own little silos. And one of the reasons we got into the mess we are in is because they were all so busy looking at their own little bit that they totally failed to understand how it interacted with the rest of society."

By looking through a different lens, Tett was able to identify the factors that were driving Western financial institutions to their default future. She was able to identify the driving forces and assess their impact in a way others could not, or would not. She defined a default future for an industry that its leaders, regulators and politicians did not want – or chose not to hear. In 2009, she published a book called *Fool's Gold*[43] in which she gives a detailed analysis of the factors and forces that led to the crash of 2008.

Our objective is to help you develop skills similar to Tett's. To help you look differently at strategy and change, identify the forces that cannot be ignored and plan a course of action that will lead your organization to a future that is not only better, but achievable.

AN ORGANIZATION'S TRAJECTORY IS DETERMINED BY ITS NAVIGATING FORCES

An organization does not follow a particular trajectory by accident. Its path is determined; it's the result of a number of factors, some within its leaders' control, others not. These factors – which we call 'navigating forces' – collectively act like 'tramlines' taking an organization to its default future. In certain circumstances these navigating forces can be so strong that it feels as though the organization has been programmed, or hard-wired, and no matter what actions management tries to take, it continues to travel on the same trajectory. If strategy is about changing an organization's trajectory, then a key aspect of developing strategy must be to identify these navigating forces and assess their level of influence. Only then can informed choices be made about what actions to take to alter their level of influence.

Some of these navigating forces, such as economic trends and regulation, are exogenous, originating outside the organization, while others, such as systems, processes and capabilities, are endogenous, originating from within. Some navigating forces are easy to observe, such as technology and structure, while others, such as values and culture, are often hidden deep within the organization and are not apparent to the untrained eye.

EXOGENOUS NAVIGATING FORCES

Navigating forces that originate from outside the organization typically include such things as Central Bank interest rates, currency exchange rates, regulatory controls, demographics, government policy, oil price and climate change.

These exogenous navigating forces also include customer behaviour. For example, in recent years the major supermarket chains in the UK have seen a significant shift in customer behaviour. Whereas a few years ago their customers would do one big weekly shopping trip to a large supermarket, they now prefer to do more frequent shopping at their local convenience store or, increasingly, online. As a result, the major super-markets are being forced to close some of their larger stores, abandoning plans to open new ones and opening up more, smaller, convenience stores.

Another example of changing customer behaviour is in the do-it-yourself (DIY) world. The early 1980s saw enormous growth in large – typically out-of-town – DIY stores like B&Q and Homebase in the UK. This trend to do things yourself was fuelled by popular tele-vision shows that made it all look so fun and easy. More recently, as people became time-poor but cash-rich, and as practical skills are no longer passed down from one generation to the next, it has become the norm to 'get a man in to do the job' rather than doing it yourself. As a result, major DIY chains are realizing their default future is dramatically different from what they thought it would be a few years ago, and are hurriedly developing strategies to shift their trajectory. In one case, the UK's Home Retail Group decided the DIY consumer market had become so competitive that in 2016 it sold its Homebase DIY chain to Austral-ian retail giant Wesfarmers for £340 million.[44] Later that year, also as a result of changing buying habits, it sold Argos, its catalogue and online retail business, to supermarket chain Sainsbury's for £1.4 billion.[45] It can only be assumed that the Board and shareholders of Home Retail Group concluded that the default future of the two businesses was unacceptable, and in confronting this reality decided that the best option would be for them to be acquired by larger organizations.

The essence of exogenous navigating forces is that the decision power to change their influence resides outside the organization, and therefore outside the direct control of management. In such situations, organiza-tions can only respond to these navigating forces rather than change them.

ENDOGENOUS NAVIGATING FORCES

These are the forces that originate from within the organization, and to a large degree are the result of past management decisions and actions. Examples include organizational structure, roles and responsibilities, process design, sourcing agreements, recognition and reward systems, performance management systems, IT systems, governance and organizational culture.

It's worth remembering that all organizations are designed, either explicitly or implicitly. Whichever is the case, the resultant design is a product of past decisions and actions aimed at achieving objectives that were relevant to the context and management thinking at the time. Embedded in the resulting operating model is a set of endogenous navigating forces that are determining the current trajectory.

Whether through design or evolution, the reality is that most organizations are complex – particularly those comprising multiple divisions operating across multiple territories. Complexity is a result of the number of components in a system and their degree of interaction. The greater the number of divisions, business units, departments, distribution channels, territories, customer segments, regulators, suppliers and partners, the greater the organizational complexity. Organizational complexity can manifest itself in many ways, the most common being slow and inconsistent decision-making, myopic planning, unsynchronized thinking, silo management and dysfunctional executive behaviour. Employees across the organization can feel frustrated, disillusioned and unable to contribute to their full potential. It's not unusual in these situations to see staff – including senior executives – 'hunker down' and pursue their own agenda. Complexity is a symptom of the interaction between the different navigating forces at play across the organization.

Another example of an endogenous navigating force is the capabilities that an organization has developed over time. These organizational capabilities act like muscles – the more they are used, the stronger they become, and the more they shape organizational culture and establish organizational habits. Understanding and changing organizational capabilities is key to changing a trajectory, as we will explore further in the next chapter.

The decision-making power necessary to alter the influence of endogenous navigating forces resides within the organization, and therefore within direct control of management.

VISIBLE NAVIGATING FORCES

Some navigating forces, whether exogenous or endogenous, are easily observable. As a result they can be identified and documented relatively easily, communicated, assessed and understood. Examples include organizational structure, supplier contracts, IT architecture and market trends.

One of the most powerful, visible navigating forces defining the trajectory of organizations today is digital technology, specifically legacy systems. This is particularly the case for information-intensive organizations, like banking and insurance, where entrenched IT systems have become so complex after years of incremental enhancements that the effort and risk associated with further changes are significant. There have been many examples in recent years of banks routinely upgrading their systems only to find that the upgrade failed and their customers were unable to access their money or make payments. In some cases, it took several days or even weeks before the problems were rectified. But complexity is not the only issue. Many of the IT systems still in use today were designed to support operating models of the past – for example, supporting business functions and products as opposed to processes and customers. This lack of alignment between the architecture of the IT systems and the desire of the business to operate in different ways can significantly constrain leaders' choices regarding the future trajectory of their organization. Past technology choices – made with the best of intentions in a different context – have created a legacy that is difficult and expensive to change. The challenge is that these legacy systems are often at the very core of the organization and therefore driving it to its default future.

But, as we've said, visible navigating forces can be easily identified, documented and assessed, and their influence on defining an organization's trajectory understood.

HIDDEN NAVIGATING FORCES

The good thing about visible navigating forces is that they are clearly evident, for all to see. The bad thing is that by focusing on what you can see you risk missing what's hidden. It's a bit like an iceberg – you can see what's above the waterline but not below. And just like an iceberg there are often greater, more impactful navigating forces below the waterline than above. Examples of hidden navigating forces are values, beliefs and, of course, culture.

In his early work, Peter Scott-Morgan described these hidden navigating forces as "the unwritten rules of the game".[46] He later developed this thinking into a field of study he called cryptonomics,[47] which offered a practical way of diagnosing even the most obscure organizational misalignments in sufficient detail to simulate, understand and act upon them. His methodology provides ways to decode the rationale behind behaviour – and the resulting culture – and then replicate the control logic of the organization. He believes it's then possible to simulate the organization's real operations and forecast how it will evolve.

Another example of a hidden navigating force is what Tracy Goss calls "winning strategies". In her book *The Last Word on Power*[48] she argues that all organizations, and individuals, have a winning strategy, which consists of the set of behaviours that have delivered success in the past. We may not recognize that we have them or be able to describe them, but we act in the belief that these behaviours will contribute to delivering success. This may be true if the context does not change, but when it does – as with Blockbuster and so many others – a winning strategy can fail to deliver the anticipated future. The reality is that it's often difficult, and sometimes impossible, for individuals, groups or organizations to adapt their tried-and-true winning strategy to the new context. It's important to recognize that what has made you successful in the past will not necessarily make you successful in the future.

By definition, hidden navigating forces are not readily apparent to the untrained eye. Yet the fact that they are hidden does not mean they should be ignored, as they can be a powerful force in defining an organization's trajectory.

The four types of navigating forces are depicted in figure 2i.

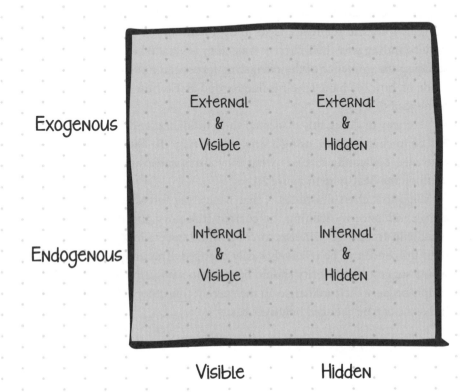

FIGURE 2i:

Framework for making an organization's navigating forces explicit

ASSESSING THE INFLUENCE OF AN ORGANIZATION'S NAVIGATING FORCES

The reality is that most leaders instinctively know the navigating forces that are controlling their organization's trajectory, but they are not always articulated in a way that can be easily understood by others. Furthermore, the tendency is to jump to solutions, rather than fully understanding why their current trajectory is what it is. Only by understanding the influence of the navigating forces can informed choices be made on how to change their influence and assess how much effort will be needed to do so.

One way of doing this is to map their influence, and how difficult it will be to change them, using a simple heat-map. To illustrate this we've taken ten navigating forces – what they are is irrelevant – and plotted them on the heat-map in figure 2ii.

What this chart illustrates is that navigating forces 2, 5 and 7 have a high influence in defining the current trajectory and their influence is difficult to change, whereas forces 3 and 8 have a low influence and their influence can be relatively easily changed. This simple assessment would suggest that priority should be given to navigating forces 1 and 4, simply because their influence on the current trajectory is high and their influence can be changed relatively easily.

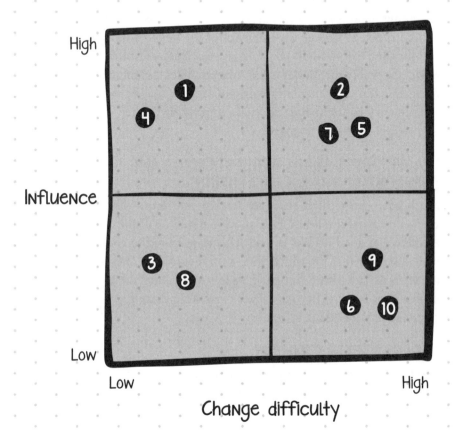

FIGURE 2ii:

Navigational forces heat-map

STRATEGY MUST REFLECT THE ART OF THE POSSIBLE

Although this simple assessment offers insight into where a strategy needs to be focused, it must also take into consideration how difficult it might be to change the influence of the navigating forces that are determining the organization's current trajectory. This involves 'sizing the effort' needed to change the influence of the targeted navigating forces and the time that it might take to do so. Such an assessment should also reflect the reality that under some circumstances the influence of certain navigating forces, particularly exogenous forces, may be so strong – and, by their very nature (being external), impossible to alter – that a trajectory simply cannot be changed.

LEADERSHIP IS ABOUT UNDERSTANDING AND CONFRONTING THE DEFAULT FUTURE

Much has been written about leadership, and more will inevitably be written on what it takes to be a good leader. One of the essential characteristics of good leaders is that they are prepared to confront the default future of that for which they are accountable. They may not use the term 'default future', but good leaders understand the likely outcome if no action is taken beyond what's currently planned, and they accept responsibility for taking action.

THE CHAPTER IN SUMMARY

An organization's default future is where it will end up if no action is taken, other than that which is currently planned. As depicted in figure 2iii, the default future could be better than the current state, or it could be worse, depending upon the organization's trajectory. Furthermore, while the diagram may suggest it, organizations do not travel to their default future in a straight line, or indeed along a smooth curve. The purpose of this simple diagram is to illustrate the spectrum of default futures that are possible.

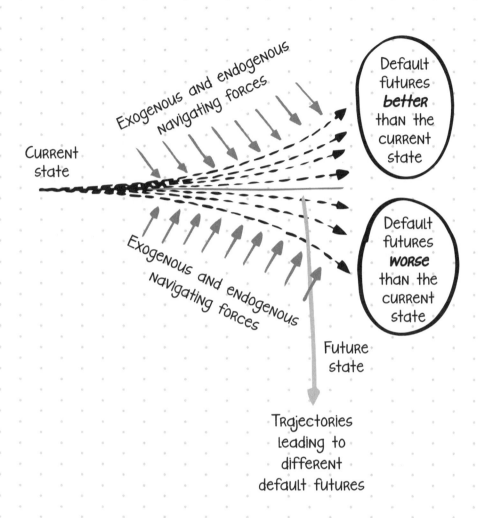

FIGURE 2iii:

Navigating forces define an organization's
trajectory, thereby determining
its default future

An organization's default future is determined by its trajectory, and its trajectory is determined by a set of navigating forces. Some of these forces are exogenous in nature – originating from outside the organization. As a consequence their influence is difficult, if not impossible, to change. Other navigating forces are endogenous by nature – they originate from within the organization, and their influence can potentially be altered through the actions of management.

Meanwhile, some navigating forces are easily observable, while others are not apparent to the untrained eye. Altering an organization's trajectory therefore involves changing the influence of some or all of the navigating forces at play – at least those that are discernible.

Furthermore, if the exogenous navigating forces change significantly – resulting in a radical change of context – it's possible that an organization's trajectory, and its resultant default future, can change without management doing anything at all.

FIVE QUESTIONS FOR REFLECTION

1. Is there a shared understanding of the current default future – in terms of outcomes – for your organization?

2. Are you, or your management colleagues, confronting this default future (assuming it's perceived to be worse than the current state)?

3. What are the top five exogenous (external) navigating forces – in terms of their level of influence – that are defining your organization's trajectory?

4. What are the top five endogenous (internal) navigating forces – in terms of their relative influence – that are defining your organization's trajectory?

5. Where would you place these navigating forces on a heat-map, like the one illustrated in figure 2ii?

CHAPTER 3

HOW ORGANIZATIONAL CAPABILITIES DETERMINE AN ORGANIZATION'S TRAJECTORY

"*The difficulty lies not so much in developing new ideas as in escaping from old ones.*"

John Maynard Keynes (1883–1946)
British economist

In the previous chapter, we argued that all organizations are on a trajectory to their default future, which is where they will end up if no action is taken, other than that which is currently planned. If the default future is judged to be better than the current state, there may be no need to take any action, other than that which keeps the organization on its current path. Alternatively, if the default future is worse than the current state, then leaders need to make choices and take action that will change the trajectory – charting a course to a better future. We also explored how an organization's trajectory is determined by a set of navigating forces, be they exogenous or endogenous. Exogenous factors such as demographic trends, interest rates and regulatory controls, aren't under management's control and their influence is therefore difficult, if not impossible, to change. Conversely, we looked at endogenous influencing factors, such as organizational structure, IT infrastructure and culture, which are, in theory, under management's control and could conceivably be changed.

We also argued that only by understanding the influence of these navigating forces can informed choices be made on the actions needed to change an organization's trajectory. In this chapter we will build upon this idea and argue that endogenous navigating forces are largely a result of capabilities an organization has built up over time.

We call these 'organizational capabilities' simply because they reside within the organization, and not with individuals, although individuals of course shape, contribute to and exercise them. Some examples of organizational capabilities include:

- Cost management
- Product development
- Customer service delivery
- Process management
- Innovation
- Acquisition integration
- Vendor management
- Regulatory compliance
- Risk management
- Data analytics
- Talent acquisition
- IT service management.

In many respects, these are examples of generic organizational capabilities, as they need to exist to some degree. At the same time, organizations need capabilities that are specific to their industry, like exploration in the oil and gas industry, merchandising in retail, fleet management in car rental, patient care in health services, fundraising in the charity sector and relationship management in investment banking. It's the combination of the generic and industry-specific capabilities that enables an organization to achieve what it sets out to do, whatever that may be.

THE NOTION THAT ORGANIZATIONS HAVE CAPABILITIES IS NOT NEW

In their 1990 *Harvard Business Review* article "The Core Competencies of the Corporation",[49] C.K. Prahalad and Gary Hamel argue that to remain competitive, corporations need to perceive themselves as "a portfolio of competencies versus a portfolio of businesses". They also suggested that in the coming decade, "corporations will be judged on their ability to identify, cultivate, and exploit the core competencies that make growth possible" and as a result they would need to "rethink the concept of the corporation itself". They defined a competency as "a bundle of skills and technologies that enables a company to provide a particular benefit to customers". In their later book, *Competing for the Future*,[50] they made no distinction between competency and capability, but again emphasized the need to identify those competencies/capabilities that are core to future success.

In their 2004 *Harvard Business Review* article "Capitalising on Capabilities",[51] Dave Ulrich and Norm Smallwood make a clear distinction between competency and capability. In fact, they go further and make three distinctions – competency, capability and ability. They describe organizational capabilities as "the collective skills, abilities, and expertise of an organization". They also argue that they "form the identity and personality of the organization by defining what it is good at doing and, in the end, what it is". Furthermore, they believe organizational capabilities are difficult to copy, and "as they aren't easy to measure, managers often pay far less attention to them than to tangible investments like plant and equipment". In their view, organizational capabilities emerge when a company delivers on the combined competencies and abilities of its individuals.

More recently, Paul Leinwand and Cesare Mainardi, in their book, *The Essential Difference – How to Win with a Capabilities-Driven Strategy*,[52] define capability as "the ability to reliably and consistently deliver a specified outcome, relevant to your business". They assert that capability "is ensured through the right combination of processes, tools, knowledge, skills, and organization, all focused on meeting the desired outcome". In addition, they argue that for any organization to be successful it needs between three and six distinctive capabilities that reinforce one another, forming what they describe as an interlinked "capability system".

Organizational capabilities are all of these things, and more. In the rest of this chapter we will explore how they determine an organization's trajectory, and what leaders must do to change their portfolio of organizational capabilities if they want any chance of successfully changing their trajectory.

ORGANIZATIONAL CAPABILITIES EXIST FOR A REASON

It's important to remember that the dominant organizational capabilities are present for a reason: to maintain the current trajectory. When an organization thinks about changing its trajectory, it usually does this by establishing a set of change initiatives. These might include creating a new business unit, launching a new product, entering a new market, introducing a new distribution channel, acquiring a competitor, implementing a new IT platform, reengineering processes or moving production to a lower-cost geography. As we've previously discussed, organizations generally don't have a good track record in successfully undertaking these types of initiative. One of the major reasons is that the influence of their current capabilities is either underestimated or ignored. The reality is that when a change initiative comes up against organizational capabilities that are not in line with the target trajectory, the initiative will fail – particularly if the influence of existing organizational capabilities is not addressed. In these situations, the organizational capabilities that contributed to past success often act as 'antibodies' to change.

When changing an organization's trajectory, it's highly likely that new and different capabilities will be required, and the influence of others may need to be reduced or 'retired'.

ORGANIZATIONAL CAPABILITIES VERSUS INDIVIDUAL COMPETENCIES

It's important to make a distinction between organizational capabilities and individual competencies. Whereas competencies are possessed by individuals, capabilities reside within organizations. Obviously, it's not possible for an organization to have capabilities without having competent people. But not everyone in an organization needs to be highly intelligent, as organizational capabilities develop over time, through application and practice. As we've said, in many respects they act like muscles that become stronger with exercise. Also, the more embedded they become, the greater their impact on organizational culture. They are also the source of what Charles Duhigg calls an organization's habits,[53] where employees instinctively and collectively do things in a particular way without consciously knowing how or why. As we will explore later, their impact can be profound when developing and executing strategy, as existing organizational capabilities can make it very difficult for an organization to change its trajectory.

Organizational capabilities are formed from a combination of shared mental models and frameworks, common language, beliefs and mindset, processes and practices, conventions and norms, shared experiences and individual skills developed over time. Significantly, as they become embedded within an organization, they are not lost when key individuals leave.

It's worth taking a moment to distinguish between organizational capabilities and other types of capabilities. For example, IT departments have recently shifted their focus from developing technical capabilities to building business capabilities – for example, the capability to run a credit check on an individual. This shift of perspective is aimed at encouraging IT professionals to think more in terms of what the business needs, rather than what IT solutions they can provide. But these IT-enabled business capabilities should not be confused with organizational capabilities, as they provide only one component of an organizational capability – a technology platform on which they can be executed.

ORGANIZATIONAL CAPABILITIES CAN ANCHOR AN ORGANIZATION TO ITS CURRENT TRAJECTORY

Organizational capabilities create organizational habits that become the source of what organizations instinctively do. It's often assumed that since an organization's capabilities have been the source of its success in the past, they'll be the source of its success in the future. But if future success depends upon changing trajectory, then this is certainly not the case. As Tracy Goss argues in her book *The Last Word On Power*,[48] it's natural for people and organizations to fall back on what they know and do best when the going gets tough. She calls this their "winning strategy". It's a bit like doing more of the same but at a higher volume. As Goss puts it, "we may not recognize that we have our winning strategies, and we may not be able to describe them, but we instinctively act in the belief that they will continue to deliver us success". Over time, our winning strategies become part of who we are. It's the same with organizations; when the going gets tough, the default reaction is to fall back on its winning strategy, a strategy that's enabled by existing organizational capabilities. To put it another way, if a winning strategy is the mindset, then the combination of individual competencies and organizational capabilities is the muscles that bring the mindset to life.

The world of IT offers a common example of existing organizational capabilities anchoring an organization to its present trajectory. Most IT organizations deliver what is expected of them; they keep the systems running, fix faults when they arise, deliver enhancements when requested and manage the risks that come with a complex – often legacy – installed base. They do everything they can to prevent the systems from going down. Continually meeting these same, unwavering expectations results in a set of organizational capabilities that are entirely appropriate for the context as the IT team sees it – keeping the business running and minimizing the risk. Should the context change – for example, following a decision to replace core legacy systems with a modern, more integrated platform – existing organizational capabilities are likely to be out of line with those that are needed. Add to this a decision to use an offshore IT services provider, and you create a context where most IT organizations struggle, particularly when they are also expected to maintain legacy systems during the transition. It's therefore not surprising that a vast number of IT transformation projects overrun budgets and miss deadlines, with many ultimately failing to deliver their intended outcomes.

By their very nature, organizational capabilities become omnipresent as they pervade the organization, so much so that it can be hard to recognize that they exist. In many respects, they act like invisible currents, keeping the organization on its current trajectory. The challenge comes when an organization acknowledges that it needs to change its trajectory, but existing organizational capabilities are so strong that it's difficult, if not impossible, to achieve a course correction.

CHANGING TRAJECTORY REQUIRES DIFFERENT ORGANIZATIONAL CAPABILITIES

In chapter 2 we looked at Blockbuster and how the organizational capabilities it developed in its early years led to tremendous success. But the rapid development of broadband changed its context, and as a result its default future significantly changed for the worse. Whereas its existing organizational capabilities of locating, opening, customizing and running stores supported its original trajectory, they were not the ones needed for an online, video-streaming future. Unfortunately for Blockbuster, it was not able to acquire these new capabilities fast enough to change its trajectory.

Further examples of this trap can be seen along any high street, where online sales have continued to grow year on year and traditional 'bricks and mortar' retailers are finding it increasingly difficult to compete. Industry commentators were quick to point out that these companies failed because they didn't recognize the threat from online competitors and were too slow to change their business model. Easy to say, but the organizational capabilities of these companies were those needed for high-street retailing. It's therefore not surprising that they failed to recognize and acquire the organizational capabilities needed for e-tailing.

During our research, we interviewed the CEO of a very successful builders' merchants and DIY chain. It had grown significantly in recent years, principally through acquisition. As it acquired companies it chose to keep their brands intact, as each addressed a different segment of the market. Its online presence across all its brands consisted essentially of electronic catalogues where customers could browse available products. However, there was little facility for customers to check stock availability or order online for either delivery or in-store collection.

Recognizing that newer entrants to the market were offering customers an omni-channel shopping experience, the CEO instigated a project to transform the company's online presence. Initially, he thought it was essentially an IT project, so the head of IT was asked to lead it. As the CEO and his executive team understood more clearly what they were trying to achieve, they realized that neither their IT organization, nor the business units involved, had the capabilities necessary to deliver a successful outcome. What was being asked of them was completely outside their field of experience. What's more, they soon realized that it would take far too long to develop this capability in-house. As the CEO put it, "We shouldn't be surprised, as over the years we've developed the capability to understand the industry, our customers and manage cost… but innovation, particularly technology-enabled innovation, is not in our DNA."

The CEO chose to get the omni-channel shopping capabilities he needed by acquiring a company that already had them. He purchased a relatively new start-up in the sector whose business model was based entirely upon digital retailing. It was only after he'd bought the company that he and his colleagues fully understood and appreciated what had been acquired. It wasn't just the omni-channel technology itself, but a whole set of organizational capabilities that were different from those in the other businesses. Not only did the business operate differently but its people also thought differently and acted differently. The subsequent challenge for the CEO and his colleagues was to bring these organizational capabilities into their other brands, and do it in a way that did not dilute or destroy what they had acquired, which often occurs with acquisitions.

Another example we came across was a successful household and motor insurance company that had recently been divested by a major financial service organization. Becoming an independent company had removed many of the constraints that had kept the CEO from realizing his vision of taking the organization to the 'next level of digitization'. He now had more freedom, but realized that his organization didn't have the capabilities needed to do 'cool things' digitally and give his customers an easy-to-use, compelling and differentiated online and mobile experience.

The company already had a website that was no better or worse than any of its competitors'. While the IT function was perfectly capable of updating the site, and managing the legacy IT applications that sat behind it, they lacked a fundamental understanding of what the next-generation digital experience would look and feel like. What's more, the CEO felt that the major consultancies and IT system integrators had little to offer in this respect and, as he put it, "I needed to go to Shoreditch."

Shoreditch is an inner-city district of London, northeast of the financial centre. Together with Hoxton and Old Street, it forms an area known as 'Silicon Roundabout'. It's one of a growing number of high-tech business hubs that have emerged around the world – urban concentrations of small-tech businesses that are young, hip and have a 'digital edge'. Those who work in these districts are innovative, agile and unconstrained by the traditional thinking that permeates most large corporations and government agencies. This CEO knew that the best way of gaining access to the digital organizational capabilities he needed was through collaborating with these types of organizations, particularly those with online gaming and social media capabilities.

When A.G. Lafley became CEO of Procter & Gamble (P&G) in 2000 its share price was $52, down from $118. Furthermore, only about 15% of its innovations were being successfully commercialized, and in order to grow faster than the overall economy – which investors expect – he needed to find $4 billion of new revenue, and even more every year. At the time, P&G's default future did not look good, and with a 66% drop in share price its investors knew this all too well. Despite a string of acquisitions from 1998 to 2000, Lafley knew that P&G's current trajectory was one he didn't want, and that making further acquisitions alone was not the answer. In confronting P&G's default future, he knew that he needed to put the organization on a different trajectory, one based upon accelerated organic growth, fuelled by innovation.[54]

Traditionally, innovation in P&G came from its 7,500 researchers, but they hadn't been delivering the results the company needed. Lafley knew that spending more and more on research and development (R&D), for less and less payoff, was not the answer. What the company needed was an entirely different approach to innovation. At this point it's worth noting that the R&D organizational capabilities that P&G had built over the years had served them well in the past, but their focus – and measure of success – was on the number of patents registered, not the proportion that generated new revenue and profits. In fact, these R&D capabilities were anchoring P&G on a trajectory to a default future that was starved of sources of new revenue. A different approach was required – one that built upon the company's strong R&D organizational capabilities, but also focused more on innovations that generated new revenue.

P&G's eventual change in trajectory came from a radical idea: for every researcher there were at least 200 scientists or engineers elsewhere in the world, a total of perhaps 1.5 million people whose talents the research organization could potentially use. The challenge was to find them and connect with them. The solution was enabled in part by the growth of the internet, which provided access to external pools of talent around the world. The subsequent innovation initiative became known as Connect + Develop (C+D).[55]

The success of C+D was predicated on changing P&G's innovation capabilities. Specifically, the company needed to get better at identifying external sources of new ideas and collaborating with external bodies and individuals to bring innovations to commercial reality. To support the development of these capabilities it established a number of global networks and six C+D hubs, located in China, India, Japan, Western Europe, Latin America and the US. By 2006, more than 35% of new products had elements that originated from outside P&G, up from about 15% in 2000. And, 45% of the initiatives in the product development portfolio had key elements that originated externally. Furthermore, R&D productivity had increased by nearly 60% and the innovation success rate had more than doubled, while the cost of innovation had fallen. R&D investment as a percentage of sales was down from 4.8% in 2000 to 3.4% in 2006. And, from 2003 to 2005 alone, more than 100 new products were launched, with some aspects of execution coming from outside the company. In the five years immediately following the company's stock collapse in 2000, its share price doubled.

The organizational capabilities built as a result of the C+D initiative undoubtedly put P&G on a different trajectory, and carried it to a better future. But, not satisfied with its initial success, P&G wanted to build on its achievements by establishing what it called 'new-growth factories' that would identify and bring disruptive innovations to market.[56] These virtual factory operations comprise new-business creation groups, focused project teams and entrepreneurial guides who help teams rapidly prototype and test new products and business models in the market. The teams follow a step-by-step business development manual and use specialized project and portfolio management tools. Innovation and strategy assessments, once separate, are now combined in revamped executive reviews.

When GE CEO Jeff Immelt announced in that 2015 Wall Street analysts' call[40] that he was selling many of the conglomerate's biggest businesses, it was as much a move to divest core organizational capabilities as it was to shed core businesses. Such a bold move could only have been taken as a result of his decision some five years earlier to build a new set of organizational capabilities geared towards 'digitizing in the industrial space'.

Immelt and his colleagues realized that GE was in the information business, whether it wanted to be or not. And many of its products, such as jet engines, locomotives and MRI scanners, had hundreds of sensors capable of capturing continuous data about performance, usage and need for repair. For example, on a single flight between New York City and Chicago, one of GE's jet engines alone produces a terabyte of data. (As a frame of reference, one terabyte is equal to 16 days of continuously running DVD movies or 8,000 times more data than the human brain retains in a lifetime.)

This realization put GE on a different trajectory, one based on data analytics.[13] In 2011 Immelt declared that GE needed to become a software and analytics company or risk seeing its hardware products become commodities as information-based competitors took over.[57] As Marco Annunziata, GE's chief economist, put it, "We're no longer selling customers just a jet engine, a locomotive, or a wind turbine; we're bringing data and actionable solutions along with the hardware to reduce costs and improve performance."[57] GE's intent was to build an analytics-based industrial 'internet of things' on which it and third parties could build, use and sell applications. By 2015, this new stream of revenue was generating $5 billion per annum[13] and approaching $500 million in measurable productivity gains per year.

In order to successfully make this shift in trajectory, GE needed to not only build up its existing organizational capabilities, but also develop new ones. As Immelt put it, "We went through a process of 'make versus buy', 'in versus out'. We basically said, 'Look, do we want to make a big acquisition in analytics or IT?' Furthermore, we don't have the foundation inside the company to do a big acquisition. Do we want to partner, or do we want to do it ourselves?"[13] In the end, the industrial giant decided to see if they could do it themselves. That was 2010.

In deciding to go it alone, GE embarked on building data analytics as a core organizational capability, similar to what material science had been over the past 50 years. They brought in people from outside GE and built an innovation centre in California, and then another in Boston. But building the capabilities was not simply about hiring data scientists. As Immelt put it, "This is something I got wrong. I thought it was all about technology. I thought if we hired a couple of thousand technology people, if we upgraded our software, things like that, that was it. I was wrong. Product managers have to be different; salespeople have to be different; onsite support has to be different."

Early success in 'digitizing in the industrial space' gave Immelt the confidence to make his startling transformation announcement and put GE on the road to becoming a coherent whole. It was a significant shift in trajectory, and not without considerable risk. The trajectory he chose was for GE to become an industrial infrastructure business, underpinned by a data-analytics-based internet platform.

ORGANIZATIONAL CAPABILITIES DETERMINE HOW AN ORGANIZATION OPERATES

If we accept that organizational capabilities are based upon shared mental models, frameworks, language, skills, mindset, beliefs, conventions and experiences, it's reasonable to assume that they have a major impact on how things get done – thereby shaping the organization's operating model. To put it another way, an organization's operating model is a manifestation of its organizational capabilities.

It's interesting to note that in most transformation programmes one of the first questions consultants ask is, "What's the target operating model?" If the people defining the target operating model are the same as those who operate and manage the current model, then the best one can expect is an improvement of the current model. If true innovation and transformation are to be achieved – as in the examples above – then the new operating model needs to be defined and built by people who collectively possess the organizational capabilities needed for the target future.

UNDERSTANDING THE INFLUENCE OF ORGANIZATIONAL CAPABILITIES

While some organizational capabilities are easily recognizable, others only become apparent when they are experienced. And, not all organizational capabilities will exert the same influence on the current or targeted trajectory. For example, if an organization wanted to pursue a target trajectory that gave its customers an omni-channel shopping experience – like the builders' merchant example – a new 'being digital' capability is required, as without it the trajectory simply will not change. Yet, the capability to provide a positive customer experience in their stores is no less important. But its influence is neutral when it comes to changing the organization's trajectory. The only exception to this would be if there were a decision to close all its stores and only offer its customers the online option – which is hardly omni-channel!

The challenge is that organizational capabilities are often difficult to identify, particularly for those in the organization who are so close to them that they may not be able to see them. It's a bit like being in a hot air balloon; you don't feel the wind because you are travelling with it. It's only when you come to land, and the wind drags the basket along the ground, that you notice its strength. The idiom 'can't see the wood for the trees' is also acutely true in this case. Very often, organizational capabilities are only noticed when they are not aligned with the direction the organization wants to travel. One way of identifying the most critical organizational capabilities is to ask the following two questions:

- Which existing capabilities are anchoring your organization to its current trajectory?
- What new capabilities are needed to pull your organization onto its target trajectory?

It's important to note that some of the most influential anchoring organizational capabilities are often hidden – not intentionally hidden, but so embedded in how the organization operates that they are difficult to identify. Furthermore, many are pervasive, and drive the way everything is done. That makes it difficult for people within the organization to appreciate that they exist, and equally difficult for them to appreciate the need to introduce new ones, strengthen existing ones and reduce – or 'retire' – the influence of others.

ASSESSING THE INFLUENCE OF ORGANIZATIONAL CAPABILITIES

Organizational capabilities can be assessed in many ways; we advocate assessing their level of influence. The greater their influence, the more they will anchor an organization to its current trajectory or pull it onto its target trajectory.

When assessing anchoring capabilities, consider the following two questions:

1. To what degree is the organizational capability anchoring the organization to its current trajectory?
2. How difficult – in terms of level of effort – would it be to weaken the influence of the organizational capability?

When assessing pulling capabilities, consider the following:

1. To what degree is the required pulling organizational capability currently in place?
2. How difficult would it be, in terms of degree of effort, to strengthen the influence of the organizational capability?

For each question, a simple grading of 1 to 5 is sufficient, where 1 is low and 5 is high.

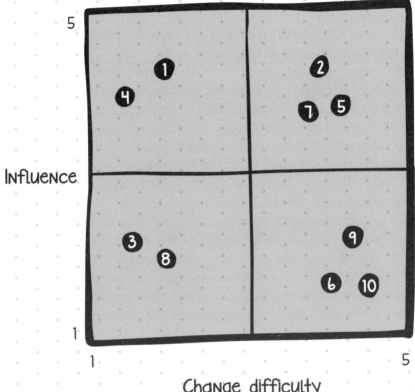

FIGURE 3i:

Assessment of anchoring
organizational capabilities

Ideally, the assessment would be done by a number of individuals and groups, including outside advisors who are able to give an external perspective. The goal is to create insight and align thinking through dialogue, rather than through scientific analysis of how the organization operates. To illustrate this technique we've taken ten anchoring organizational capabilities (1 to 10) and ten pulling organizational capabilities (A to J) – what they are is irrelevant – and mapped them onto the frameworks given in figures 3i and 3ii, respectively.

These heat-maps are similar to the one we introduced in chapter 2, which assessed the influence and change difficulty of navigating forces. All we are doing here is using the same technique to better understand the influence and change difficulty of organizational capabilities. In figure 3i, we see that the anchoring organizational capabilities that are believed to have the greatest influence and that are most difficult to change are 2, 5 and 7. The organizational capabilities that are having the greatest influence but seem to be relatively easy to change are 1 and 4. In figure 3ii we see that none of the organizational capabilities has much pulling power, and that A, D, G, I and J are more difficult to change.

The aim of these assessments is to create dialogue rather than find the 'scientific truth'. We call them 'dialogic assessments' rather than audits. We often find that the paradox with these types of assessments is that people don't like being assessed, but they love being part of an assessment process! By and large, people like to know how they and their organization are doing, especially from a capabilities perspective. But they are sceptical (and rightly so) of outside consultants who parachute in and assess them or their organizations. We therefore believe that self-assessments, supported by an expert facilitator – who can bring experience and act as an impartial arbiter to resolve differences of perspective, opinion or interpretation – work best. Not only do they allow those involved to retain ownership, they also motivate resultant action.

Furthermore, the assessment must be transparent and repeatable. Like any meaningful study, the process should lend itself to being repeated periodically with consistent, comparable results. In fact, repetition over time is important in order to track progress.

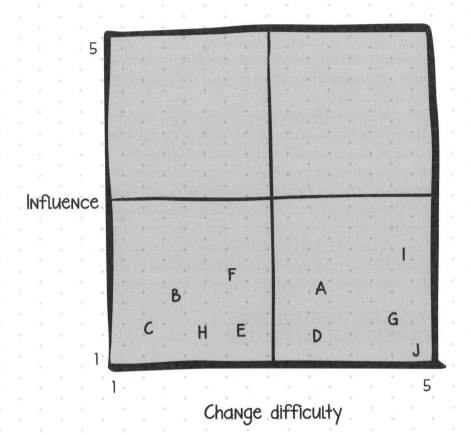

FIGURE 3ii:

Assessment of pulling organizational capabilities

CHANGING THE INFLUENCE OF ORGANIZATIONAL CAPABILITIES

The above assessments identify those organizational capabilities whose influence needs to be strengthened in order to pull the organization onto its target trajectory and those whose influence needs to be weakened in order to reduce their anchoring effect. It's important to remember that today's organizational capabilities were the source of past success, and assumed by many who currently practise them to be the key to future success.

The challenge is changing the relative influence of the pulling and anchoring organizational capabilities, while at the same time maintaining those whose current influence should not be changed. This can only be done by understanding the competing commitments and underlying assumptions. What we mean by this is that while people might be committed to increasing the influence of pulling organizational capabilities, they might also remain committed to existing ones that are anchoring the organization to its current trajectory. The potentially disruptive impact of these competing commitments should not be underestimated, as they can consume considerable management time and resources.

APPROACHES TO ESTABLISHING ORGANIZATIONAL CAPABILITIES

Establishing, or strengthening, those organizational capabilities needed to pull the organization onto its target trajectory is dependent upon two criteria: urgency and difficulty. As illustrated in figure 3iii, there are essentially four approaches that can be taken.

DEVELOP

In-house development is often considered the default option, where the targeted pulling organizational capabilities are developed through training. The limitation of this approach is that it's difficult for people to understand what these new capabilities are until they've experienced them. And, as training develops personal competencies, as opposed to organizational capabilities, it only partly solves the problem. One way of overcoming this is for key individuals and groups to experience the target organizational capabilities first-hand in other organizations, possibly through some form of exchange programme or by participating in experiential learning journeys.

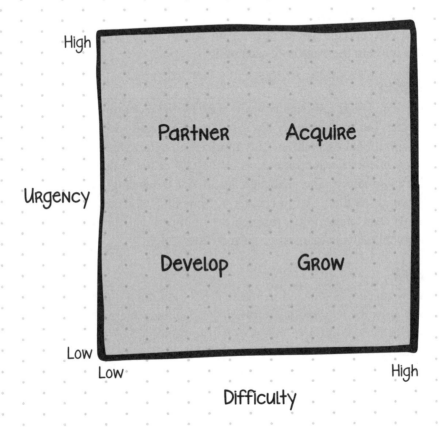

FIGURE 3iii:

Different approaches to putting targeted organizational capabilities in place

PARTNER

If the urgency is high and the difficulty of bringing them into the organization is low – in the sense that they are readily available through outside service providers such as consultancies – then the best approach is to source the capability through some form of partnership, as was the case with P&G and the insurance company. Ideally these partnerships would also result in the transfer of capability.

ACQUIRE

The acquisition approach typically assumes the recruitment of new employees, but, as previously discussed, people possess competencies, not organizational capabilities. This approach therefore involves the acquisition of entire organizations, as in the case of the builders' merchants discussed above. The challenge lies in not destroying what has been acquired. As discussed in chapter 1, some 80% of acquisitions destroy rather than create value, through the unintentional elimination of the acquired entity's organizational capabilities.

GROW

If the urgency is low and the difficulty is high, then the best approach is to grow the required organizational capabilities internally. As was the case in the GE example, this process can be seeded by recruiting individuals who possess the targeted capabilities. Their role is to grow such capabilities through experimentation, practice and application. But care must be taken. The risk is that in their enthusiasm to build the new capability, they inadvertently destroy organizational capabilities that need to be preserved.

All four approaches work, but each needs to be applied appropriately. They must be calibrated according to how urgently the target pulling capabilities are required and how difficult it will be to put them in place. An organization can use a combination or a portfolio of these approaches depending upon what they are, their availability and the urgency of the situation. For instance, P&G not only partnered with outside organizations and individuals but also developed the necessary collaboration capabilities and grew the capabilities needed for its 'new-growth' factories.

MANAGING ORGANIZATIONAL CAPABILITIES AS A PORTFOLIO

Portfolio management is not new; it has been practised in financial, investment and fund management for decades. Its essence is building, balancing, sustaining and rebalancing a portfolio of assets to achieve a desired outcome. For example, when it comes to managing a financial investment portfolio, younger people want growth and are prepared to accept more risk. As one approaches retirement, on the other hand, less risk is tolerated and lower returns are acceptable, so funds might be shifted from equities to government bonds or cash. Managing the portfolio is therefore based upon a set of criteria that changes as circumstances change.

Similarly, consumer product companies actively manage their portfolio of brands and products. They frequently exchange and trade brands and product categories with competitors as they rebalance and refocus their market presence. Capital-intensive industries such as mining and steel also manage their portfolio of assets – things like mines or factories – to ensure long-term profitable growth at an acceptable risk.

Another example of portfolio management involves selecting and managing the portfolio of change initiatives that individually and collectively contribute to changing an organization's trajectory. These could be product investments, IT enhancements, change programmes, or M&As. Over the years, we have found that this is something all organizations understand at a conceptual level, but few have actually mastered its application. One notable exception is GE Power Systems in Atlanta, Georgia, which makes large power-generating turbines. We came across this organization when asked to plan and deliver an experiential learning journey for a group of executives from a European oil company. One of the topics they wanted to learn more about was leading practices in portfolio management. During our visit we asked then-CEO John Rice how he went about building the balanced portfolio of initiatives in GE Power Systems.

He replied, "It's very simple. We are a growing business and we have three very clear strategic objectives. We need to do things that support our *growth*. We need to be *profitable*. We need to build *connectivity* with all our partners, customers and suppliers as we collaborate to build our power-generating turbines. So, when someone proposes a new initiative, I ask how does this contribute to *growth*, *profitability* or *connectivity*? If it does not contribute to at least one of these strategic objectives, it does not make it onto the list."

We also asked him why he personally chaired the Portfolio Management Steering Group. At first he seemed bemused, even amused, by the question, and then answered: "Why would I delegate some of the most important strategic discussions in the company to someone else at this stage of our development?"

On a quarterly basis, Rice and his executive team reviewed the portfolio; assessed the progress of initiatives; killed, cancelled or redirected those that were not going where they wanted; and assessed the potential contribution of proposed new initiatives.

We talked to several other executives during our visit and one made a telling remark about portfolio management in GE Power Systems: "You can tell exactly where the priorities are in this business – they're simply where the best resources are committed at any one time."

Without question, Rice and his team recognized the importance of portfolio management and developed it as a core organizational capability.

Organizational capabilities can, and should, be managed as a portfolio. They are, after all, a type of asset. And like all portfolios, each element has a current and future role to play: some are needed to pull the organization onto its target trajectory, some must be maintained, some need to have their influence reduced and others should be retired.

PORTFOLIO MANAGEMENT IS ITSELF AN ORGANIZATIONAL CAPABILITY

The general principles and practices of portfolio management can be applied to organizational capabilities. However, when managing a collection of organizational capabilities as a portfolio, particular attention needs to be given to:

1. Identifying and defining the most influential organizational capabilities – an organization comprises many capabilities and they don't all have the same importance or influence at a given point in time
2. Defining the role (pulling, anchoring or maintaining) of each organizational capability
3. Assessing the influence of each capability
4. Increasing the influence of targeted pulling capabilities
5. Reducing the influence of – or retiring – targeted anchoring capabilities.

The desired outcome is to have a portfolio of capabilities in place that enables an organization to pursue its chosen trajectory. As it travels along that trajectory, the role of each capability in the portfolio will change. Equally, new ones may need to be introduced and others retired.

RETIRING ORGANIZATIONAL CAPABILITIES THAT ARE NO LONGER REQUIRED

As in all portfolios, the time will come when some assets – in this case organizational capabilities – are no longer required, and need to be removed from the portfolio. However, unlike other assets, organizational capabilities cannot be simply divested, eliminated or stopped. And unfortunately, if no action is taken to reduce their influence, they could continue to anchor the organization to its current trajectory.

The complication in retiring organizational capabilities that are no longer required is that this involves people, often the same ones who made the organization successful in the past. They may have become such an integral part of the organizational capability that they're unable or unwilling to appreciate that a particular capability is no longer required. While there is no easy solution to this, the focus needs to be on the future and finding ways for individuals to repurpose their competencies in ways that support the development and application of more important organizational capabilities.

THE ENTERPRISE VIEWED AS A PORTFOLIO OF ORGANIZATIONAL CAPABILITIES

If we accept the argument that existing capabilities determine how an organization operates, it could also be argued that an organization consists of a portfolio of capabilities. And, like any portfolio, it needs to be managed – dynamically. Not all organizational capabilities will be of equal importance and their relative contribution will change and shift over time. Tension is also likely between employees who value the old organizational capabilities and those who see the need for new ones. As one CEO put it: "We know cost control is our strongest organizational capability, and it's also the one that stops us from innovating and thinking long term." If this argument is accepted, then the role of leaders is to identify and acquire new organizational capabilities, nurture the ones that are most needed today and retire those whose influence prevents the organization changing its trajectory to an improved future.

THE CHAPTER IN SUMMARY

Organizational capabilities are an important class of endogenous navigating forces that help determine an organization's trajectory. Formed over time – from a combination of shared mental models and frameworks, common language, beliefs and mindset, processes and practices, conventions and norms, shared experiences and individual skills – they embody that muscle-memory we've mentioned. If an organization decides to change its trajectory, then it needs to consider which capabilities it needs to introduce or strengthen, and which should be weakened or retired. Assuming that an organization's trajectory can be successfully changed without changing its portfolio of capabilities is a sure-fire recipe for failure.

FIVE QUESTIONS FOR REFLECTION

1. Which organizational capabilities are exerting the most influence in determining your organization's current trajectory and thereby taking it to its default future?

2. What capabilities need to be introduced or strengthened in order to change your current trajectory to the targeted improved future?

3. How could these pulling organizational capabilities be introduced or strengthened?

4. How could the influence of those organizational capabilities that anchor your organization to its current trajectory be reduced or retired?

5. How would you approach managing your collection of organizational capabilities as a portfolio?

CHAPTER 4

UNDERSTANDING YOUR TRAJECTORY OF STRATEGIC OPPORTUNITY

"We always overestimate the change that will occur in the next two years and underestimate the change that will occur in the next ten."

Bill Gates (1955–)
Philanthropist, co-founder of Microsoft

If the purpose of strategy is to change an organization's trajectory for the better, then how is that target trajectory decided? How are the choices made, and how can they be best communicated by management and understood by those who are expected to implement them? In this chapter, and the next, we'll look at how to explore and understand what's strategically possible and, by doing so, be better positioned to define an organization's *trajectory of strategic opportunity*.

We've already laid out the basic premise that all organizations are on a trajectory to their default future. Going forward we'll call this the *trajectory of strategic reality*, because it is in fact the reality of the current strategy – whether or not it's intentional, well defined or well executed. As illustrated in figure 2iii in chapter 2, some organizations' trajectory of strategic reality is taking them to a default future that is better than their current state. For others it's taking them to a future that is undeniably worse – one that its leaders have the accountability to avoid. But why is understanding the trajectory of strategic reality – and the default future it will bring – so important? As discussed earlier, it is a result of the influence exerted by exogenous and endogenous navigating forces. Collectively, they create a context within which an organization operates and they define the feasible future trajectories, taking into account the navigating forces and the influence they have on an organization's ability to change.

THE TRAJECTORY OF STRATEGIC OPPORTUNITY IS AN ENVELOPE OF OPPORTUNITIES

Deciding which new trajectory to take depends not only on understanding the current trajectory of strategic reality, but also what opportunities are strategically possible. We call this the trajectory of strategic opportunity, which, as illustrated in figure 4i, is not one trajectory but an 'envelope' of trajectories – the spectrum of opportunities open to an organization. In this example, we've intentionally shown the trajectory of strategic reality leading to a slightly worse default future than the current state. We've shown the trajectory of strategic opportunity improving over time, both in terms of the possible outcomes and the spectrum of opportunities the expanding envelope offers. We've also illustrated how some strategic opportunities exist now (in the current state).

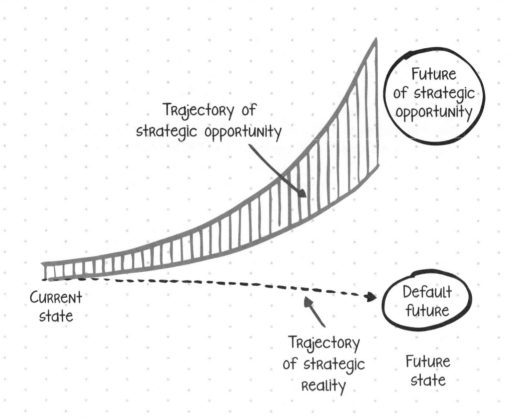

Trajectory of
strategic opportunity

Future
of strategic
opportunity

Current
state

Default
future

Trajectory
of strategic
reality

Future
state

FIGURE 4i:

An expanding and improving
trajectory of strategic opportunity

The horizontal axis in the diagram represents time, spanning a period from the current state to a future state. The period of time is entirely dependent upon the industry and the pace at which the exogenous navigating forces are changing. The vertical axis represents outcomes, which, as we have said, are entirely context-specific and dependent upon the particular circumstances of an organization at a given point in time. These outcomes could be: improved profitability; increased cash flow; a stronger competitive position; a better performing asset portfolio; greater market share or a more ethical culture. It's entirely up to you, in your leadership role, to decide.

The diagram is a simplified representation of the complex reality within which organizations operate. Its purpose is to illustrate the rationale and concepts behind the framework. However, to really put this framework into practice – for a specific organization – it's important that the trajectories and their relative positions are represented as accurately, and in as much detail, as possible.

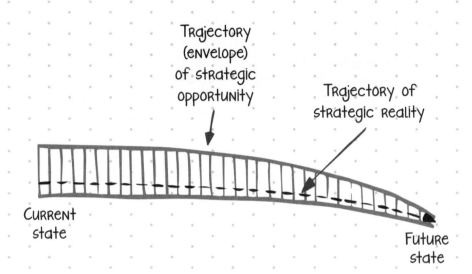

Trajectory
(envelope)
of strategic
opportunity

Trajectory of
strategic reality

Current
state

Future
state

FIGURE 4ii:

A narrowing and deteriorating
trajectory of strategic opportunity

It should also be noted, as illustrated in figure 4ii, that in some cases the envelope of strategic opportunity could narrow over time and also lead to outcomes that are worse than the current state. Such a scenario is possible when the context within which an organization operates changes significantly – for example, as a result of changing regulation or the advent of disruptive new technology.

Some might argue that the envelope of strategic opportunity lies between the upper boundary of the trajectory of strategic opportunity and the trajectory of strategic reality, as illustrated in figure 4iii. We'd suggest that this is not the case. Yes, there is a spectrum of opportunities for improvement between these two trajectories, but not all of these positions are strategic.

As noted previously, future trajectories are only strategic if they're virtually impossible to reverse. It is for this reason that the lower boundary of the trajectory of strategic opportunity is not the same as the trajectory of strategic reality, as is the case in figure 4iii. That's not to say that an organization is wrong if it chooses to pursue a trajectory that is positioned between the lower boundary of the trajectory of strategic opportunity and the trajectory of strategic reality; it's just that it's not strategic, and therefore represents lower risk and less upside opportunity.

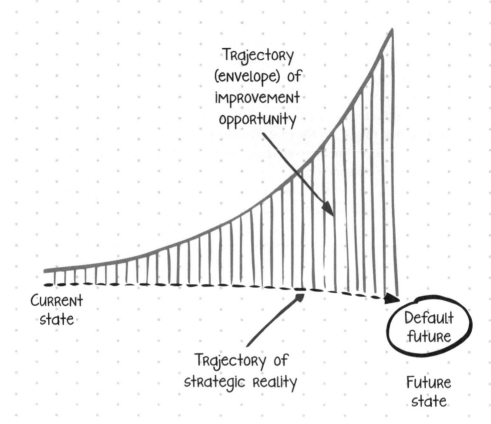

Trajectory (envelope) of improvement opportunity

Current state

Trajectory of strategic reality

Default future

Future state

FIGURE 4iii:

Trajectory of improvement opportunity

YOUR TRAJECTORY OF STRATEGIC OPPORTUNITY IS DEFINED FOR YOU

The first thing to remember about your trajectory of strategic opportunity is that it is defined for you, not by you. It's a result of the exogenous navigating forces. Some of those external factors – such as legislation, regulation and trade agreements – potentially constrain strategic opportunity, while others – such as globalization and digital technology – potentially enable it. As we've established, exogenous navigating forces in effect change the context within which an organization operates.

In the next chapter we'll explore five exogenous navigating forces that directly, or indirectly, impact the trajectory of strategic opportunity for all organizations around the globe, to a greater or lesser degree. These *global exogenous navigating forces* are population dynamics, globalization, energy, climate change and the internet. But in this chapter, we'll focus on the non-global exogenous navigating forces that may be specific to your organization, your industry or the regions in which you operate. While there are many such navigating forces at play, we have selected the following five:

- Trajectory of other organizations
- Regulatory controls
- Trade agreements
- Regional and local economic conditions
- Talent availability and accessibility.

TRAJECTORY OF OTHER ORGANIZATIONS

The first thing to appreciate is that your trajectory of strategic opportunity is defined largely by the trajectories of organizations other than your own. You may be familiar with some of these entities; they may include your fiercest competitors. Others you may never have heard of; they could be operating in a completely unrelated industry. For example, when Amazon first came on the scene in 1994 as an online retailer of books – and later CDs, videos and DVDs – it was not considered a threat to the vast majority of established retailers around the world. It certainly wasn't seen as a source of future opportunity for the tens of thousands of businesses and individual sellers who now trade via the Amazon website. We now know that Amazon, from the start, was not just aiming to be another online retailer of books, CDs and DVDs; it was building an online retail platform that became known as Amazon

Marketplace. When it was launched in 2000, Amazon Marketplace changed the context of retailing forever, and redefined the trajectory of strategic opportunity of literally millions of businesses, small and large, worldwide.

When Apple launched its App Store in 2008, it was in many ways very similar, but this time the product was software. In return for providing both a development platform and a distribution channel for app developers, Apple collects 30% commission on all revenues. As of June 2016, there were more than 2 million apps available on Apple's App Store and more than 130 billion had been downloaded in the eight years since its launch.[58] This not only generated a new and growing stream of revenue for Apple, but it also opened up new revenue-generating opportunities for software developers and businesses everywhere. Significantly, the Apple Store platform also provides an opportunity for companies of all types and sizes to connect with their customers in ways that simply weren't feasible before. Whether in the hospitality, travel, online betting or gaming sectors, the Apple App Store and others, like Google Play, have redefined the trajectory of strategic opportunity for thousands of organizations.

GE's Predix platform is very similar, but in a very different space. As described in chapter 2, Predix is a purpose-built platform-as-a-service for developing, deploying, operating and monetizing internet applications in the industrial space. It allows developers to unlock an industrial app economy that delivers more value from the machines, fleets and factories to which it connects. One of the early applications on Predix monitored the wear and tear on GE's jet engines and calibrated their maintenance schedules based on real, airline-specific data rather than the average for the entire fleet across multiple airlines. Another application created smart wind turbines that tell each other how to adjust their blades to catch more wind, thereby increasing their power generation output by as much as 20%. GE not only provides the machines and equipment, including the sensors within them – which it has traditionally done – it now provides an entirely new data-analytics capability, technology platform and supporting ecosystem for internal and external application developers. In many respects, GE is driving the creation of a new industry that is digitizing the industrial space. Like Apple, GE receives a commission from the use of third-party-developed applications. But, unlike Apple, it also generates new revenue based on the efficiency gains of the machines that the Predix platform and its analytics applications deliver. In 2016, the Predix industrial internet generated approximately $5 billion of new revenue for GE[13], and by 2020 this figure is expected to reach $15 billion.

The trajectory that GE has chosen, along with similar ones taken by Apple, Amazon and many others, has significantly changed the trajectory of strategic opportunity for thousands, if not millions, of organizations of every description.

REGULATORY CONTROLS

Regulation, or more specifically, deregulation, became very common in advanced industrial economies in the 1970s and 1980s. This was both as a result of new trends in economic thinking and the realization that excessive government control ultimately led to inherent inefficiencies. In the UK, deregulation was accompanied by the privatization of many state-owned industries, a move pioneered by Prime Minister, Margaret Thatcher. These companies included British Telecom (1984–93), British Gas (1986), British Airways (1987), the electricity companies (1990–93) and British Rail (1994–97). A more recent example of deregulation, again in the UK, is that of Royal Mail, which on 1 January, 2006, lost its 350-year monopoly on mail delivery to business and residential customers. Since then, any licensed operator has had the right to compete for this business. The regulatory change opened up new strategic opportunities for companies that became Royal Mail's competitors, and at the same time redefined the trajectory of its strategic opportunity.

As we discussed in chapter 2, the financial services sector became heavily regulated following the Great Depression of the 1930s, most notably with the introduction of the 1933 Glass-Steagall Act in the US. Some 50 years later, bankers and governments alike concluded that the time had come to ease regulation, ushering in an era of greater industry self-regulation. As a result, in 1986 the UK financial services industry was significantly deregulated, with what was known as the 'Big Bang'. This, along with the 1999 repeal of Glass-Steagall, redefined the trajectory of strategic opportunity for the financial services industry and enabled banks in particular to pursue very different trajectories. However, many now argue that the decision to deregulate so sweepingly was naive, and had serious unintended consequences – namely the financial crisis that started in late 2007. Subsequent government action to tighten up regulation following the 2008 crash has again redefined the trajectory of strategic opportunity for the financial sector, and in doing so restricted what organizations can and cannot do. For example, after 2019 UK banks will have to run their retail banking operations as independent banks, almost entirely separate from their investment banking and overseas operations.

While there is currently no significant global trend towards deregulation or increased regulation, all organizations need to be cognizant of local or regional trends. For example, India's attempts to reform its financial services sector through deregulation – and China's intent to partially privatize its state-owned enterprises, as well as focusing on a small number of 'strategic' sectors for the future – are examples of national trends that could transform the trajectory of strategic opportunity for organizations competing or seeking to compete in these areas.

TRADE AGREEMENTS

When it comes to selling products and services, the global playing field is anything but level. While many countries are open to free trade, others are not, and some are quite keen to protect their indigenous industries. But trade is an important component of economic development and trade agreements are a way of bringing clarity and stability to who can trade with whom, and under what conditions. The ultimate intent of trade agreements is to establish free trade between two or more nations, where commerce in goods and services can be conducted across their common borders without tariffs or hindrances. Under such agreements, member countries usually impose a uniform tariff – called a common external tariff – on trade with non-member countries. Unlike in a common market – the European Union (EU), for instance – capital and labour may not move freely across borders. According to the World Trade Organization (WTO):[59] "As of 1 July, 2016, some 635 notifications of Regional Trade Agreements (RTAs) – counting goods, services and accessions separately – had been received by the WTO. Of these, 423 were in force. These figures correspond to 460 physical RTAs – counting goods, services and accessions together – of which 267 are currently in force."

The UK referendum decision on 23 June, 2016 to leave the EU will have a profound impact on the trajectory of strategic opportunity for many organizations, both within the UK and across the EU. For UK organizations it will impact the ease with which they can trade with their former EU partners and, for some, whether they can continue to get access to EU research and funding. Many believe that leaving the EU – and with it, access to the so-called single market – will have a detrimental effect on the UK, in terms of its future economic prosperity. Others believe that it opens up new opportunities to establish trade agreements with countries that have faster-growing economies, particularly those in Asia. Until the UK's new trade arrangements with the EU are established – and the extent to which it is allowed access to the EU single market – it will be difficult to predict what the full implications will be. But one thing is certain: the trajectory of strategic opportunity for organizations within the UK, and the UK economy as a whole, will be very different following its departure from the EU.

REGIONAL AND LOCAL ECONOMIC CONDITIONS

While it's important to track global economic trends, it's equally important to understand the economic conditions and trends within which an organization operates. More importantly, it's necessary to understand the factors that are shaping these conditions. That insight is critical because economic conditions can vary significantly across regions, and within regions. And, of course, they can change rapidly.

A recent example is that of China, whose growth in GDP, according to the World Bank,[60] slumped from 7.7% in 2013 to a projected 6.7% in 2016. It is expected to decline further, to 6.3% in 2018. While 6.7% GDP growth is still impressive, this sudden decline took many organizations by surprise as they'd perhaps become over-reliant on the Chinese economy for their own growth. The most obvious of these were commodities such as iron ore at one end of the spectrum and luxury goods, including fashion accessories, at the other end.

Before the 2008 global recession, mining companies were only too keen to open up whole new iron ore deposits, lay down new railway tracks, build new harbours and establish new communities for their workers in remote regions of Australia, South America and Africa. This was driven by huge, growing demand from China to fuel its steel production and construction boom. However, when China's demand for iron ore and other minerals and metals began to decline, commodity prices fell to all-time lows and mining companies suddenly became exposed, given the massive capital expenditure commitments they'd previously made. Furthermore, during the boom, most of the world's dry-bulk ships were fully commissioned in moving these commodities to China, with the Baltic Dry Index (cost of shipping index) hitting an all-time high. Since then, demand has slumped and the Index has dropped an astounding 96% from its 2008 high. According to the Shanghai International Shipping Institute's Q1 2016 *Prosperity Index* report,[61] 'the profitability situation of shipping transport enterprises is worrisome' and 'profitability overall was down a further 10% from Q4 2015, and for dry-bulk shipping it was down 11.34%'. They also reported that 'most ship-owning companies expect the government to provide or improve financial tax policies support to ease business operation pressures on shipping enterprises'. In January 2016, Reuters reported[62] that more than 60% of China's dry-bulk shipping firms were struggling with long-term losses, while about 40% faced liquidity problems.

Luxury goods companies like Burberry, LVMH, Prada, Kering and Salvatore Ferragamo also saw a slowdown in sales in 2016. Burberry alone saw its shares tumble 8% as a result of diminishing sales growth. The challenges that companies like Burberry face are not confined to China. For example, in Russia sales have also slumped, partly attributable to trade sanctions, but more significantly due to the dramatic fall in oil prices. Russia's economy shrank by 3.7% in 2015, and is expected to contract a further 1.2% in 2016.

According to the World Bank,[60] the US is expected to grow by 1.9% in 2016, the Euro Area 1.6%, Japan 0.5%, East Asia and the Pacific 6.3%, South Asia 7.1%, India 7.6% and Sub-Saharan Africa 2.5%. Latin America and the Caribbean are expected to shrink by 1.3%, and Brazil 4.0%. These differences are significant and can, over a few short years, open up an organization's trajectory of strategic opportunity. Just as quickly, however, they can torpedo that trajectory.

TALENT AVAILABILITY AND ACCESSIBILITY

In chapter 3 we discussed how existing organizational capabilities can anchor a company to its current trajectory and how new ones are often needed to pull an organization onto its chosen trajectory. We also talked about the different options available for establishing these capabilities, namely acquisition, growth, development or partnering. What we did not talk about was accessibility, specifically having access to people with the necessary skills and experience.

The availability of these people – and how easily they can be accessed – plays a significant role in defining an organization's trajectory of strategic opportunity. Simply put, if they are available and readily accessible, they can help open up strategic opportunities. Yet, if they are scarce or difficult to access, they can significantly constrain opportunities.

For example, when GE was looking at its strategic opportunities to digitize in the industrial space, it knew it could not do this without recruiting thousands of data scientists and software engineers.[57] It also realized it had little chance of attracting them in sufficient numbers to its headquarters in Fairfield, Connecticut. It therefore chose to locate its new software centre in San Ramon, California, close to Silicon Valley. But location alone was not all it took, as GE had no brand recognition in software development. To overcome this barrier, the company hired a talent acquisition leader, someone who knew the industry and understood what it would take to attract top talent. GE knew that the talent it needed was available – but also that it was in great demand – and did everything it could to increase its access to this talent pool.

Virtually every organization today is dependent upon IT, and their trajectory of strategic opportunity – whether as a developer or user of software – is defined by their access to affordable IT talent. For many, this means turning to locations such as India, which over the last 25 years has built up a vast pool of IT talent. It's estimated[63] that in 2013 the Indian IT industry provided employment to 3 million people directly and a further 10 million indirectly. In 2013, this represented 8% of India's GDP and in 2015 it generated around $120 billion of revenue, doubling from $60 billion in 2009. In support of this industry the Indian government has invested heavily in education and its universities are now producing more than 5 million English-speaking IT and engineering graduates each year. While the Indian IT industry has traditionally focused on providing lower-cost talent – typically some three to four times cheaper than the US – it is increasingly attracting large amounts of inward investment into tech start-ups. It's now not unusual to see global IT organizations locate centres of innovation in India. The trajectory of strategic opportunity for most organizations in advanced economies is being defined by the availability of IT talent in places like India.

The reality is that there will always be demand for suitably qualified talent, and the degree to which this talent is accessible defines an organization's trajectory of strategic opportunity.

KNOWING WHERE TO LOOK

It's human nature to focus on and seek information that confirms what we think we know, understand and believe. This can be very dangerous, particularly when defining your trajectory of strategic opportunity, because the future is unlikely to be a direct continuation of the past, or align with what we think we know and understand. While this may have been the case in the past, the increasing influence of exogenous navigating forces is creating discontinuities that will make planning our futures more challenging and, in many ways, tremendously exciting. The risk is that we – either intentionally or unintentionally – miss these discontinuities and the different futures they could bring.

This is illustrated by the story of a man who had lost his car keys. The story goes that one dark evening a passer-by saw an elderly man searching through the grass under a lamp post. He asked, "Have you lost something? Can I help?" The man replied, "I've lost my car keys." Feeling sorry for the old man, the good-hearted stranger joined the search. After a while, and with no success, he asked, "Where were you when you lost your keys?" "Over there by my car," the man gestured. The passer-by was puzzled and asked, "If you lost your keys over there, why are you looking for them over here?" The old man replied, "It's dark over there, and the light's much better over here."

We may laugh at this foolishness, but we all have a tendency to operate in a space that we know and understand – in effect where the light is shining and where we feel more comfortable. The danger is that in doing so we miss things that are happening in places where we're not looking, whether it is the emergence of new technologies, global economic trends or the growth of a competitor we've not yet heard of. Any one of these variables could radically change the context within which we operate and have a profound impact on both our default future and our trajectory of strategic opportunity.

The risk of focusing on what we know and understand is that we assume the future is a straight extrapolation of the past, even if we should know from history that that's just never going to be the case.

THE FUTURE IS ALREADY HERE
– IT'S JUST NOT VERY EVENLY DISTRIBUTED

While there is some debate as to when the writer William Ford Gibson first said, "The future is already here, it's just not very evenly distributed", we've attributed it to a radio interview he gave in 1999.[64] When we first came across it a few years later, it immediately resonated with us and helped us make sense of a lot of what we'd been experiencing and observing. What he was saying was that as a science fiction writer he was not able to predict the future, and in many respects didn't need to, as it's already happening. His point is that the future doesn't happen overnight; it evolves over time and there are clues out there for us to find and interpret. This is particularly true when the future is shaped by advances in technology. For example, today's so-called disruptive digital technologies were actually developed in the laboratories of technology companies years, even decades, ago.

In our research we uncovered an early reference to Big Data in the proceedings[65] of an October 1999 Institute of Electrical and Electronics Engineers (IEEE) conference on visualization. In another example we found an article[66] by Kevin Ashton claiming to have first used the term internet of things (IoT) in a presentation he gave at P&G in 1999. Cloud computing has evolved through a number of disguises over the years, including grid and utility computing, application service provision and software as a service. The notion of machines having intelligence goes all the way back to antiquity, where the Greek myths of Hephaestus and Pygmalion incorporated the idea of intelligent robots (such as Talos) and artificial beings (such as Galatea and Pandora). Back in 1950, Alan Turing developed a test[67] of a machine's ability to exhibit intelligent behaviour equivalent to, or indistinguishable from, that of a human.

What we know is that reality follows invention, usually with a lag in time. The ideas of today's technologists will become tomorrow's reality. What's difficult to predict is exactly when. Some organizations such as Accenture,[68] Consumer Technology Association,[69] *Harvard Business Review*,[70] Gartner Research,[71] EY,[72] Goldman Sachs[73] and Leading Edge Forum[74] produce regular reviews that forecast the growth and application of emerging technologies. Futurists such as Ray Hammond[75] and Patrick Dixon,[76] to name just two, regularly publish newsletters, post videos and give keynote presentations on developments that are shaping our tomorrow. While we may not be able to predict the future, there's sufficient information out there to help us understand the direction it is taking.

KNOWING IS NOT THE SAME AS UNDERSTANDING

In today's world, where an abundance of information is readily available, it's all too easy to believe we understand something when actually we don't. But, if we really want to make informed choices about the trajectory we want to take – decisions based on a thorough understanding of the strategic opportunities open to us – how can we gain that understanding?

First, we need to appreciate what understanding something really means and how as human beings we best learn. In order to do this we can draw upon the words of three philosophers.

> *"Experience is the child of thought, and thought is the child of action – we cannot learn from books."* – Benjamin Disraeli[77]

> *"For the things we have to learn before we can do them, we learn by doing them."* – Aristotle[78]

> *"I hear and I forget. I see and I remember. I do and I understand."* – Confucius[79]

Each of these quotes tells us something we already know: that we only really learn through our experiences. It's impossible to understand the culture and buying behaviour of customers in an emerging market on the other side of the world unless you've personally experienced it. It's impossible to know how best to deal with suppliers in emerging economies without experiencing first-hand how they operate. And, it's difficult to appreciate how a new technology can be used until you've actually used it. To paraphrase Confucius, "You may remember something if you observe it, but you'll only understand it when you experience it."

It's the same when we look at how people learn. This can be illustrated using a technique adapted from Steve Kerr[80] when he was Chief Learning Officer at GE and head of its Crotonville leadership education centre. Try it for yourself by asking:

> *What have been your most powerful learning experiences? What were the experiences that led you to believe you truly understood something?*

Over the years that we have asked this question, no one has ever mentioned their time at university, a conference they attended or training they went through. Without exception, they referred to times when they faced a really challenging situation, one that took them way out of their comfort zone and stretched them intellectually and emotionally. They will often refer to the fact that they were learning with others while being challenged to deliver something important – for example, launching a new product, integrating a new acquisition, opening up a new market or dealing with a difficult client situation.

We now know this as 'experiential learning'[81] and the work of David Kolb in the 1980s taught us that we learn continuously through a four-stage cycle: Concrete Experience > Reflective Observation > Abstract Conceptualization > Active Experimentation. In other words, we experience something, we think about it, we consider how we might apply it to our situation and we try it. In short, we learn through our experiences.

SHARED UNDERSTANDING LEADS TO COLLECTIVE LEADERSHIP

While individual learning and understanding are important, shared understanding is critical when it comes to collective leadership. Collective leadership is when a leadership team's thinking is so aligned that its members act collectively, as opposed to individually. Alignment is particularly important when it comes to strategy, as people are quite astute at picking up the different signals that members of a leadership team send out. Leaders often lose sight of the fact that employees interpret the organization's strategy by observing management's decisions and actions. Differences are quickly spotted, and if management's lack of alignment is obvious, employees can think, "If they can't get their act together, why should I?" Alignment is therefore important, not only when it comes to deciding an organization's future trajectory, but also in understanding the trajectory of strategic opportunity. And alignment comes from shared understanding.

DEVELOPING SHARED UNDERSTANDING THROUGH EXPERIENTIAL LEARNING JOURNEYS

Learning journeys are a means of accelerating both the process of learning and gaining alignment. They are based upon the principles of experiential learning[81] and are designed to achieve specific learning outcomes that will have a profound impact on how we do business or the capabilities needed to execute a given strategy. Through shared experiences and reflective discussion, participants begin to see the world differently, their perceptions change, new insights are gained and greater alignment is achieved.

Depending upon the challenges faced by a leadership group, a learning journey could take several weeks or span a number of months. Its duration depends entirely upon the urgency of gaining the necessary understanding and the time participants are willing to dedicate to the journey.

By their very nature, learning journeys need to be adaptive. Yes, they have to be planned from the outset, but like any journey, unforeseen things happen: participants experience the unexpected; their perceptions change as a result of insights gained; and business priorities impact timelines. Learning journeys are most effective when they not only impart knowledge but also change the participants' perception of the world and the role they need to play in it. In fact, learning journeys can be life-changing if participants embrace the possibilities they offer.

Below are four examples of learning journeys, three that we were personally involved in organizing and delivering, and one that came from our research.

UNDERSTANDING THE IMPACT OF EMERGING TECHNOLOGIES

Over the years, we've organized and facilitated many learning journeys. The most common type of these involved helping both business and technology executives understand how emerging technologies would impact the future of their organizations. Learning journeys were particularly popular in the 1990s, when the nascent internet was seen as both a threat and an opportunity. On one particular occasion, we took a group of executives from a UK logistics and distribution company to California's Silicon Valley to visit a selection of research centres, technology vendors and start-up companies whose business models were internet-based. These visits took the form of workshops rather than presentations, where the disruptive impact of current and future internet technology on existing business models was explored and debated.

The initial reaction of participants was one of polite interest and mild disbelief, as they thought the technology was interesting but that it would not have a big impact on their business. But as the visits and discussions progressed you could see how their views were changing and the conversations were shifting to what they needed to do when they got back from their trip. This was particularly apparent after visiting the start-up companies whose business models were totally internet-based.

What they experienced during this learning journey helped them understand how the internet was changing the context of their organization and thereby its trajectory of strategic opportunity. Following the learning journey, their feedback was that, without it, it would have taken them much longer to get the depth of understanding they now had – and some said they may never have got there. This learning journey let them meet and talk with people who, in effect, were shaping their future.

Many organizations offer similar learning journeys, including technology vendors and independent research firms. Often called 'technology study tours', they're designed to provide insights into the potentially disruptive impact of emerging technologies.

GAINING INSIGHT INTO CREATING A COMPELLING CUSTOMER EXPERIENCE

Our second example involved the CEO of a financial services organization realizing that his company could no longer compete on product and pricing alone. He knew that his organization operated in what had become a commodity market; differentiating through product features alone was increasingly difficult, and his marketing team – while not short of ideas – had no clue whether their strategies would have any real impact on revenue and profits. It was then that he realized the only way to differentiate his organization in a very crowded market was through the experience it gave to its customers.

The only problem was that while his colleagues thought it was a great idea, they didn't actually know what delivering a compelling customer experience involved. Nor could they make the distinction between delivering a compelling customer experience and providing exceptional customer service. Furthermore, they didn't really know how to shape and deliver a game-changing customer experience initiative.

Our role was to help the CEO and a few senior colleagues understand the strategic opportunities that customer experience thinking and practice had to offer. We did this by helping them fully appreciate the art of the possible and experience first-hand some exemplary companies that had developed customer experience as a core organizational capability. The learning journey that we designed and facilitated took the group to the US, where they made a number of 'observational visits' to banks and retail stores. They met with executives and front-line staff from organizations in businesses similar to their own and participated in a customer experience learning workshop at the Ritz-Carlton Leadership Center.[82]

The experiences gained through the learning journey gave them insight into the strategic opportunities that delivering a compelling and consistent customer experience had to offer. It also helped them better understand the link between employee experience, employee engagement and customer experience – and how strongly interconnected they are.

DEVELOPING COLLECTIVE LEADERSHIP

In our third example, the CEO of a major German insurance company was helped to develop collective leadership across his extended leadership team. While he was happy with the recent work that had been done on his company's strategy by outside consultants, he recognized that it would not be successfully implemented unless his extended leadership team – some 35 executives – really understood the strategic shifts that were required. The learning journey spanned three years and focused on the principles and leading practices in the key strategic shifts they needed to make, including horizontal enterprise integration, shared services, IT transformation and innovation.

Over the course of their journey, some 20 different organizations from within and outside their sector were visited. Immediately after each visit, participants reflected on their individual and collective insights and experiences, and challenged themselves on how what they had learned could best be applied in their particular context. They then used this understanding – and resulting confidence – in what became one of the largest transformation programmes in their industry, which itself became part of their ongoing learning journey.

The 35 leaders created a powerful community that continues to meet several times a year to challenge current strategies and develop new ones in a safe environment. They also developed levels of trust and confidence that enabled them to ask one another for help, which was unprecedented in the context of a traditional, conservative German insurance company.

ALIGNMENT ON A TARGET TRAJECTORY

The fourth example began when, as we discussed in chapter 2, the chairman of a mid-sized UK hospital confronted the default future of his organization – a world-class centre of excellence for cardiac and thoracic research and treatment. He and his chief medical officer recognized that if the hospital wanted to take patient care to the next level, an altogether different strategy was required.

Having spent some time working in the US and being familiar with the work of several clinics – most notably the Mayo Clinic in Minnesota,[83] which has been featured in the *Harvard Business Review*[84] – the chief medical officer felt that the hospital's new strategy should be 'patient-centric'. You might think this would be an obvious conclusion but, as they found out, turning this strategic intent into operational reality required significant change for all involved. In order to develop greater understanding and alignment, the chairman took a group of senior colleagues on a learning journey to see first-hand how leading patient-centric clinics operated. On their return, the insights they had gained enabled them to develop and implement a patient-centric strategy that worked for them. The hospital is now widely acclaimed and regarded as one of the best UK healthcare providers.

THE CHAPTER IN SUMMARY

Before an organization can decide on its target trajectory, it needs to understand two other trajectories, namely the *trajectory of strategic reality* and *trajectory of strategic opportunity*. The trajectory of strategic reality is the path that's taking an organization to its default future. Furthermore, its direction and speed are determined by the combined influence of the exogenous and endogenous navigating forces. The trajectory of strategic opportunity is actually not one trajectory, but an envelope of trajectories that collectively defines the spectrum of strategic opportunities open to an organization. This trajectory is also determined by the influence of exogenous navigating forces, both industry-specific and global, the latter of which we'll discuss in the next chapter. Only by understanding these two trajectories can informed choices be made on the target trajectory, taking into account what's strategically possible and what's realistically feasible. At the same time, fully understanding the strategic opportunities open to an organization requires a different approach to learning and leadership: learning that is experientially based, and leadership that is based upon alignment and collective action.

FIVE QUESTIONS FOR REFLECTION

1. To what extent does your organization define its trajectory of strategic opportunity as part of the strategy development process?

2. What are the top ten exogenous navigating forces that are defining your organization's trajectory of strategic opportunity?

3. Which of these exogenous navigating forces are opening up strategic opportunities (e.g., digital technology, globalization, urbanization) and which are closing down opportunities (e.g., tighter regulation, demographic shifts, economic downturns)? How would you rate their influence on a scale of 1 to 5?

4. How does your organization go about identifying and assessing the influence of the exogenous navigating forces that are defining its trajectory of strategic opportunity? For example, has your leadership group recently participated in some form of experiential learning journey with this intent?

5. How is your trajectory of strategic opportunity shared with colleagues?

CHAPTER 5

HOW GLOBAL EXOGENOUS NAVIGATING FORCES SHAPE YOUR TRAJECTORY OF STRATEGIC OPPORTUNITY

"The one thing we know about the future is that it will be different."

Peter Drucker (1909–2005)
Management educator and author

In this chapter, we will concentrate on five global exogenous navigating forces that directly or indirectly impact the trajectory of strategic opportunity of all organizations worldwide, to some degree or another. These global exogenous navigating forces are:

- Population dynamics of growth, demographics, urbanization and international migration
- Globalization and international trade
- Energy usage and availability
- Climate change
- The internet revolution.

While there are other global exogenous navigating forces at play, these are the ones that are most relevant today. In this chapter we describe each of them and explore how they individually and collectively redefine the trajectory of strategic opportunity of all organizations, regardless of whether they operate globally, internationally or locally. We don't claim to be futurists and certainly don't have all the answers, but what we do know is that if you're serious about changing your organization's trajectory of strategic reality then you need to know how these forces – and others – are defining your future trajectory of strategic opportunity.

POPULATION DYNAMICS

In mid-2015, the world's population reached 7.3 billion, and it is expected to hit 8.5 billion by the year 2030. While the population is growing, a greater proportion is also getting older. In 2015, 901 million people (12% of the population) were aged 60 or over, and the figure is expected to increase to 1.4 billion (16%) by 2030. Furthermore, the population is continually moving, both through urbanization and international migration.

Recent United Nations publications on the world population,[85] population ageing,[86] urbanization[87] and international migration[88] paint the following picture.

Population growth. The world's population continues to grow, though more slowly than in the recent past. Ten years ago, the world population was growing by 1.24% per year. Today, it is growing by 1.18% per year, adding approximately an additional 83 million people annually. The global population is expected to reach 8.5 billion by 2030, 9.7 billion by 2050 and 11.2 billion by 2100.

Population distribution. Of the global population, 60% lives in Asia (4.4 billion), 16% in Africa (1.2 billion), 10% in Europe (738 million), 9% in Latin America and the Caribbean (634 million), and the remaining 5% in Northern America (358 million) and Oceania (39 million). China (1.4 billion) and India (1.3 billion) remain the two largest countries in the world, representing 19% and 18% of the world's population, respectively. In 2022, India is expected to overtake China as the world's most populous country.

Fastest-growing countries. More than half of the global population growth between now and 2050 is expected to occur in Africa. Africa has the highest rate of population growth among major regions, growing at a rate of 2.55% annually in the period 2010–2015. Consequently, of the additional 2.4 billion people projected to be added to the global population between 2015 and 2050, more than half – 1.3 billion – will be added in Africa. Asia is projected to be the second-largest contributor to global population growth, adding 0.9 billion people between 2015 and 2050. Europe is expected to have a smaller population in 2050 than in 2015.

Fertility rates. Global fertility is projected to fall from 2.5 children per woman in 2010–2015 to 2.4 in 2025–2030 and 2.0 in 2095–2100. Fertility rates across European, North American and 20 Asian countries are now below the level required (around 2.1 children per woman, on average) for full replacement of the population in the long run.

Life expectancy. Globally, life expectancy rose by three years between 2000–2005 and 2010–2015, from 67 to 70 years. The greatest increases were in Africa, where life expectancy rose by six years in the 2000s. Life expectancy in Africa in 2010–2015 stood at 60 years, compared to 72 years in Asia, 75 years in Latin America and the Caribbean, 77 years in Europe and in Oceania, and 79 years in North America. Globally, life expectancy is projected to rise from 70 years in 2010–2015 to 77 years in 2045–2050, and to 83 years in 2095–2100.

Population ageing. Globally, the median age is projected to increase from 30 to 36 years between 2015 and 2050 and to 42 years in 2100. In 2015, there were 901 million people aged 60 or over, comprising 12% of the global population. The population aged 60 or above is growing at a rate of 3.26% per year. Currently, Europe has the greatest percentage of its population aged 60 or over (24%), which is expected to reach 34% by 2050. The number of older people in the world is projected to be 1.4 billion by 2030 and 2.1 billion by 2050, and could rise to 3.2 billion by 2100.

Population ageing is projected to have a profound effect on the number of workers per retiree, as measured by the Potential Support Ratio (PSR). The PSR is defined as the number of people aged 20 to 64 divided by the number of people aged 65 and over. Currently, African countries, on average, have a PSR of 12.9, while in Asian countries it is 8.0, in Latin America and the Caribbean 7.6, and in Oceania it is 4.8. In Europe and North America it is 4 or under, and Japan, at 2.1, has the lowest PSR in the world. Europe has seven countries with PSRs below 3. By 2050, seven Asian countries, 24 European countries, and four countries in Latin America and the Caribbean are expected to have PSRs below 2.

Urbanization. Globally in 2014, more people lived in urban areas (54%) than in rural areas. In 1950 this figure was 30%, and by 2050 it is expected to be 66%. By 2030, the world is projected to have 41 mega-cities with more than 10 million inhabitants each.

International migration. The number of international migrants worldwide has continued to grow rapidly over the past 15 years, reaching 244 million in 2015, up from 222 million in 2010 and 173 million in 2000. In 2015, two thirds of all international migrants were living in just 20 countries. The largest (47 million) resided in the US, equal to about a fifth of the world's total. Germany and the Russian Federation hosted the second and third largest numbers of migrants worldwide (12 million each), followed by Saudi Arabia (10 million). From 2000 to 2015, average annual net migration to Europe, Northern America and Oceania averaged 2.8 million persons per year. From 2014, numbers travelling to Europe increased significantly as a result of the conflict in Syria, ongoing violence in Afghanistan and Iraq, abuses in Eritrea and poverty in Kosovo. In 2015, Germany alone accepted more than 1 million migrants.

Whether our planet becomes over-populated is not only dependent upon the size and distribution of the population, but also on the ratio of population to available sustainable resources, including clean water, clean air, food, shelter and other resources necessary to sustain life. If the quality of human life is to be improved in the developing countries, and at least maintained in developed countries, then additional resources, such as medical care, education, proper sewage treatment, waste disposal and energy supplies, are also needed.

The most important of these resources is water. Without clean water, good health is not a viable option. According to the *United Nations World Water Development Report 2015*,[89] some 748 million people lack access to an improved drinking water source, while billions more lack drinking water that is really safe. At least one fifth of the world's population – about 1.2 billion people – live in areas where water is physically scarce and a quarter of the global population live in developing countries that face frequent water shortages. In addition, global water demand for manufacturing is expected to increase by 400% between 2000 and 2050. In 2012 some 2.5 billion people did not have access to improved – as opposed to basic – sanitation facilities.

Another challenge is providing enough food for the growing population. According to the 2015 *United Nations State of Food Insecurity in the World Report*,[90] about 795 million people globally are undernourished. While this is a strikingly high number, that is in fact 167 million less than a decade ago. The *United Nation's World Water Development Report 2015*[89] forecasts that by 2050 agriculture will need to produce 60% more food globally, and 100% more in developing countries.

The evidence indicates that the number of people occupying our planet will continue to increase for the foreseeable future. This growth will not only open up new opportunities, it will also place an increasing strain on our natural resources and our ability to provide clean water, food, healthcare, shelter and safety for all. As the population gets older it will also place an increasing burden on the younger working population, on whom we will become increasingly dependent to generate the wealth needed to fund the healthcare and support services needed during older age.

GLOBALIZATION

According to the World Bank,[91] 896 million people (12.7%) lived on or with less than $1.90 a day in 2012. This was compared with 1.95 billion people in 1990 and 1.99 billion in 1981. In China alone between 1981 and 2011, 753 million people moved above the $1.90 a day threshold. While this is a remarkable achievement, there is still much more to be done. For example, in 2011, 21.25% of India's 1.3 billion people lived on less than $1.90 a day and in Madagascar, with a population of 23 million, it was more than 80% in 2010.

Many argue that one of the most effective ways of lifting people out of poverty is through greater international trade and economic integration – what's commonly called globalization. The term globalization became popular in the 1980s, reflecting the technological advances that made it easier to complete international transactions – both trade and financial flows. The International Monetary Fund[92] describes globalization as "an extension beyond national borders of the same market forces that have operated for centuries at all levels of human activity – village markets, urban industries, or financial centres". Globalization is therefore not a new phenomenon, as during the late 19th and early 20th centuries the global economy operated in a very open environment, with goods, services and people able to move across borders with little if any difficulty. But as Martin Wolf, *Financial Times* columnist and author of *Why Globalisation Works,*[93] puts it, "Anti-liberal pressures, two world wars and huge policy mistakes by the US in the 1920s and 1930s brought about a catastrophic implosion between 1914 and 1945."

While globalization drives economic growth, it also creates a vulnerability as global linkages have increased the economic interdependence between countries, as illustrated in the 2008 financial crisis. What started with payment difficulties in the US sub-prime mortgage market quickly spread around the world, resulting in dramatic falls in stock markets and deterioration of business and consumer confidence. The resulting fall in demand drove a contraction in international trade and inward investment (including M&As), causing the crisis to spread throughout the entire global economy. As a result, trade in the Organization for Economic Co-operation and Development (OECD) area fell by 25% on average between October 2008 and June 2009.[94]

Nevertheless, the growth of 'global value chains' continues to makes us more globally interconnected, and thereby increasingly interdependent in all that we do. Firms that implement global value chains seek to optimize the production process by locating various production stages across different regions according to the rule of comparative advantage. In addition, multinational enterprises (MNEs) transfer capital, highly-skilled labour, technology and products internationally, and shift activities within their multinational networks according to changing demand and cost conditions.

The latest statistics from the World Trade Organization (WTO)[95] – an organization that was formed only in 1995 – paint the following picture.

World exports of commercial services. These grew by more than 400%, from $1,179 billion in 1995 to $4,872 billion in 2014.

World merchandise exports. These grew by more than 350%, from $5,168 billion in 1995 to $19,002 billion in 2014.

World trade and GDP. From 1995 to 2000, world merchandise exports grew annually by an average of 7% in volume terms, while world

GDP grew by an average of 3%. From 2000 to 2005, exports grew more significantly, with an average growth of 5% per year, while the average annual GDP growth was 3%.

GDP is highly influenced by international trade. The average share of exports and imports of goods and commercial services in world GDP increased significantly, from 20% in 1995 to 30% in 2014 (in value terms).

Global value chains (GVC). In 2011 49% of world trade in goods and services took place within GVCs, up from 36% in 1995.

Growth of IT services. From 1995 to 2014, world exports of computer and information services expanded much more rapidly than any other services sector, with an average annual growth of up to 18%. In 2014, world exports of these services reached an estimated $302 billion.

Leading importers. Europe has been the leading destination of exports over the past 20 years, followed by Asia, which has greatly increased its importance as a trading region. In 2014, world merchandise exports to Asia amounted to $5,465 billion, almost a third of the total of world merchandise trade.

Developing economies. Share of exports in world trade increased from 26% in 1995 to 44% in 2014, while the share of developed economies' exports decreased from 70% to 52%.

China. Overtook Japan as the leading Asian exporter in 2004, three years after its accession to the WTO. China surpassed the US in 2007 and Germany in 2009 to become the world's leading exporter.

Regional trade agreements (RTAs). The EU has consistently been the leading exporter within the RTAs over the past 20 years, with exports of $6,162 billion representing 33% of world trade in 2014. The North American Free Trade Agreement (NAFTA), covering Canada, Mexico and the US, comes second with exports of $2,493 billion, accounting for 14% of world trade in 2014. While increasing in value terms, the percentage shares of the EU and NAFTA in world merchandise exports have slightly decreased.

2008 financial crisis. The sub-prime lending crisis in the US led to a global recession between 2008 and 2011. The volume of world exports plunged 12% in 2009 while worldwide GDP dropped 2%.

Global debt crisis. Following the financial crisis of 2008, and with an escalation of geo-political tensions, world trade slowed to a crawl from 2012 to 2014, with global merchandise trade growth averaging just 1% per year.

Whatever the merits of increased international trade, globalization for some represents capitalism at its worst, leading to income inequality and poverty. While per capita incomes have risen across virtually all regions, even for the poorest segments of population, incomes for the relatively well-off have increased at a faster pace. As Martin Wolf[93] put it, "Inequality might have to be the price we pay if, in the long run, it leads to advances for everyone."

Some would argue that the results of the 2016 US presidential election are a stand against greater globalization, where the people of America's once-thriving rust belt made it known that they wanted their industries and jobs back. For them, the fact that many goods are cheaper as a result of globalization is of little comfort if they have no income to pay for them.

Globalization is an exogenous navigating force that is unlikely to go away, but its influence on shaping the trajectory of strategic opportunity for many organizations could be very different to that envisaged before the US election.

ENERGY

At the present time, there are approximately 7.5 billion people on the planet, of which some 1.2 billion – about 16% of the population – have no access to commercial energy, particularly electricity. This lack of access to electricity negatively impacts their lives. It makes the provision of basic social services, such as healthcare and education, more difficult and hinders both economic and social development.

Yet, according to the World Energy Council (WEC), there are more available energy resources than ever before. In its 2013 survey of energy resources,[96] the WEC reported that "the main fossil fuels: coal, oil and natural gas are plentiful and will last for decades". The report also notes that as a result of continued global population growth – coupled with economic growth – global, primary energy demand could increase by 50% by the middle of the 21st century. At least 80% of this increase is expected to come from developing countries, with China alone expected to increase its energy use by 100% by 2035. Over the same period, India is expected to increase its usage by almost 150%.

The WEC's assessment of the different energy sources is summarized as follows.

Coal. This is most widespread fossil fuel around the world, with more than 75 countries having coal deposits. Currently, coal is used to generate more than 40% of global power. While this proportion is expected to decrease in Europe and North America, any reductions will be more than offset by the large developing economies, primarily in Asia. Today, China alone uses as much coal as the rest of the world. While the global reserves of coal decreased by 14% between 1993 and 2011, production went up by 68% over the same time period. In 2011 the world total R/P (reserves to production) ratio for coal was more than 100 years.

Oil. Global reserves are almost 60% larger today than 20 years ago, and oil production has gone up by 25% over that period. In 2011, the world's total R/P ratio for oil was more than 56 years. If unconventional oil resources, including oil shale, oil sands, extra-heavy oil and natural bitumen, are taken into account, the global oil reserves are four times larger than the current, conventional reserves.

Natural gas. The cleanest of all fossil-based fuels. Reserves have grown by 36% over the past two decades and production by 61%. In 2011, the world total R/P ratio for natural gas was more than 60 years. Shale gas resources alone are estimated to be 456 tcm (thousand million cubic feet) situated in some 700 locations worldwide.

Nuclear. The first nuclear reactor was commissioned in 1954 and in the late 1980s nuclear's contribution to global electricity production peaked at 17%. In 2012, this dropped to 13.5%, but in absolute terms output remains broadly the same as it did in the late 1980s. The relative share of nuclear power generation continues to decrease, primarily as a consequence of the Fukushima Daiichi nuclear disaster. Before this accident, nuclear energy accounted for 30% of Japan's electricity generation. Today, none of that country's 54 reactors are in operation. Following the Fukushima incident, Germany, Italy, Belgium, Spain and Switzerland also decided they would be nuclear-free. Furthermore, many of the world's ageing nuclear power stations will be decommissioned in the coming two decades.

Hydro power. Water-driven turbines account for approximately 15% of global electricity production, across more than 100 countries. The largest of these is China with 24% of global-installed capacity. Over the past two decades, the total global-installed hydro power capacity has increased by 55%, and the actual generation by 21%. Since the WEC's survey in 1993, the global-installed hydro power capacity has increased by 8%, but the total electricity produced dropped by 14%, mainly due to water shortages.

Wind. According to the Global Wind Energy Council,[97] at the end of 2014 there were 26 countries with more than 1,000 MW (megawatt) installed capacity, the largest being China with 145,362 MW. Furthermore, the WEC estimates that the capacity installed in 2015 was 63,467 MW, compared with 3,760 MW in 2000 and 39,058 MW in 2010. The cumulative installed capacity in 2015 was an estimated 432,883 MW.

In the UK alone, 6,680 wind turbines were in operation in 2015, accounting for 11% of capacity demand in an industry that employed some 30,000 people. In comparison, the US and China, have 48,500 and 92,981 turbines, and employ 88,000 and 280,000 people, respectively.

Solar PV (photovoltaic). Solar is the most abundant energy resource and it is available for use in its direct (solar radiation) and indirect (wind, biomass, hydro, ocean) forms. Even if only 0.1% of this energy reaching the Earth could be converted at an efficiency of 10%, it would be four times larger than the world's total electricity-generating capacity of about 5,000 GW (gigawatts). From 2008 to 2011, solar PV capacity increased in the US from 1,168 MW to 5,171 MW, and in Germany from 5,877 MW to 25,039 MW.

It is estimated that more than 1,000 new solar systems were installed around the world in the first half of 2016. Continuing at this rate, the current total of 1.1 million solar systems – which took 40 years to reach – will grow to more than 2 million by 2018.

Bioenergy and waste. Bioenergy is a broad category of energy fuels manufactured from a variety of feed-stocks of organic origin, and by numerous conversion technologies, to generate heat, power, liquid biofuels and gaseous biofuels. Conventional incinerators are primarily designed to dispose of growing volumes of societal waste material, not for production of electricity. Therefore, waste's contribution to primary energy supply is minimal. In 1990, the share of bioenergy was estimated to be about 10%. Between 1990 and 2010, bioenergy supply increased from 907 to 1240 Mtoe (million tonnes of oil equivalent).

According to a special report by *The Economist* in 2015 on energy and technology,[98] the energy landscape has significantly shifted in recent years and is likely to continue to change. The decision of Saudi Arabia and its Gulf allies not to reduce production in the face of falling demand – and the growth of oil and gas production from hydraulic fracturing ('fracking') in the US – has broken the power of OPEC and led to a spectacular plunge in oil prices. As the US shale revolution continues and that country's exports of liquefied natural gas increase, they will create a more global gas market and greater resilience of supply. It will also undermine Russia's pipeline monopoly in Europe.

The report also illustrates how we are getting more for less, citing the US, whose economy has grown by around 9% since 2007 as its demand for finished petroleum products has dropped by nearly 11%. And in Germany, household consumption of electricity in now lower than it was in 1990. Transmission costs for electricity are also dropping.

The challenge for the energy industry is the pressure to reduce greenhouse gasses and become less reliant on fossil fuels. While modern coal-fired power stations are far cleaner and more efficient than those of the past, the vast majority still emit enormous amounts of CO_2 gas. By all accounts this will continue even with the average investment of $260 billion a year on renewable energy over the past five years.

The availability of different forms of energy shapes the trajectory of strategic opportunity for organizations and countries alike. In the UK the last deep coal mine – in Kellingley, North Yorkshire – closed in December 2015, and in the US more than 200 coal power plants have shut down, eliminating more than 50,000 jobs over the past five years. Meanwhile, the growth of solar and wind energy has opened up opportunities for many organizations and led to the growth of entire new industries.

CLIMATE CHANGE

We've all seen and read about the devastating floods in Bangladesh in 2013, 2015 and 2016, and China in 2016; the drought in southern and eastern Africa in 2016 that left more than 36 million people facing starvation; the forest fires in Indonesia in 2005, California in 2015 and Canada in 2016; and the extreme heatwaves in China in 2013, India in 2015 and 2016 and Korea in 2015. Though some people simply do not agree that these events are a direct result of climate change, the evidence presented by NASA[99] is overwhelming.

Rising sea levels. Global sea levels are rising on average 3.4mm per year and since 1993 have risen by 81.2mm (3.2 inches). This puts a number of coastal cities, low-lying Pacific Ocean islands and countries (like Bangladesh) that are essentially built on floodplains at greater risk of flooding and subsequent loss of life.

Warming oceans. The oceans have absorbed much of the increased heat associated with climate change, with the top 700 metres (about

2,300 feet) of ocean showing warming of 0.302°F since 1969. We know from basic physics that when water heats up, it expands – hence, the rising sea levels.

Rising global temperature. The Earth has warmed significantly since the 1970s, with the 20 warmest years having occurred since 1981 and all ten of the warmest years on record occurring since 2000. The average global temperature has risen 1.4°F since 1980. The year 2015 ranks as the warmest on record.

Shrinking and growing ice sheets. The Greenland and Arctic ice sheets have decreased in mass. Data from NASA's Gravity Recovery and Climate Experiment[100] shows that Greenland lost 150 to 250 cubic kilometres (36 to 60 cubic miles) of ice per year between 2002 and 2006. However, Antarctic sea ice has grown in recent years. Between 2012 and 2014 it reached record highs, growing to 7.78 million square miles in September 2014, the largest increase since satellites started keeping accurate measurements in 1979.

Declining Arctic sea ice. Unlike the Antarctic, the Arctic sea ice in September – when it reaches its minimum – is now declining at a rate of 13.4% per decade, relative to the average recorded between 1981 and 2010. Both the extent and thickness of Arctic sea ice have declined rapidly over the last few decades.

Glacial retreat. Glaciers are retreating almost everywhere around the world, including in the Alps, Himalayas, Andes, Rockies, Alaska and Africa.

Ocean acidification. Since the beginning of the Industrial Revolution, the acidity of surface ocean waters has increased by about 30%. This increase is a result of humans emitting more CO_2 into the atmosphere and, as a result, more being absorbed into the oceans. The increase in ocean acidity has a significant impact on the viability of many marine organisms, including coral, shellfish, sea urchins and other calcifying species.

Extreme events. The number of record-high-temperature events around the world has been increasing in recent years, while the number of record-low-temperature events has been decreasing since 1950.

Decreased snow cover. Satellite observations reveal that the amount of spring snow cover in the Northern Hemisphere has decreased over the past five decades and that the snow is melting earlier.

Furthermore, there is increasing consensus among the scientific community that the main cause of climate change is the 'human expansion of the greenhouse effect' caused by emissions of greenhouse gasses, including CO_2, methane, nitrous oxide and chlorofluorocarbons (CFCs). Of these, CO_2 generated by the burning of fossil fuels, such as coal and oil, is seen as the major contributor. The clearing of land for agriculture, industry and other human activities has also had an impact, but to a lesser extent. In 1995, the atmospheric concentration of CO_2 was 360.67 parts per million (ppm); in late 2016 it reached 404.93 ppm. In 1950 it was 311.3 ppm and in 1850, at the height of the Industrial Revolution, it was 285.2 ppm. NASA's projections are that by 2020 it could reach 408.7 and by 2040 in excess of 457.8 ppm.[101]

While there is agreement among climate scientists on the causes and effects of climate change, politicians continue to struggle with what action needs to be taken. The body charged with negotiating agreement is the United Nations Framework Convention on Climate Change (UNFCCC). It was formed in 1992 and comprises 197 member parties. Its most significant achievement was the Kyoto Protocol. Although this was adopted on 11 December, 1997, it took another seven years for it to be ratified by members, and came into force on 16 February, 2005. In late 2015, the UNFCCC meeting in Paris reached a historic agreement to "combat climate change and to accelerate and intensify the actions and investments needed for a sustainable low carbon future by governing climate change reduction measures from 2020". By late December 2016, 118 countries had formally signed up to the agreement.

If the case for reducing greenhouse gasses is so compelling, why are governments so slow to take action? It's simple: their economies are dependent upon fossil fuels. Since the beginning of the Industrial Revolution in the mid-1800s, the economic growth of developing countries has been almost totally dependent upon fossil fuels. And not only in developing countries. In 2014, 83.3% of the energy consumed in the US was fossil fuel. In the UK it was 82.8%, down from 90.1% in 2008, and 88.4% in 2000.

While most developed countries are committed to phasing out their coal-fired power stations, the same cannot be said for developing countries. That's particularly so in India, with 455 coal-burning plants accounting for 519,396 MW of installed generating capacity due to come online, and China, which has 363 coal-fired power plants in the pipeline. Developing countries need energy to grow their economies and coal is both the cheapest and often the most geographically convenient fuel.

Our dependence on fossil fuels is also driven by our love of the automobile,[102] which is unlikely to diminish in the near future, even as our cities become ever more congested. According to the Organisation Internationale des Constructeurs d'Automobiles,[103] in 2014 there were 1.2 billion vehicles of all types on the road – up from 892 million in 2005, an increase of 38%. The total production of cars in 2015 was 68.6 million, plus 22.1 million commercial vehicles, up from 41.2 million and 17.7 million, respectively, in 2000. Nearly one third of worldwide automobile production – 21 million cars – took place in China alone, which is twice that of the US and four times that of Germany. The worldwide production of electric vehicles was expected to be 1.6 million in 2016. While cars are becoming more efficient, and electric and hybrid models becoming more popular, it's difficult to see the end of the car as we know it in our lifetime.

If climate change is a result of our past actions – rather than a natural periodic cycle that the planet experiences – then our actions are defining the trajectory of our planet's future climate. If the resulting default future is unacceptable – as many believe it is – then action has to be taken to change the trajectory, and that action will in turn redefine the trajectory of strategic opportunity for most organizations on the planet.

THE INTERNET

On 24 October, 1995, the Federal Networking Council unanimously passed a resolution defining the term 'internet'.[104] At that time, there were estimated to be some 16 million internet users, representing 0.4% of the world's population.[105] By the end of 2015 this number had risen to an estimated 3.4 billion, or 46.4% of the world's population. Of these, 872.9 million were English-speaking and 704.5 million Chinese-speaking. The highest number of users was in North America, at 87.9%, followed by Europe at 73.5%, Asia at 40.2% and Africa at 28.6%. In September 2016, the number of internet users exceeded 50% of the world's population.

In 20 short years, the growth of the internet has been staggering – so much so that an entire generation has grown up knowing nothing else. Some say that we're only at the beginning of the internet revolution and that it will continue to change the way we are entertained, work and manage our lives. In order to get a better perspective on its expected growth – and insight into what it means for our individual and collective futures – let's take a look at the research.

Recently Cisco, an internet equipment provider, predicted[106] the following:

The number of devices connected to IP (internet protocol) networks will be three times as high as the global population in 2020. Cisco estimates that there will be 3.4 networked devices per capita by 2020, up from 2.2 in 2015.

Smartphone traffic will exceed PC traffic by 2020. In 2015, PCs accounted for 53% of total IP traffic, but by 2020 PCs will account for only 29% of traffic. Smartphones will account for 30% in 2020, up from 8% in 2015.

Traffic from wireless and mobile devices will account for two thirds of total IP traffic by 2020. By 2020, wired devices will account for 34% of IP traffic, while Wi-Fi and mobile devices will account for 66%. In 2015, wired devices accounted for the majority of IP traffic, at 52%.

Global internet traffic in 2020 will be equivalent to 95 times its volume in 2005. Globally, internet traffic will reach 21 gigabytes (GB) per capita by 2020, up from 7 GB in 2015.

Global IP traffic will increase nearly threefold over the next five years, and will have increased nearly 100-fold from 2005 to 2020. Overall, IP traffic will grow at a compound annual growth rate of 22% from 2015 to 2020.

One of the drivers of this growth is the availability and affordability of mobile networks. In its *Global Internet Report 2015*, the Internet Society[107] states that 192 countries have active 3G mobile networks and that these cover almost 50% of the world's population. Furthermore, the Internet Society predicts:

- 3G- and 4G-capable phone and mid-screen device connections are forecast to reach global penetration of 71% in 2019, up from 28% in 2013
- Mobile internet device penetration in North America, Western Europe, and Central and Latin America is expected to rise above 100% by 2017. In the developed Asia-Pacific region it already exceeds 100%, indicating that many people have multiple subscriptions. In developing regions, penetration is significantly lower, with individuals or households sharing access to devices
- Affordability is critical to mobile internet uptake, as measured by the percentage of per capita GDP required for a mobile internet subscription (at least 3G). Out of the 129 countries surveyed, 30 had subscription costs less than 1% of per capita GDP, 81 had a subscription below the UN Broadband Commission target of 5%

of per capita GDP, leaving a number of countries where the subscription was more than 10% of per capita GDP. In two countries the cost of a subscription was more than 100% of per capita GDP

- The average price of a smartphone is decreasing. In 2013, the average global selling price was $337, down 12.8% from $387 in 2012. The price in North America and Europe remained relatively high, reflecting the popularity of higher-end smartphones in these geographies.

As a consequence of the growth of mobile internet technology, it is estimated that literally millions of apps are currently available, and they've been downloaded more than 100 billion times.

All the evidence strongly indicates that the internet will continue to grow, in terms of both user penetration and traffic. Its capacity and speed will continue to increase and cost of usage will decrease. Furthermore, what we will be able to do online will continue to transform our lives and as a result we will undoubtedly become more and more dependent upon 'the net'.

GLOBAL EXOGENOUS NAVIGATING FORCES DO NOT ACT IN ISOLATION

While each of the global exogenous navigating forces described above will continue to redefine the trajectory of strategic opportunity for most organizations – as will others not covered here – their true influence is seen when they act in combination. In doing so, they will open up new opportunities for some organizations and eliminate opportunities for others.

For example, the world's growing population is consuming more energy, which is having a negative effect on climate change. It's also driving globalization and urbanization as more people in developing countries move from rural villages to work in urban factories. In addition, it's creating greater demand for food and clean water, which in turn creates new opportunities in the field of 'smart farming', with GPS (global positioning systems) fitted to farm equipment to improve uniformity and effectiveness of fertilizer, insecticide and pesticide spraying. The internet is also enabling farmers to access farm-management systems that help them optimize production, and in developing countries small farmers can use these internet-enabled platforms to sell their livestock and produce without having to travel miles to market.

These developments are also driving investment in agri-tech start-ups. According to AgFunder,[108] an organization that helps connect investors with agricultural companies, $704 million was invested in IT-based start-ups in 2015. These comprised drones and robotics, decision-support technology, and smart equipment and hardware, representing some 15.3% of the $4.6 billion invested in the industry that year. As many of the traditional seed and fertilizer companies take an increasing interest – for instance, Monsanto now has its own venture capital operation – developments in the sector will increase rapidly. As discussed previously, the trajectories that these large organizations take will in turn redefine the trajectory of strategic opportunity for many other organizations.

They also create new institutions and markets, for example those supporting carbon trading, where countries that have higher carbon emissions can purchase the rights to release more CO_2 into the atmosphere from countries that produce lower emissions.

The influence of these navigating forces can have serious consequences for some companies. For instance, Germany's drive to renewable fuels, and its decision in 2011 to turn its back on nuclear power following the Fukushima disaster, has had a devastating impact on its big power companies, E.ON and RWE. The prospect of lost future business in nuclear energy, coupled with the cost of decommissioning and subsequent clean-up, led these energy companies' share prices to drop 34.26% and 45.99% respectively between mid-2013 and mid-2016. In 2015 both companies announced big losses – E.ON's net loss was €7 billion, the largest in its history.

Of all the exogenous navigating forces currently at play, the one that will have the greatest impact on the trajectory of strategic opportunity for most organizations is the internet. It is the platform on which new business models can be built. As we discussed earlier, an example of this is the emerging IoT, comprising computing devices, mechanical and digital machines, objects, natural resources and people that are provided with unique identifiers that enable the transfer of data over a network without requiring human-to-human or human-to-computer interaction. As previously discussed, an example of an organization aggressively pursuing this opportunity is GE, with its $1 billion-plus commitment to the development of its Predix 2.0 Industrial Internet platform.[13]

A further example is that of blockchain – a peer-to-peer network of distributed databases that sits on top of the internet. In their best-selling book *Blockchain Revolution,*[109] Don Tapscott and his son Alex describe it as the technology most likely to have the greatest impact on the enterprise and the global economy. As they put it: "The first generation of the digital revolution brought us the internet of information. The second generation – powered by blockchain technology – is bringing us the internet of value: a new, distributed platform that can help us reshape the world of business and transform the old order of human affairs for the better."

They argue that the impact of blockchain will be revolutionary as the technology can transform the very nature of the corporation, animate the internet of things, recast the role of government and change content industries. Without question, blockchain technology has the potential to open up new strategic opportunities for most organizations and close others for some. For many, it is already having profound implications for their operating model strategy, technical architecture and leadership. Organizations will need to rethink how they access talent outside their boundaries, how their supply chains will be transformed, how triple-entry accounting works and how contracts will be evidenced by distributed databases rather than paper. According to Don and Alex Tapscott this second era of the internet will have a bigger impact than the first, and there is no reason to think otherwise.

HOW EXOGENOUS NAVIGATING FORCES DEFINE AN ORGANIZATION'S TRAJECTORY OF STRATEGIC OPPORTUNITY

Exogenous navigating forces determine an organization's trajectory of strategic opportunity by closing down current opportunities and opening up new ones. This may be relative to changing markets, resource and talent availability, technological developments or changing customer demographics. The challenge is understanding their impact – both negative and positive – along with the likely timeframes. One way of doing this is to develop a number of *scenario futures* that provide insight into emerging strategic opportunities.

One of the greatest exponents of this approach is Royal Dutch Shell, which has been developing scenarios for the energy sector and its business since the 1970s.[110,111] The power of scenarios is that they affect the way people perceive the world around them, bringing invaluable insight and influencing choices. At Shell, scenarios play a crucial role in developing strategy by asking important 'what if?' questions.

AN APPROACH TO DEVELOPING SCENARIO FUTURES

There are many ways of developing scenario futures; the one we favour is based upon the following seven-step approach.

1. **Identify** the exogenous navigating forces – including those covered in this and the previous chapter, plus others relevant to your industry – that have the potential to define the trajectory of strategic opportunity for your organization.
2. **Understand** these forces through data gathering and analysis. Assume you know nothing, seek out original research, talk to relevant experts and get first-hand experience of how these forces are shaping today.
3. **Assess** their potential influence in terms of what future opportunities they could open up and what current opportunities they could close down.
4. **Select** a small number of possible scenarios (three to five) that collectively define the envelope of your trajectory of strategic opportunity.
5. **Develop** the selected scenarios in terms of possible futures that your organization would want to achieve. Remember, these are possible futures that assume your organization would not be constrained in realizing them.
6. **Present** the scenarios in ways that are meaningful to those who ultimately decide on strategy. Ideally, present them as stories that enable people to mentally model the futures being presented. Also present them as a journey and describe how the future will unfold.
7. **Decide** which future you intend to aim for, and this is the topic of the next chapter.

THE CHAPTER IN SUMMARY

In this chapter we selected five global forces that we believe will have a profound influence on shaping all our futures. Understanding the influence of these forces – and relevant others – enables informed choices to be made on an organization's trajectory of strategic opportunity, from which its *trajectory of strategic intent* can be chosen. A powerful way of getting the insight and understanding needed is through the development of a small, tightly focused number of scenario futures.

FIVE QUESTIONS FOR REFLECTION

1. Which of the five global exogenous navigating forces discussed in this chapter will have the greatest influence in shaping the trajectory of strategic opportunity for your organization?

2. Are there other global exogenous navigating forces that you feel your organization should also consider?

3. What approaches is your organization taking to understand these navigating forces and the influence they could have?

4. Does your organization use techniques such as developing scenario futures? If so, how effective are they in shaping strategy? If they are not used, why not?

5. What combination of global exogenous navigating forces do you think will have the greatest influence in opening up opportunities for your organization, and which will have the biggest influence in closing down current opportunities?

CHAPTER 6

DEFINING YOUR TRAJECTORY OF STRATEGIC INTENT

*"Destiny is no matter of chance.
It is a matter of choice.
It is not a thing to be waited for,
it is a thing to be achieved."*

William Jennings Bryan (1860–1925)
41st US Secretary of State

When leaders think about their strategic intent, they are essentially thinking about where and how they would like their organization to operate in the future. They are thinking about how current sources of value could be maximized and where new ones could be established. We call these sources of value the *strategic axes* of the organization. Strategic axes define not only what an organization does but also, equally importantly, the extent to which it does it.

For example, in retail banking there is a recognizable set of strategic axes. One of these is the service a bank provides that allows its customers to pay bills and transfer money. This axis is often called a current or cheque account. This strategic axis includes a spectrum of choices, in terms of what the customer is able to do, and where a bank chooses to position itself on this spectrum defines its strategic intent along this particular axis. At one extreme, it could provide a full range of payment facilities through its branch network, by post, over the telephone, or via a computer, smart phone or tablet. At the other, it could choose to offer a limited set of payment services, for example only via the internet or smart phone.

If a bank also provides mortgages it would be operating on an additional strategic axis, pursuing an additional source of value. The spectrum on this axis ranges from basic repayment mortgages through to offset mortgages linked to current accounts. Equally, if it offered insurance products it would operate on an additional strategic axis. Where an organization aims to operate along its chosen strategic axes defines its strategic intent – a strategic intent that is positioned within the trajectory of strategic opportunity.

But strategy is not just about defining strategic intent; it's also about making choices on the trajectory an organization needs to follow in order to realize that intent. We call this the *trajectory of strategic intent*, which is illustrated in figure 6i. In essence, the purpose of strategy is to take an organization away from its trajectory of strategic reality – headed towards its default future – to a trajectory that will realize its strategic intent. Obviously, figure 6i is a simplified representation of the complex reality within which organizations operate. The purpose of the diagram is simply to illustrate the rationale and concepts behind the framework.

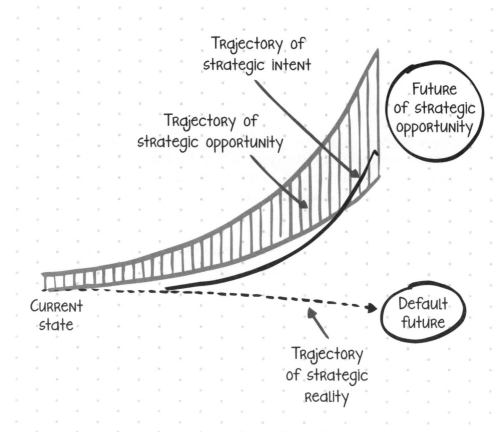

FIGURE 61:

The purpose of strategy is to change the trajectory of the organization from its trajectory of strategic reality to its trajectory of strategic intent

The choice of a trajectory of strategic intent needs to be based on a thorough understanding of the organization's trajectory of strategic opportunity, discussed in chapters 4 and 5, and its current trajectory of strategic reality, discussed in chapter 2. Whereas the trajectory of strategic opportunity presents the spectrum of possible strategic intents, the trajectory of strategic reality is what needs to change and be brought in line with the trajectory of strategic intent. It's therefore important when deciding on this change of course to assess the time and effort needed to bring the trajectory of strategic reality in line with the trajectory of strategic intent. This assessment involves understanding the influence of the exogenous and endogenous navigating forces that are anchoring the organization to its current trajectory of strategic reality. Choosing the right trajectory of strategic intent is important for a number of reasons. First, if the gap between the trajectories of strategic intent and strategic reality is too wide, the time and effort needed to bring strategic reality in line with strategic intent could be too great, and execution of the strategy is more likely to fail. Second, if the gap is too narrow, it may be easier to bring the trajectory of strategic reality in line with the trajectory of strategic intent, but many of the strategic opportunities will be missed. To put it another way, the closer the trajectory of strategic intent is to the upper boundary of the trajectory of strategic opportunity, the more ambitious the strategy, but the more difficult it will be to successfully execute. Correspondingly, the closer the trajectory of strategic intent is to the trajectory of strategic reality, the less the current trajectory needs to change and the less ambitious the strategy must be.

If you look at the framework more closely, you'll see that there are actually two gaps, not one, and both need to be closed. The first gap – between the trajectory of strategic opportunity and the trajectory of strategic intent – is closed by building the capability to define a trajectory of strategic intent that maximizes strategic opportunities. The second gap – between the trajectories of strategic intent and strategic reality – is closed by developing the capability to execute the strategic intent. Both of these are organizational capabilities that can be developed. It's important to remember that a strategy is only successful if it changes the trajectory of strategic reality to the extent that it becomes coincident with that of the trajectory of strategic intent.

Understanding these three strategic trajectories is important as they provide the framework within which strategic choices can be made.

In the next two chapters we offer ideas and approaches to increase the chances of successfully executing a trajectory of strategic intent. For the remainder of this chapter, we will focus on how best to define strategic intent.

Deciding on the trajectory of strategic intent involves making choices about which strategic axes an organization intends to operate on, *and* where along each strategic axis it intends to position itself. It also involves deciding how to establish new strategic axes and/or acquiring the capability to operate at a different strategic position along existing strategic axes. This could involve making acquisitions, establishing partnerships, building new organizational capabilities, divesting certain assets or some combination of these. For example, when Apple launched iTunes in January 2001 it introduced a new strategic axis – one that enabled users to rip CDs onto MP3 players and organize their music through an easy-to-use interface. Three releases later, in April 2003, it launched the iTunes Music Store, which offered individual songs for $0.99 apiece. Back then, it may not have fully understood the complete spectrum of possibilities along this strategic axis, but over time it has continually extended the strategic axis and repositioned itself accordingly, from offering a simple music player to becoming the sophisticated multimedia content manager, hardware synchronization manager and e-commerce platform of today.

NEW STRATEGIC AXES CAN BE CREATED

On 1 August, 2013, the UK and the Republic of Ireland saw the launch of two new TV channels, both dedicated to sport. The channels represented a £2 billion investment by the BT Group, formally known as British Telecom. At the time, Gavin Patterson, the CEO of BT Group, was quoted in an interview[112] as saying that the launch of BT Sport "was not a bet for the faint-hearted".

BT Group launched BT Sport because it had outbid ESPN for the rights to broadcast 38 English Premier League football matches in the 2013–14 and 2015–16 seasons. The £2 billion deal was only the start of their investment, as the company went on to acquire ESPN's UK channels and broader sports' broadcasting rights. BT Sport has since also acquired the broadcasting rights for other sports, including rugby, basketball, MotoGP and World Rally Championships. In launching BT Sport, the BT Group chose to go head to head with Sky Sports, which had dominated sport broadcasting in the UK and Ireland for many years.

Why did the BT Group make such a bold move into a market where it had very little experience or capability? BT Group is the world's oldest telecommunications company, dating back to 1846. As early companies amalgamated and were taken over or collapsed, the survivors were eventually transferred to state control under the old General Post Office. In 1980, the telecommunications division of the General Post Office became known as British Telecom and in 1984 the UK government sold more than 50% of the shares to the public. It sold the remainder in 1993. While the technology had undoubtedly changed, BT's business as a provider of telecommunication networks had remained fundamentally unchanged. Its only experience with television was BT Vision, a service it launched in 2006 to provide access to TV channels over the internet. BT Sport was very different – it involved the production and delivery of live programmes, which in turn required TV studios, presenters, production staff and outside broadcasting capability. In short, the company needed to establish an entirely different set of organizational capabilities from those traditionally found in the rest of BT Group.

Why did BT Group make such a big bet? Without question, the company had confronted its default future and concluded that it was not acceptable. As Patterson said in *The Sunday Times*,[112] "Revenues in the retail arm had been in decline and urgent action was required. Radical change was overdue."

BT Group understood its trajectory of strategic reality and the resulting default future. It also understood its trajectory of strategic opportunity, which shaped an informed choice on its strategic intent to establish a new, completely different strategic axis.

Most start-ups begin by establishing a business based on a single strategic axis, a case in point being Hailo.[113] Founded in London in 2010 by three taxi drivers and three internet entrepreneurs who initially raised more than $100 million in investment, Hailo is a digital platform that provides taxi drivers with a better view of potential passengers, how to attract these fares and how to track their overall performance. Customers can order a taxi via a smartphone app, and their digital confirmation includes the taxi's registration number along with the name, photo and mobile number of the driver. This new business, based on a clearly focused, innovative and digitally enabled strategic axis, now operates in a number of major cities around the world. Hailo and Uber – its more successful California-based competitor, which currently operates in more than 540 cities worldwide – operate on the same strategic axis and are seen as a significant threat to the traditional taxi companies, such as London's black cabs. In late 2016, Hailo was absorbed by mytaxi, a German e-hailing company belonging to Daimler Financial Services.

Another example is Airbnb.[114] Founded in San Francisco in August 2008, the company provides 'a trusted community marketplace for people to list, discover and book unique accommodation around the world – online or from a mobile phone or tablet'. Its value proposition also enables people to 'monetize their extra space'. As of mid-2016 it had more than 2 million properties listed, across 34,000 cities in 191 countries. At the time it claimed to have found accommodations for more than 60 million guests.

TripAdvisor was founded in 2000 on a strategic axis that provided a forum for travellers to post reviews of their travel experiences.[115] Its initial success allowed it to launch an additional strategic axis that gave users the ability to book hotel rooms, restaurant reservations and museum admissions. More recently it extended this strategic axis by offering flight bookings. TripAdvisor currently boasts 350 million visits a month and claims to be used by 70% of all millennials.

When a trajectory of strategic intent involves building a new strategic axis, it inevitably includes the development of new organizational capabilities. In some cases these are known and exist in other organizations in the same sector, as was the case with BT Sport. In other instances, completely new capabilities have to be developed while the new strategic axis is established, as was the case with Apple iTunes, Hailo, Airbnb and TripAdvisor. Developing new strategic axes can take time and requires substantial investment. Amazon took ten years from its inception in 1994 to turn a profit; even today it generates very little income from its $110 billion-plus in revenue, choosing to reinvest in growth instead. Ocado, a British online grocery distributor, took 14 years and more than £350 million in investment before becoming profitable.

Something all these examples have in common is that their strategic axes are based on a technology platform – one that then enables existing strategic axes to be extended, or new ones added. Uber,[116] for example, recently launched UberEATS, a restaurant delivery service.

NEW STRATEGIC AXES CAN ALSO BE ACQUIRED

In early 2016, BT Group established an additional strategic axis to its business through its £12.5 billion acquisition of EE, Britain's largest mobile phone group at the time.[117] The deal added more than 25 million customers to BT's business and re-established it in the mobile phone space, which it had exited more than a decade earlier following the demerger and subsequent £18 billion sale of its Cellnet business (later rebranded O2) to Telefónica.

Over the last 30 years, there have been a number of instances where large and successful IT service companies have launched a new strategic axis, with the intention of offering their customers higher-value management consulting services. Many realized this strategic intent by acquiring established management consulting firms. Examples include Computer Science Corporation's (CSC) acquisition of Index Group in 1988, Electronic Data Systems' (EDS) $596 million acquisition of AT Kearney in 1995, Cap Gemini's $11 billion acquisition of the consulting arm of Ernst & Young in 2000, and IBM's $3.5 billion acquisition of PwC Consulting in 2002.

As discussed previously, few acquisitions are truly successful and IT service companies' acquisition of management consulting firms is no exception. Following its acquisition by CSC in 1988, CSC Index was allowed to operate virtually independently until around 1997, at which point CSC decided to integrate it into its mainstream IT services business. As a result, it lost its distinctiveness and only a few Index consultants remained, with many going on to establish their own independent consulting firms. EDS's acquisition of AT Kearney in 1995 was no more successful, and in 2005 it once again became an independent company.[118]

After divesting their management consulting businesses, PwC and Ernst & Young (now EY) each went on to re-establish a management consulting strategic axis. In 2014, PwC strengthened this axis by merging with the strategy firm Booz & Co to form Strategy&.

More recently, on 13 June, 2016, Microsoft announced its $26.2 billion bid for LinkedIn, the professional social network.[119] As LinkedIn reported a 2015 loss of around $165 million on revenues of $3 billion, one can only assume that the rationale for the acquisition – the third largest in the history of the tech industry – was to establish a new strategic axis that will enable Microsoft to compete with the likes of Google and Amazon.

In all these examples, leadership confronted the default future of their organization and concluded that a different trajectory was needed, one that involved establishing one or more new strategic axes. How they chose to achieve this was to acquire a business that already operated on the target axis, thereby gaining the necessary organizational capabilities and market presence. How successful they were in integrating and preserving what they acquired is another matter.

NEW STRATEGIC AXES ESTABLISHED THROUGH PARTNERSHIPS

New strategic axes can also be established through partnerships or joint ventures. One example is that of Wm Morrison Supermarkets plc (Morrisons), the UK's fourth-largest supermarket chain. Unusually for a chain of its size, for some time it did not offer an online purchase and delivery service. This changed in 2013 when it announced[120] a £216 million, 25-year contract with Ocado, an independent online grocery distributor. The partnership gave Morrisons access to Ocado's online ordering technology, distribution warehouses and organizational capabilities, all of which would have taken considerable time and investment to build in-house.

Ocado had been launched as a concept in January 2000 and started trading as a business, in partnership with the food retailer Waitrose, in January 2002. It floated on the London Stock Exchange in 2010 and turned its first profit in 2014. Waitrose, which had 5.2% of the UK grocery market in 2014, was its first customer and initial investment partner. Part of the John Lewis Partnership, Waitrose is often known as the 'up-market grocer'. In 2011, Waitrose launched its own online delivery service in direct competition with its Ocado partnership.

In early 2016, Morrisons went one stage further through a deal to supply Amazon's[121] customers with thousands of items from its fresh, chilled and frozen food line. Although Amazon already offered relatively small-scale grocery services through Amazon Fresh (in the US) and Amazon Pantry (in the UK), its deal with Morrisons extensively broadened the range of products available to high-volume subscribers to the Amazon Prime service, and established a new strategic axis for Morrisons as a wholesaler. In June 2017, Amazon announced a $13.7 billion deal to aquire Whole Foods Market.

On 3 August, 2012, the Bank of Ireland and the UK Post Office announced[122] that they had agreed to continue their financial services joint venture until 2023. Through that partnership the Bank of Ireland is responsible for product development and delivery, and the Post Office for product marketing and sales through its network of 11,500 branches. The partnership, formed in 2004, allowed the Post Office to offer a new source of value to its customers and established a new strategic axis for the organization. Rather than build this capability in-house, or acquire its own bank (which, being owned by the UK government, it was not able to do), it chose to realize its strategic intent through partnership with a financial services organization that already had a banking licence in the UK. In 2012 this partnership served 2.8 million customers, had a savings book of more than £17 billion and had a loan book of more than £3 billion.

In 2004 Nike came up with an idea to establish a new source of value for its customers, one that would allow them to get more from the running experience. But in order to make it happen the sportswear company needed a technology partner, so CEO Mark Parker called a friend, Apple CEO Steve Jobs. As a result, a collaboration to bridge the gaps between sports, electronics and entertainment was born. Some two years later, on 23 May, 2006, the first jointly developed product was announced.[123] The Nike+iPod sports kit had an electronic sensor inserted under the inner sole of a new Nike running shoe that communicated with a wireless receiver attached to Apple's iPod nano music player. The device gave voice prompts, interjected while music was playing, that told runners how far they'd gone and at what pace. The iPod kept track of duration, distance and other information on each run, and the data could then be uploaded to a Mac or PC, and from there to a website called Nikeplus.com, where users could track progress, set goals and share results. The collaboration continued with the 2012 launch of the Nike+ FuelBand activity tracker, which was worn on the wrist. However, in 2014 Nike ceased development of these wearable devices, prompting speculation on whether the collaboration with Apple would continue. When Apple launched the iWatch2 in 2016 it also launched a Nike+ version, signalling that the collaboration remained in place.

EXISTING STRATEGIC AXES CAN ALSO BE EXTENDED

In the examples above, the trajectory of strategic intent was to establish new strategic axes, either through acquisition, through partnership or by building capability in-house. But strategic intent could also include repositioning the organization along one or more of its existing strategic axes.

When GE concluded it was already in the information business, and that it could deliver greater value to its customers through the data its machines generated, it extended an existing strategic axis rather than creating a new one. GE, like many other industrial companies, traditionally made its money from the sale of its machines and after-sales service. In more recent years, it had repositioned itself along this strategic axis by leasing rather than selling its machines and being paid 'by the hour' for their use. It was also responsible for all planned maintenance and repairs. The added value is that customers get the use of the machines with none of the hassle associated with ownership. The model is also attractive to GE, as the more the machines are used, the greater their revenue generation. But this model only works when the machines are well maintained and serviced during periods of planned downtime. This requires a level of planning that can only be achieved with constant performance monitoring through built-in sensors.

GE then took this model a step further by offering to manage the performance of the machines, and in return get paid for their power output and efficiency. In order to do this, it needed not only access to the data provided by the onboard sensors – which it already had – but also a powerful analytics capability to derive value from the data. For example, increasing the average number of miles that a locomotive travels each day can be worth millions of dollars in additional annual profit for the operator.

As described earlier, GE then made the technology available to others, creating an industrial data-analytics internet platform on which third parties could build, and sell, industrial apps. In return, GE charged a commission for the use of this platform. By offering this platform to third parties, the company created for itself a new strategic axis and offered a new source of value to new and existing customers. Significantly, it was able to do this as a result of the technology and the organizational capabilities it had built while continually extending and repositioning itself along its existing strategic axes.

The strategic intent of BBVA, Spain's second-largest bank, is to become a 'digital bank' by extending its existing strategic axis through digital transformation.[124] It has spent around $200 million in the last three years acquiring and investing in new digital banks and fintech start-ups. It also set up a separate venture capital subsidiary based in San Francisco and London to attract new businesses that are wary of dealing with major global banks. Many of BBVA's 66 million customers are in emerging markets in Latin America, and in 2015 just under 30% of consumer loans in Mexico were issued digitally, up from 2% the previous year. BBVA's strategic intent is to make mobile banking so attractive that in these countries it does not have to invest in the bricks and mortar of traditional bank branches.

STRATEGIC AXES CAN ALSO BE EXITED

IBM has repeatedly reinvented itself by establishing new strategic axes, extending existing ones and exiting others. When it launched its first personal computer on 12 August, 1981, it not only established a new strategic axis within the IBM Corporation but also launched a whole new industry. The PC Convertible, IBM's first laptop computer, was introduced on 3 April, 1986, extending its PC strategic axis. It was without question a successful strategic axis for IBM that delivered great value for both its customers its and shareholders. But in 2005, after only 19 years, the company decided that the potential for PCs to drive more value was coming to an end. As a result, it sold the business to a Chinese manufacturer, Lenovo. In 2014 IBM made a similar decision when it sold its x86 server unit, also to Lenovo, for $2.3 billion, removing another strategic axis from its business.

Sometimes an organization has to exit strategic axes as a result of past strategic decisions – which turned out to be bad ones – and the subsequent need to repair its balance sheet. One such example is the UK's Co-operative Group,[125] whose banking division got into difficulty in 2013, resulting in a £2.5 billion loss. As a result, the company sold its life insurance and pensions business for £219 million, its pharmacy business for £620 million, its farms for £249 million and Sunwin, its cash and valuables transportation business, for £41.5 million. It also sold 80% of its banking division to a number of US investors, and in February 2017 the bank was put up for sale.

As discussed previously, the UK supermarket retailer Tesco exited some strategic axes and scaled back others in order to return to profitability and improve its balance sheet. This included selling businesses that had operated in the UK, Turkey and Asia.

OPTIONS FOR REALIZING STRATEGIC INTENT

What these examples show is that an organization has essentially four options open to it when considering how best to realize its strategic intent: making an acquisition, establishing partnerships, building new organizational capabilities, divesting certain assets – or some combination of these. Each option has its advantages and disadvantages, and together they define the organization's trajectory of strategic intent.

AN ORGANIZATION'S STRATEGIC SIGNATURE IS UNIQUE

All organizations in the same sector could potentially operate on the same strategic axes, but where they choose to position themselves on each axis is likely to be different. We call this uniqueness their *strategic signature.*

An organization's strategic signature can be represented in a number of ways. Figure 6ii illustrates the use of 'slider bars' to represent the strategic signature of a retail bank, where each slider bar represents a strategic axis and the position of the slider indicates the strategic positioning along the spectrum of strategic possibilities on each axis. Typically, the left of the slider bar represents the less ambitious or more limited strategic intent and the right the more ambitious, often in terms of its range of products or services.

Strategic signatures are an effective way of defining an organization's strategic intent, as they define not only what an organization intends to do – its strategic axes – but also the extent to which it intends to do it. It also helps to define explicitly which strategic axes an organization chooses *not* to pursue.

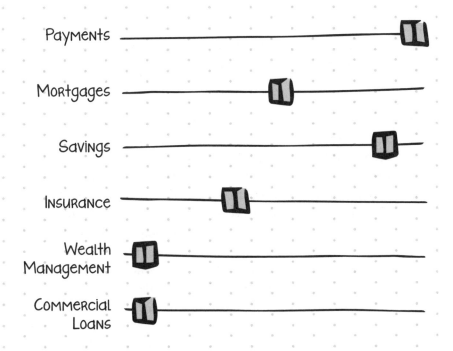

FIGURE 6ii:

Strategic signature represented
as a set of slider bars

HOW STRATEGIC SIGNATURES CHANGE OVER TIME

When Amazon was launched in 1994, it had only one strategic axis: that of e-retailing, initially focusing on books. Over the years, it continually repositioned itself along this strategic axis to sell CDs, DVDs, online music and many other products provided by third-party suppliers. Today it is possible to get virtually anything from Amazon.

In 2002, Amazon chose to establish a new strategic axis when it launched Amazon Web Services. Over the years it has repositioned itself along this 'web services' axis by launching Amazon Simple Storage Service (Amazon S3) in 2006 and Mobile Ads API for developers in 2013.

On 7 September, 2006, it launched Amazon Unbox, a video-streaming service that it renamed Amazon Video-on-Demand in September 2008. On 22 February, 2011, this was again rebranded as Amazon Instant Video when it added access to 5,000 movies and TV shows for Amazon Prime members. On 16 November, 2010, it launched Amazon Studios, a production unit that develops television shows, movies and comics from online submissions and crowd-sourced feedback. On 30 July, 2015, Amazon announced it had hired Jeremy Clarkson, Richard Hammond and James May – the three presenters previously of BBC's globally popular motoring programme *Top Gear* – to produce a motoring show called *The Grand Tour* for Amazon Prime Video. The reported budget for an initial 36 episodes was £160 million, making it Amazon's most expensive TV production to date. The first show became globally available on 18 November, 2016, and was well received by fans and critics alike.

In 2007, Amazon established another strategic axis when it launched the Kindle e-book reader. Over the next nine years it continually repositioned itself on this strategic axis and in April 2016 the eighth-generation Kindle was released.

In 2010, the company started work on a new strategic axis, that of a mobile phone it had designed and developed, known as the Amazon Fire. This innovative 3D-enabled smartphone had four front-facing cameras and a gyroscope to track the user's movements. It also included X-Ray, used for identifying and finding information about media; Mayday, a 24-hour customer service tool; and Firefly, a tool that automatically recognizes text, sounds and objects, then offers a way to buy recognized items through Amazon's online store. The smartphone was announced on 18 June, 2014, and launched as an AT&T exclusive on 25 July, 2014.

In addition to establishing new strategic axes, Amazon has continued to extend its existing strategic ones and the value they deliver. For example, in 2000 it launched Amazon Marketplace, where businesses and sole traders can sell their products directly on the Amazon website. In 2012 it launched Amazon Supply, targeting the B2B (business-to-business) market, which it relaunched in 2015 as Amazon Business. And, as we discussed earlier, in 2016 Amazon extended its online grocery business in the UK through its partnership with Morrisons.

Amazon's strategic signature has certainly changed from the time it was launched in 1994. Its continued success is a result of pursuing new sources of value by introducing new strategic axes and repositioning itself along its existing strategic axes in order to generate greater value.

WHEN CHOICES ARE STRATEGIC

If the essence of strategy is making choices on the trajectory of strategic intent, how can we be sure that the choices are informed rather than 'shots in the dark'? Making informed choices involves having a good understanding of the implications of those choices, knowing what outcomes they are likely to bring and what subsequent action will be needed. An effective way of achieving this is to have a good understanding of your organization's trajectory of strategic reality and trajectory of strategic opportunity. But is this sufficient? In reality, no – while the uncertainty can be reduced, it cannot be eliminated entirely. Therefore, some choices are truly strategic in that once implemented they are difficult, if not impossible, to reverse or undo.

WHEN CHANGING YOUR STRATEGIC SIGNATURE DOES NOT WORK OUT

There are many examples where organizations tried to change their strategic signature and it didn't work out as they intended. Some of these we discussed in chapter 1. Here are a few additional examples.

In July 2005, Rupert Murdoch's News Corporation (News Corp) bought the social networking site Myspace for $580 million,[126] outbidding rival Viacom. Within a year Myspace's value had tripled, and between 2005 and early 2009 it was the largest social networking site worldwide. But in 2009 it was overtaken by Facebook and its visitor numbers and revenue began to decline. By June 2011 its number of employees had fallen from a peak of around 1,600 to a mere 200. In late February 2011, News Corp officially put the now-struggling business up for sale at an estimated value of between $50 million and $200 million. Losses in the last quarter of 2010 were $156 million, more than double the previous year's, which dragged down the otherwise strong results of News Corp. On 31 May, 2011, the deadline for bids passed with none above the reserve figure of $100 million. In June 2011, Specific Media and pop singer Justin Timberlake bought MySpace for $35 million.

The acquisition of MySpace established a new strategic axis for News Corp, one intended to complement its other strategic axes by engaging a sector of the market that consumed news, information and entertainment differently. Why did News Corp fail in what appeared to be a straightforward acquisition of a successful and rapidly growing business? While we don't have a definitive answer – although the popularity of Facebook was certainly a factor – our view is that News Corp did not have the organizational capabilities we talked about in chapter 3. In the end, it lacked the capabilities it needed to run and grow a social-media-based business.

As previously mentioned, in 2011 HP acquired 87.3% of UK-based Autonomy for $10.3 billion. It did this to establish its position in the rapidly developing field of Big Data, also known as data analytics. After the acquisition, most of Autonomy's senior team left and just one year later HP wrote off some $8.8 billion of its value. The due diligence process was subsequently questioned and lawsuits followed. Why did HP fail to realize the potential of what it had acquired? Again, we don't have the complete answer, but at the time the press reported that Autonomy staff felt stifled by HP's bureaucracy and HP didn't know how to nurture a relatively new, fast-growth business.

Earlier we mentioned that in 2010 Amazon established a new strategic axis focused on the smartphone market. In 2014 it announced a $170 million write-down of costs associated with the phone and in August 2015 withdrew it from the market.[127] By any measure, Amazon is seen as a successful organization, but even the best and brightest sometimes get it wrong.

In 2014 Microsoft attempted to reposition itself on one of its existing strategic axes, namely its mobile phone business, through the acquisition of Nokia's phone production unit for $7.2 billion.[128] Its aim was to strengthen its position against Apple's iPhone and those powered by Google's Android operating system. Its strategic intent was to move into the device manufacturing business, so that it could design both the software and hardware of its products. It was a move that Microsoft's CEO, Steve Ballmer, hoped would bring the kind of success that Apple had traditionally enjoyed.

Unfortunately, Microsoft's strategic intent did not turn into strategic reality and 18 months later the company announced it would eliminate 7,800 jobs and take a restructuring charge of $750–$850 million related to the layoffs, plus a $7.6 billion impairment charge.[129] In Q1 2016 the global market share of Windows smartphones fell below 1% and the company sold its entry-level feature phones business for $350 million. It also announced a further 1,850 job losses and the closure of its Finnish mobile phone unit, including a major R&D site.

A TARGET STRATEGIC SIGNATURE CAN HELP STEER A TRAJECTORY OF STRATEGIC INTENT

A target strategic signature can be an effective way of steering an organization along its trajectory of strategic intent. If articulated in a way that employees across the organization can understand, it is a powerful tool for pulling the organization to its target trajectory. It's important to remember that organizations are not like machines – they cannot be programmed, but they can be guided and managed onto a trajectory that leads to a target future. Strategic signatures are a way of making that guidance explicit, as they define where and how the organization wants to operate in the future. They give guidance on what needs to be done to pull the organization away from its current trajectory of strategic reality to its target trajectory of strategic intent.

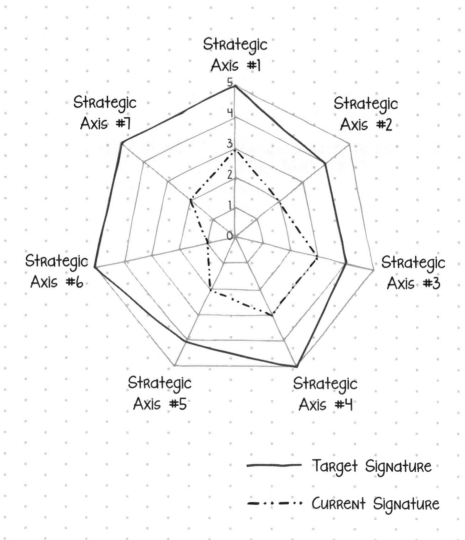

FIGURE 6iii:

Example of current and target strategic signatures presented as a spider diagram

STRATEGIC SIGNATURES CAN ALSO DESCRIBE CURRENT STRATEGIC REALITY

Our focus up until now has been on using strategic signatures as an expression of what leaders want their organization to be in the future. But in reality, all organizations also have a *current* strategic signature, which defines how they operate today. The current strategic signature may not be explicitly defined – or widely understood – but it is a representation of an organization's current strategic reality.

Understanding the current strategic signature helps inform what needs to be done to make the target strategic signature a reality. Yet, most leaders focus on the wrong future – the one they hope to achieve rather than the one they're likely to get. As a result, they're often surprised and disappointed when the organization doesn't respond in the way they had hoped, and they continue on the same trajectory as if nothing had happened. What they often do not appreciate is that their trajectory is determined by a set of powerful navigating forces that define the current strategic signature and, as described earlier, act as invisible tramlines carrying it to its default future.

By describing the current strategic signature and comparing it with the target signature, it is possible to assess the magnitude of the gap and formulate actions to make the target signature a reality. The bigger the gap, the greater the challenges associated with implementing the strategy. It's worth remembering that a strategy that is not achievable and sustainable can be as damaging as having no strategy at all.

Figure 6iii illustrates the gap between current and target strategic signatures. It also provides an alternative to the slider bars in figure 6ii as a way of representing a strategic signature.

DELIVERING STRATEGIC SIGNATURES THROUGH A BALANCED PORTFOLIO OF INITIATIVES

As we discussed in chapter 1, the majority of strategies do not deliver their strategic intent. One of the principal reasons is that organizations try to do too much, too quickly. Attempting to introduce new strategic axes while extending existing ones and exiting others typically results in a portfolio of change initiatives that is not balanced. We can look at this from four perspectives. First, the portfolio of change initiatives might not be prioritized over time. Second, the resources available to execute the change initiatives don't always match those required. Third, the resultant level of change is often greater than the organization can reasonably absorb. And fourth, leadership and management may not have the bandwidth to deal with the inevitable governance, prioritization and decision issues that will arise.

How can a better balance be achieved? While such an exercise is context-specific and depends upon each organization's capacity and capability for change, our experience is that an assessment based upon a few key criteria can be quite effective. If an organization is engaged in one strategic initiative, it's reasonable to assume that inititative should be achievable; if it's involved in two it will be a stretch; three will pose a challenge; and four or more will almost certainly be unfocused and likely to fail. The logic is that each strategic change initiative requires levels of resources, time, effort, money, leadership and management time that are typically underestimated. Furthermore, the risk profile increases exponentially, rather than linearly, as additional initiatives are added to the change portfolio.

In undertaking such an assessment it's important to make a clear distinction between truly strategic initiatives and those aimed at implementing incremental change. As previously discussed, strategic initiatives are those aimed at changing an organization's trajectory of strategic reality to align with its trajectory of strategic intent. They are strategic because once implemented they're difficult, if not impossible, to reverse or undo, while incremental change can be reversed. Furthermore, delivering incremental change is something that's expected of all managers.

Leaders of organizations are ambitious, and rightly so, yet it is this ambition that often makes achieving such a balance quite challenging. Successfully developing and implementing strategy requires *collective* leadership, which means taking a shared position on the target strategic signature and making choices that balance what is best for the organization with what is collectively achievable. Unfortunately, it's often wrongly assumed that a successful strategy for the organization is the sum of individual, divisional or functional strategies. That's rarely the case.

STRATEGIC SIGNATURES ARE AN EFFECTIVE TOOL FOR ACHIEVING ALIGNMENT

Strategic signatures can be a powerful way of ensuring that leadership is aligned around the organization's trajectory of strategic intent. Strategic signatures can be used to facilitate debate and discussion in order to create shared understanding of, alignment around, and collective commitment to, the target future.

Furthermore, non-executive directors are often asked to validate the strategy developed by the executive team, while not having been involved in formulating the strategy and perhaps not being as informed about it as they should be. We argue that strategic signatures are a powerful way of creating informed debate and discussion between executives and non-executives about the choice of those axes, the positioning on each axis and the organizational capabilities needed to deliver success.

THE CHAPTER IN SUMMARY

Defining a trajectory of strategic intent involves making informed choices about the organization's strategic signature and the means by which the strategic axes are established or strengthened. This could be achieved through acquisition, partnership or building the necessary organizational capabilities internally. The strategic axes define not only what an organization does but also, of equal importance, the extent to which it does it.

While being appropriately ambitious, the choices that define the trajectory of strategic intent should be informed through a thorough understanding of the trajectories of strategic reality and strategic opportunity. And, the organizational capabilities needed to establish a new strategic axis or to extend an existing one must be understood and plans developed to put them in place.

A strategic signature is a powerful way of communicating strategic intent. It's a simple representation of something that for many can seem quite theoretical and complex. It's also an effective tool for aligning stakeholders by building a shared understanding of, and commitment to, the strategic shifts needed to change their organization's current trajectory.

An important implication of operating on a new strategic axis – or repositioning the organization on an existing axis – is that it inevitably requires very different organizational capabilities.

FIVE QUESTIONS FOR REFLECTION

1. What are the key strategic axes of your organization? How would you describe the value that each of them delivers?

2. What is your strategic intent for each of these strategic axes, in terms of repositioning your value proposition along each of them?

3. Does your strategic intent include establishing new strategic axes? If so, by what means – build, acquire or partner?

4. Is it your strategic intent to exit one or more strategic axes?

5. Is the change portfolio to deliver your target strategic signature balanced?

CHAPTER 7

MAKING STRATEGIC INTENT MEANINGFUL TO OTHERS

*"Life is really simple, but we insist
on making it complicated."*

Confucius (551–479 BC)
Chinese teacher, politician and philosopher

In the previous chapter we talked about how strategic intent can be defined in terms of a strategic signature – the goal being to communicate your strategic choices and resulting strategic shifts along each of your organization's strategic axes, in a way that's understandable to everyone.

But is this enough? Will the target strategic signature make the choices behind the strategic intent meaningful to others? Is it enough to help employees understand what they need to do differently to bring about the change of trajectory? We don't think so, and what's more we don't think that it's reasonable to expect people – particularly those who have not been involved in the strategy development process – to translate strategic intent into operational reality without appropriate guidance and support.

All too often strategies are too complicated, too detailed or too vague to be meaningful to the people who are expected to implement them. They lack meaningful definitions of how things should operate in the future, what organizational capabilities and individual competencies need to be established, and what challenges will be faced. In this chapter, we will focus on what we see as the transition point between the development of strategy and its execution. It is a pivot point that makes the strategic shifts more meaningful to those who are expected to make the strategic intent a reality – the people within the organization. We believe the best way of achieving this transition is through the use of *operating principles* and *design principles*.

OPERATING PRINCIPLES MAKE STRATEGIC CHOICES MORE MEANINGFUL

The trajectory of strategic intent is the result of a set of informed choices made during the strategy development process. These choices can be articulated through a set of operating principles, where a principle is defined as a 'conscious choice between two equally valid alternatives'. In essence they describe how the organization will operate and behave in the future.

For example, if an organization has made the strategic choice to continue growing organically rather than through acquisition, it is declaring where it intends to operate along one or more of its strategic axes. The thinking is that if this choice (along with others) is realized, the organization's current trajectory will change to one that is in line with its strategic intent. This strategic choice can be articulated as follows:

'We will grow organically.'
   as opposed to…
'We will grow through acquisition.'

Note that the operating principle not only defines the intent – *to grow organically* – but also what it intends **not** to do – *grow through acquisition*. It's as important – if not more important – to be clear about what we've decided NOT to do as what we've decided to do. Defining an equally valid alternative principle, the 'as opposed to…', does exactly this. An operating principle therefore defines two choices, not one. It defines how the organization intends to operate in the future and, just as important, how it intends *not* to operate in the future. Obviously there will be implications of acting in accordance with a new operating principle that will need to be managed, something we will talk about later.

In many respects, translating strategic intent into a set of operating principles is the first stage of executing strategy. Not only is it an effective way of articulating the strategic choices made, it's also a powerful way of engaging employees across the organization. In the example above, the strategic intent is to maintain the existing strategic axes and then to reposition the organization along one or more of these axes by *continuing to grow organically*. If this operating principle was then shared with product development, customer service, IT and finance, for example, would it have equal meaning to them all? Probably not. But if these groups of people are given the opportunity to define their own operating principles that are in line with, and supportive of, the overarching operating principles, then it will make the strategic intent more meaningful to them and bring about a greater degree of alignment, engagement and commitment.

Let's explore further how changes to an organization's strategic signature can be made more meaningful by articulating strategic intent through operating principles. We'll do this through four quite different examples.

OPERATING PRINCIPLE #1: 'WE VALUE CUSTOMERS BASED UPON THEIR LIFETIME RELATIONSHIP WITH US'

All organizations recognize that customers are valuable, but some customers are more valuable than others. An organization could operate on the basis of – at one end of the spectrum – valuing the totality of a customer's lifetime relationship or – at the other end – the value of the current transaction. If the strategic intent was to focus on maximizing lifetime customer value, the operating principle could be:

'We value customers based upon their lifetime relationship with us.'
as opposed to...
'We value our customers based upon their latest transaction.'

As we will discuss later, every operating principle has implications, which have to be understood and managed. For example, the operating principle above is easy to articulate, but, as many organizations have found, it is difficult to realize without having the systems in place to provide front-line staff with an integrated view of the products and services that the customer has received over time.

OPERATING PRINCIPLE #2: 'WE ARE SELF-SUFFICIENT WITHIN OUR SUPPLY CHAIN'

An organization's supply chain is critical to its success. If it fails, then its customers will be let down; if it's over-engineered, it will drive up costs. A strategic choice is therefore to determine the degree to which an organization is self-sufficient, in terms of what it owns and controls, across all stages of the supply chain. One option could be to become self-sufficient; another would be to partner with outside suppliers to the maximum extent possible. If the strategic intent was to be as self-sufficient as possible, the operating principle could be:

'We are self-sufficient in everything we do within our supply chain.'
as opposed to...
'Our supply chain comprises third-party suppliers that are individually and collectively accountable for meeting our customers' demands.'

One of the implications of this operating principle is that the organization would need all of the capabilities necessary to fulfil all steps in the supply chain, up to the required level of performance.

OPERATING PRINCIPLE #3: 'WE PROVIDE CUSTOMERS WITH AN OMNI-CHANNEL EXPERIENCE'

People like browsing online; they also like checking things out for real in stores and then buying them online. Some like to ensure the product meets their requirements by 'chatting' online with a customer services agent, while others like to talk to them directly. Others like to order online and then collect their purchase from the store. And some people, whether they're buying a fashion product, a household appliance, or an airfare and hotel accommodation for a holiday, want to be able to switch channels at any stage throughout their purchasing journey. They also expect the supplier to have a complete record of their journey, so it's not necessary to start all over again when they switch channels. As we've said earlier, this is known as providing the customer with an omni-channel experience. If the strategic intent was to provide this experience, the operating principle could be:

> 'We provide our customers with an omni-channel experience throughout all stages of their purchasing journey.'
> **as opposed to...**
> 'Our buying channels are independent of one another.'

The implications are that products and services need to be omnipresent across all channels, pricing should be consistent and the technology must be in place to allow the customer to switch channels at any point throughout the transaction.

OPERATING PRINCIPLE #4: 'EVERYONE IS ACCOUNTABLE FOR ACHIEVING CUSTOMER-FOCUSED OUTCOMES'

One of the challenges many organizations face is getting their staff to be more accountable for achieving outcomes of real value, rather than following scripted processes and waiting for instructions. If the strategic intent is to create a culture where employees are more accountable for outcomes, the operating principle could be:

> 'Everyone is accountable for achieving customer-focused outcomes.'
> **as opposed to...**
> 'Everyone follows process and focuses on the tasks they are given.'

One implication of this principle is that some staff will need to change their mindset and attitude towards the role they play, and rethink their relationships with customers and colleagues. A further implication is that training may also be needed in order for staff to be better able to do what's expected of them.

The power of articulating strategy through a set of operating principles is that it makes the strategic intent meaningful to people across the organization. It tells them which choices have been made, and which were considered but consciously rejected. It also defines how the leadership team expects the organization to operate in the future and provides guidance on how everyone, at every level, can contribute through their daily decisions and actions. Changing the trajectory of an organization is a bit like changing the direction of an ocean liner – it takes time. The more people understand that putting the target operating principles into practice will change the trajectory of their organization, the more likely they are to contribute.

The examples above illustrate individual operating principles. Obviously, more would be required (in our experience, typically between 8 and 12) to fully articulate how an organization intends to operate differently and change its trajectory. These enterprise-wide operating principles would then be supported by additional operating principles for the different functions and departments that will in turn need to change how they operate.

PRINCIPLES ARE UNDERSTOOD THROUGH THEIR IMPLICATIONS

Making choices about strategic intent and articulating them through a set of operating principles is necessary, but not entirely sufficient. As noted, it's also important to understand their implications. Understanding the implications then informs what subsequent decisions and actions must be taken to operationalize the principle. In the first example above, the implications of the principle 'we will grow organically' as opposed to 'we will grow through acquisition' could be:

- The need to build the capability to capture new customers, understand the value of different customer segments and retain a higher proportion of targeted current customers
- The need to extend the existing range of products, services and channels across existing strategic axes
- The need to de-emphasize, or redirect, resources previously assigned to acquisitions and integration.

If the implications of an operating principle are not significant, it suggests that the strategic intent is not ambitious and that the target trajectory is not significantly different from the one the organization is currently travelling along. If the implications are highly significant, it may suggest that the strategic choices, which define the strategic intent, may need to be revisited. And, an operating principle may not have the same implications across all parts of an organization. For example, the implications of the operating principle 'we will grow organically' might be quite significant for sales and marketing, but less so for product development.

Let's think about the ramifications of reversing the operating principle:

'We will grow through acquisition.'
as opposed to…
'We will grow organically.'

The implications would be quite different, as the organization would need to:

- Be capable of actively seeking suitable acquisitions and undertaking due diligence
- Have the funding available to make acquisitions
- Have the capabilities necessary to successfully integrate acquisitions without destroying their inherent value.

The first and last implications are particularly important, as all too often organizations develop a new strategy and completely ignore the organizational capabilities needed for future success. Defining the implications develops understanding of the subsequent decisions and actions that will be needed. Assessing the implications also provides insight into the degree of difficulty, time and effort that will be involved in successfully operationalizing the operating principles. Remember, the purpose of operating principles is to help the organization steer itself away from its current trajectory and onto its chosen trajectory of strategic intent. For example, if an organization has never made an acquisition, it is unlikely to have the organizational capabilities needed to:

- Identify potential acquisition targets
- Carry out appropriate due diligence
- Manage a potentially complex integration that involves the convergence of operating models, systems, technology, people and culture
- Align, rationalise and consolidate a broader portfolio of products and services, customer value propositions, customer/market segments and sales channels

- Manage a larger, more complex organization, with a new governance framework and vastly different roles and accountabilities.

The implications of an operating principle could be that new organizational capabilities are required, but also that existing capabilities need to be intentionally weakened or eliminated. Organizational capabilities are a powerful means of pulling the organization onto its target trajectory, but they are equally effective at anchoring it to its current trajectory.

In using operating principles to articulate strategic intent, it is not that one principle is right and one is wrong: both are valid choices. It's about articulating the choice, understanding the implications and moving forward with the decisions and actions needed to operationalize the principle.

This will be illustrated through three different examples of operating principles and their implications, in three different organizations. In each case the situation has been simplified to illustrate the approach.

OPERATING PRINCIPLES CASE EXAMPLE 1: ENTERPRISE HORIZONTAL INTEGRATION

Companies with multiple divisions spanning different geographies often struggle with what type of organization they should be and what role the corporate headquarters function plays. Group CEOs often ask, 'Why do we replicate everything we do across divisions and geographies? There must be synergies and opportunities for cost savings.'

While there are many possible models, the one advocated by Christopher Bartlett and Sumantra Ghoshal in their book *Managing across Borders*[130] is called the transnational organization. An initial set of operating principles for this type of entity could include:

#1: *'We operate as a horizontally integrated company, with the highest possible level of common and shared processes, systems and resources, while recognizing the need for authentic differences.'*
  as opposed to…
  'We operate as a holding company comprising independent, self-contained businesses.'

#2: 'The role of the country head is primarily one of sales, marketing and customer relationship management.'
as opposed to...
'The role of the country head is to act as the CEO of an independent business.'

#3: 'Product development, customer support and back-office functions are provided by regional shared service centres.'
as opposed to...
'Each country is self-sufficient in everything it does.'

The implications of the operating principles could include:
1. We will measure profit and loss by product and customer, rather than by country.
2. The role and decision rights of the country head will be reduced.
3. Rationalization of products and services happens at a global and regional level.
4. Rationalization and consolidation of business processes and supporting IT platforms happens at a global and regional level.
5. We will create a number of regional shared service centres.
6. Staff are viewed, managed, developed and deployed as enterprise-wide assets.

OPERATING PRINCIPLES CASE EXAMPLE 2:
AGILE IT ORGANIZATION

In many organizations, the IT function is seen as an inhibitor of change, rather than the enabler. Business colleagues get frustrated when IT gets in the way of them implementing their strategies, and IT staff feel that business colleagues don't appreciate the complexity of managing, maintaining and enhancing the core legacy IT systems.

As a result, the strategic intent of many CIOs is to make their IT organization more agile and responsive to business needs, and to spend a greater proportion of available resources on enabling business change than on maintaining current applications. The initial set of operating principles to articulate this strategic intent could include:

#1: *'Business and IT colleagues collaborate in the discovery and definition of requirements and solutions.'*
   as opposed to...
   'IT acts as an order taker.'

#2: *'IT projects are prioritized and managed as an enterprise-wide portfolio that is jointly governed by business and IT.'*
   as opposed to...
   'IT projects are prioritized by the CIO based on demands from the business.'

#3: *'IT projects follow the most appropriate software development approaches, including that of the Agile, Scrum and DevOps.'*
   as opposed to...
   'All IT projects follow the linear and sequential life-cycle/ waterfall approach.'

The implications of these operating principles could include:

1. IT colleagues need the confidence and capabilities to collaborate with business colleagues throughout all stages of a project.
2. The structure of the IT organization should reflect the project-based approach to people-resource management.
3. Flexible deployment of both internal and external resources will be necessary, using an extended workbench approach.
4. Agile development tools and techniques will coexist with more traditional development approaches.
5. Business and IT will jointly manage the portfolio of IT development.

OPERATING PRINCIPLES CASE EXAMPLE 3:
DIGITIZING IN THE INDUSTRIAL SPACE

Our third example is based on our interpretation of GE's strategic intent to digitize in the industrial space by becoming an infrastructure business underpinned by its Predix industrial data-analytics internet platform.

The operating principles to articulate this strategic intent could include:

#1: *'We deliver increasing value from machines that are managed by the applications on our Predix platform.'*
   as opposed to...
   'Our only sources of value are the machines we sell and the after-sales service we provide.'

#2: *'We operate within an ecosystem that goes beyond our traditional organizational boundaries.'*
   as opposed to...
   'We operate within the traditional life cycle of our products.'

#3: *'Our Predix platform will be open, allowing third parties to develop applications that manage our machines and those manufactured by other companies.'*
   as opposed to...
   'Our Predix platform is limited to GE-developed applications, managing only GE-manufactured machines.'

The implications of these operating principles could include:
1. The way we develop, market, sell, deliver and manage our machines needs to reflect our new value proposition.
2. We must better understand the business of our customers (and their customers) so we can deliver value through the analytics we bring to bear.
3. New capabilities will be required across the organization, beyond software engineering and data analytics.

4. New pricing models should reflect the additional value our Predix applications bring.
5. Standards will need to be defined and quality tests formulated for applications developed by third parties before they're made available on the Predix platform.

These examples illustrate three quite different strategic intents:

- Transitioning to a horizontally integrated enterprise
- Becoming an agile IT organization
- Establishing a new strategic axis based upon a platform-based value proposition.

How these strategic intents are to be realized can be expressed in terms of a small number of carefully worded operating principles. (In these examples we've kept it to three, but in practice there would invariably be more.) In turn, these operating principles have implications that must be understood. It is this understanding that drives the decisions and actions around what, at a practical level, needs to change in order to operationalize the operating principles and turn the strategic intent into operational reality.

OPERATING PRINCIPLES COMPARED TO OPERATING PRACTICES

Organizations like to benchmark themselves against other organizations, comparing how they're doing and picking up ideas on how they can improve. In many cases, such actions are an initial step towards developing a new strategy. While there is value in this approach, the danger is that too much focus is often given to identifying conventional best practices and not enough to understanding their underlying operating principles. All practices are based upon principles, and it's the application of an operating principle in a specific context – within a specific organization – that establishes the operational practices. If the context is different in two organizations, even if they are in the same sector, application of the same operating principle in both organizations could lead to quite different operating practices. It is for this reason that it's always dangerous to advocate best operating practices over best operating principles.

When the leaders of a European oil company visited GE Power Systems in Atlanta to learn how GE practised portfolio management, they observed the processes that were in place, the governance that was exercised and the IT tools that were used to manage the portfolio. While all of this impressed the group, they could not immediately see how this could be applied in their organization. It was only when they looked past the practices, to the principles, that it became apparent how they could apply what they'd learned in their context.

Similarly, the leadership team of a mid-sized UK hospital visited a number of healthcare facilities in the US to learn about the principles of being 'patient-centric'. Value was only realized when they translated these principles into the context of the NHS, which differs dramatically from the commercially minded, free-market environment of the US healthcare system.

THE TWO DOMAINS THAT OPERATING PRINCIPLES SHOULD COVER

The purpose of operating principles is to make the strategic choices that define an organization's strategic intent more meaningful. Their objective is to help people understand how the organization needs to operate differently if it is to pursue its trajectory of strategic intent. They therefore need to cover two important domains – the organization's *operating model* and its *operating state*.

OPERATING MODEL

In the late 1980s, the Massachusetts Institute of Technology's Sloan School of Management conducted research that fundamentally changed our thinking about improving organizational performance. It was a five-year, multi-million-dollar study called Management in the Nineties, and its intent was to better understand the role and impact of IT on the formulation of business strategy and structure in an enterprise. The research produced groundbreaking insights and prepared the way for what became known as business reengineering. Publications from this period include Thomas Davenport and James Short's seminal Sloan paper, "The new industrial engineering: Information technology and business process redesign",[131] published in 1990, and Michael Hammer and James Champy's best-selling book, *Reengineering the Corporation: A Manifesto for Business Revolution*,[132] published in 1993.

The enduring legacy of this early work is that we now have a better understanding of the important role that process has in organizational performance – and the need to develop IT strategies that support end-to-end business processes as opposed to vertical business functions. It was a time of revolutionary thinking about enterprise design and the powerful role that IT could play.

What followed was a period when virtually every organization reengineered all or part of its operations. Whether it was in product development, supply chain or customer services, processes were mapped, analysed and redesigned. Unfortunately, as often happens with powerful new ideas, the movement was hijacked by those who saw it as a way of giving credibility to their own ideas and initiatives. As a result, a good many change initiatives did not apply true business reengineering principles and therefore failed to deliver the expected benefits. Furthermore, business reengineering was often criticized for its lack of humanity, as it tended to focus on process over people. Unfortunately, these critics failed to understand the true nature of business reengineering – which was holistic in nature from the outset – and confused business reengineering with business process redesign.

Inevitably, the popularity of business reengineering declined, but many of the insights, principles and practices are as valid today as they were 25 years ago. One of the most powerful insights to emerge from this period was the notion of an *operating model*: an abstraction of the enterprise (or a part of an enterprise) that allows its operation to be described in a way that's understandable to others. In essence an operating model makes the implicit, explicit.

Unfortunately, the term operating model is still not well understood and much confusion remains about what it should describe, and to what level of detail. For some, it's a term used to describe structure or operational footprint, and for others, core business processes. Some executives feel the term is so overused (or misused) that it has lost all meaning and they've banned the use of it. This is unfortunate, as decisions on the design of an organization's operating model are as important as decisions on marketplace strategy.

AN OPERATING MODEL DEFINES THE 'HOW'

The purpose of an operating model is to explicitly define 'how' an organization's products and services are designed, developed, produced, delivered and supported. There are many aspects to an operating model, each describing one or more of the operational facets that work together to achieve business outcomes. While there are many frameworks available to describe an operating model, each with its own merits, they all essentially cover:

1. **Operational processes.** Most organizations have a relatively small number of core operational processes (typically 8 to 12) that are critical to delivering their products and services. For example, in the US pharmaceutical space, one of the core operational processes is obtaining Food and Drug Administration (FDA) approval, and in the courier business it's parcel collection to delivery. A company should be able to define its core operational processes on a single page, in terms of the outcomes they deliver, the principles by which they operate and the key activities they perform.

2. **Management processes.** These support the operational processes and therefore are sometimes called enabling processes. Their goal is to ensure that the organization performs as expected. Examples of management processes include performance management, HR and finance.

3. **Governance.** This defines who has what decision rights and the resultant accountabilities. Governance covers the role of the Board (including non-executive directors), the CEO and the executive team, operating committees, and steering groups. The domains covered include matters relating to policy, regulatory compliance, strategy formulation and change management.

4. **Structure.** An entity's structure delineates how resources are organized, including to what extent they're shared across different business units and geographies. It also defines how flat or hierarchical the organization is and the extent to which organizational units are self-organized. Organizational structures differ widely across industries and are often dependent upon what the organization is seeking, for example operational excellence or innovation, or both.

5. **Roles, competencies and jobs.** These are the skills and experience required for each role and how roles are combined into jobs.

Competencies are a facet of organizational capability, and organizational capabilities are formed as a result of an organization's operating model and operating state.

6. **Technology.** Tools used to support the core operational and management processes would include information, manufacturing and research technologies. In information-intensive sectors, like financial services, IT would be a core technology. In other, more production-orientated industries, core technologies could be component manufacturing or robotic assembly.

7. **Sourcing.** As organizations become increasingly virtual and global in their outlook, sourcing decisions become a critical aspect of their operating model. At the same time, as they become less self-sufficient and operate within interlinked ecosystems, finding, putting in place and managing suitable partners become increasingly important facets of the operating model.

It's highly unlikely that the trajectory of an organization can be successfully changed without altering some parts of its operating model. Defining the target operating principles is an important first step in transitioning from *strategic thinking* to *design thinking*, where the focus moves to designing (or, more accurately, redesigning) parts of the operating model to align it with the target operating principles. In many cases the redesign and rebuilding of the operating model is where most time, resources and investment are expended.

THE OPERATING STATE ADDRESSES THE 'WHO'

If an organization's operating model addresses the 'how', the operating state addresses the 'who'. It defines *who* the people in the organization think they are in terms of their identity within the workplace; their relationship with management and colleagues; how they perceive their contribution and worth; and their connectedness with what the organization is trying to achieve. The operating state is ultimately reflected in the level of employee engagement and the prevailing mindset.

As with operating models, there are many frameworks for describing an operating state. The one we've used for many years is based on the work of previous colleagues[133] and comprises four facets:

Power: The extent to which individuals up, down and across the organization feel empowered. This is a spectrum ranging from:

Resignation – where individuals are easily stopped, have little accountability, are risk-averse and are highly frustrated,

through to...

Possibility – where they are resourceful, accountable, willing to take risks and ambitious, both personally and in their work for the organization.

Identity: The extent to which individuals identify with the organization and what it is trying to achieve. This is a spectrum ranging from:

Separateness – where individuals think narrowly, act independently, finger-point at others and act sub-optimally,

through to...

Connectedness – where they think holistically, take coordinated action, feel responsible and work to optimize the whole.

Contention: The extent to which individuals effectively handle contention and conflict with colleagues. This is a spectrum ranging from:

Fear and suppression – where individuals avoid conflict, are distrustful, avoid difficult conversations and 'kill' the messenger,

through to...

Safety and resolution – where they address conflict, are trustful, engage in straight-talk and feel safe.

Learning: The extent to which individuals learn, grow and develop. This is a spectrum ranging from:

Arrogance and defensiveness – where individuals look for the fatal flaw, trust the authoritative view, don't admit failure and believe that nothing new can be invented here,

through to...

Inquisitiveness and receptiveness – where they continually look for possibilities, challenge the status quo, learn from failure and are open to new ideas.

In many respects, the operating state creates the context within which strategy can, or cannot, be executed. If the right operating state is in place, there exists a level of openness and engagement that creates the conditions for changing an organization's trajectory. Indeed, some argue that any strategy exercise should start by addressing the operating state. To an extent the operating state is one of the endogenous navigating forces, but changing the operating state alone – without addressing changes to the operating model – can lead to unsustainable change.

THE VALUE PROPOSITION ADDRESSES THE 'WHAT'

Many would also argue that we're missing an important dimension of an enterprise business model, namely the *value proposition*. It's not something we've forgotten or ignored, as an organization's value proposition is defined as a fundamental part of its strategic intent – that represented by the target strategic signature. After all, the strategic intent is a statement of 'what' an organization wants to become.

FROM OPERATING PRINCIPLES TO DESIGN PRINCIPLES

Operating principles are a tool for the strategists – a means of articulating the strategic choices and resulting strategic intent. *Design principles* are a tool for the designers – those who translate the operating principles into changes that need to be made to the organization's operating model and operating state. Let's illustrate what we mean through an example. If we go back to the following operating principle:

> 'We value customers based upon their lifetime relationship with us.'
> **as opposed to…**
> 'We value our customers based upon their latest transaction.'

If this operating principle was then shared with the IT team, and they were asked what they thought the IT implications of this operating principle could be, their answers might include:

- The need to integrate the different product-based IT applications through some form of user interface and data presentation layer
- Having a single database that provides an integrated view of the customer, showing the relationship over time
- Flags in the customer profile that announce a significant forthcoming event that may result in a change in lifestyle, for example retirement or relocation abroad
- Customers' ability to access their accounts and products online and make simple changes, for example change of address, or make

an additional investment into an existing financial fund. As you'd imagine, there are countless others.

For many financial services organizations – with their legacy, product-based systems that are not easy to change – these implications are anything but trivial.

Understanding the implications of an operating principle informs what changes need to be made to an organization's operating model. This in turn informs the formulation of a set of design principles. In the case above, the changes that need to be made to the existing IT applications and supporting infrastructure would first be articulated through a set of IT architecture design principles, which could include:

'Only use applications that are based upon service-orientated architecture and have associated application program interfaces.'
as opposed to…
'Use applications that are closed.'

'Use (and reuse) application software components that are common and shared.'
as opposed to…
'Use uniquely developed software components.'

'Integrate components via applications infrastructure and middleware.'
as opposed to…
'Point-to-point interfaces.'

'Innovate at the edge of the applications landscape and then rejuvenate the core.'
as opposed to…
'Treat every component as core.'

Don't worry if you're not technically inclined and the architecture design principles mean nothing to you. Think of an example in your own domain, and the design principles that could be applied in redesigning its operating model.

The above design principles focus on the technology facet of the operating model; other design principles would be needed for the other elements, such as process and organization. In many respects, it's a form of engineering, where the resulting artefact is the organization itself.

But what about the operating state – can this also be designed? If by designed we mean remade through conscious choices, then yes. However, the design principles for an operating state are actually the same as the operating principles. The reason for this is simply that an operating state is determined by people who work within and shape the operating model. While people cannot (as yet) be designed, their behaviour can be guided in terms of what is expected of them, through a set of operating principles.

OPERATING PRINCIPLES AND DESIGN PRINCIPLES MAKE THE IMPLICIT, EXPLICIT

Having a discussion about the operating principles by which leaders want their organization to function in the future is essential. Its value comes from surfacing the degree to which members of the leadership team – often from different businesses, functions and geographies – see the world in the same way. Inevitably, at the beginning there will be confusion, tension and possibly conflict, but defining operating principles is an effective way of resolving them and achieving alignment of both thinking and action. The problem with too many strategies is that the choices inherent in a strategy are implicit rather than explicit. Principles are conscious choices and therefore, by definition, ones that need to be articulated, debated, socialized and understood.

PRINCIPLES NEED TO BE EXPERIENCED

For operating principles to have impact, they need to be lived. Before they can be lived they need to be accepted, and before they can be accepted they need to be understood. The challenge is to articulate the principles in such a way that employees understand what they need to do differently. They can't just state the obvious, but must be aligned with what's measured – or rather, what's measured needs to be aligned with the principles. To have a principle that states, 'We focus on giving the customer a compelling end-to-end experience' as opposed to, 'We focus on driving internal process efficiency' will be meaningless if the only thing that's measured and acted upon is process efficiency.

Operating principles need to be experienced in a way that reinforces their implicit behaviour. And, most importantly, they need to provide a clear line of sight to the target future.

DEFAULT OPERATING PRINCIPLES LEAD TO A DEFAULT FUTURE

All organizations have operating principles; the only question is how explicit they are and how aligned they are with the strategic intent. Operating principles are a powerful factor in determining an organization's trajectory. If they're not explicitly managed, they can result in organizational behaviours and habits that are difficult to change. Understanding today's operating principles and replacing them with those needed to change an organization's trajectory is an essential part of operationalizing strategy.

THE CHAPTER IN SUMMARY

At the start of this chapter we argued that the purpose of any strategy is to change an organization's trajectory, steering it away from its default future to one that is judged to be better. We know that having strategic targets alone is not enough, as employees need guidance on how to translate the strategic intent into everyday action. Operating principles provide this by acting as a navigation aid. It's like having the organizational equivalent of satellite navigation, which provides continual guidance on how the organization must operate to change its trajectory. They can help ensure that change initiatives are aligned with the target future and can be a leading indicator of progress.

But operating principles alone are not enough, as changing an organization's trajectory invariably involves making changes to its *operating model* and *operating state*. Translating operating principles into (re)design principles for these two domains is an important aspect of transitioning from formulating strategy to executing strategy.

FIVE QUESTIONS FOR REFLECTION

1. Are the principles by which your organization needs to operate, in order to realize its strategic intent, clearly and explicitly articulated and understood?

2. Are the implications of each operating principle understood, and are plans in place to address them?

3. How will people learn about the target operating principles and understand what they need to do differently?

4. To what extent are the target operating principles translated into design principles for the operating model?

5. How will you know when the operating principles and design principles are bringing the organization in line with its trajectory of strategic intent?

CHAPTER 8

TURNING STRATEGIC INTENT INTO OPERATIONAL REALITY

"The secret of change is to focus all of your energy, not on fighting the old, but on building the new."

Socrates (470–399 BC)
Greek philosopher

If the purpose of developing a strategy is to define the trajectory of strategic intent, then the purpose of executing a strategy must be to turn that strategic intent into operational reality. But how should strategy execution be undertaken? How can the chances of changing an organization's trajectory be improved? Is it simply a question of articulating the strategic intent in a way that colleagues can understand? Should it be delivered as a change programme, with project charters, time-phased plans, project teams and steering group meetings? Or is there something more to it? We believe there is, and that's what we'll explore in this chapter.

IMPLEMENT OR OPERATIONALIZE?

The first question to consider is what approach to take: should a strategy be implemented or operationalized? And what's the difference? The traditional approach to strategy involves defining a vision or end-state, making the business case and executing a set of changes needed to realize the vision. The underlying assumption is that if these changes are implemented the vision will be realized and the business case achieved. For some strategies, this could indeed be the case; for others, it's not so easy. For example, if the strategy is to reduce operating costs by closing a plant or divesting a business division, implementation is relatively straightforward – plans can be developed, actions taken and progress measured against the plan. But what if the strategic intent is more transformational, where not only the structure of the organization is to change, but also its operating model and its operating state? Can this type of change really be implemented as a project – one that's organized, delivered and managed using a structured project management methodology such as PMI[134] or Prince2?[135] In our view, no. In these cases, strategic intent needs to be operationalized, not implemented.

PUSH VERSUS PULL

The difference between implementing a strategy and operationalizing one is essentially the difference between *pushing* an organization onto its trajectory of strategic intent and *pulling* it. Strategy implementation, as it's generally practised, is about pushing the present into the future, rather than pulling the present into the future. The push approach is predicated on the assumption that successful implementation is achieved through the execution of a series of steps – essentially implementation of a predefined plan, where the completion of each step takes the organization closer to its target state. The main weakness of the push approach is that it assumes organizations are deterministic and programmable. Yet we all know that organizations are not predictable, particularly at times of significant change. They are dynamic systems that respond – often in unforeseen ways – when attempts are made to change them. As a consequence, an implementation plan is always out of date. And, having such a plan can lead people to believe it is someone else's responsibility to put it into action – namely, those charged with implementing the plan.

The pull approach takes a different perspective, creating a context where employees can exercise their judgement, apply their experience and use their expertise to pull the organization from its current trajectory to the one required to achieve its strategic intent. The challenge with the pull approach is that it needs to be embedded within the organization in ways that lead to intellectual, emotional and physical engagement. And this can only be achieved if the right context is created – one where everyone can constructively contribute to *pulling the present into the future*.

So, when is it more appropriate to adopt the pull approach as opposed to the push approach?

If the required shift in trajectory is deterministic – in that the decisions and actions needed can easily be planned, executed and monitored – then the push approach is probably the better option.

If, however, the target future requires a significant shift in trajectory and, as a consequence, the outcomes of these actions are less predictable and less easy to define, then the pull approach is more appropriate.

If the push approach is chosen, then there is plenty of credible material out there on how change programmes and projects should be structured and managed. We're not going to cover this; our focus in this chapter is on the pull approach to executing strategy, which we call *operationalizing*.

THE POWER OF PULL

According to John Hagel III, John Seely Brown and Lang Davison in their book, *The Power of Pull*,[136] pull is about expanding awareness of what is possible, evolving propositions, mastering new practices and taking new actions to realize these possibilities. The authors argue that the pull journey starts with the individual and then builds outward to the institutional level, and ultimately to broader arenas like markets, industries and even society in general. They also believe that several crucial elements of the journey must be systematically created and put in place: the right *trajectory* (the direction in which you want to head); sufficient *leverage* (the ability to mobilize with passion the efforts of other people); and the best *pace* (the speed at which you progress) to make it all come together.

We agree that if these conditions are in place, pull can be a more powerful way for an organization to realize a different future than it being pushed into that future. Furthermore, what we've talked about so far – in terms of defining the strategic intent – is essentially about 'fast-tracking' the setting of the trajectory. That trajectory is both inspired by an understanding of what's strategically possible (from the trajectory of strategic opportunity) and informed by what's feasible (from an assessment of the navigating forces that are determining the trajectory of current reality). If we've already addressed the first of the conditions set out by Hagel, Brown and Davison, how then do we get leverage and pace?

CREATING THE CONDITIONS FOR TURNING STRATEGIC INTENT INTO OPERATIONAL REALITY

You will get leverage and pace if the necessary conditions for turning strategic intent into operational reality are in place. Creating these necessary conditions is about creating a context in which the organization's energy shifts from keeping it on its current trajectory to pulling it onto its target trajectory – the trajectory of strategic intent. These conditions therefore need to tap into the energy of the many, as opposed to the few.

When executing strategy – either by pulling or pushing – there are some 'always true' conditions for success that need to be in place. These include sponsorship, funding, communication, commitment and resources. These requisite conditions are well documented – although not universally or consistently applied – and therefore we will not cover them further. For the remainder of this chapter we'll focus on those conditions for success that we consider to be critical when operationalizing strategy.

GOOD GARDENERS KNOW ABOUT ESTABLISHING CONDITIONS FOR SUCCESS

One of the best ways to describe the process of establishing conditions for success is to draw upon a gardening analogy. Those of you who are keen gardeners know that certain conditions are necessary for a garden to flourish, with fertile soil being the most obvious one. Experienced gardeners know that some of these conditions can be controlled and others, like the weather, cannot. For example, they know that soil quality can be improved and that particular plants will never do well in certain types of soil. They know that some plants need good drainage and others partial shade, and that some should be pruned in spring and others in autumn.

The importance of getting these conditions in place was made clear when one of us and his wife decided to redesign their garden. Recognizing their lack of knowledge and expertise in this matter, they engaged an award-winning garden designer. A site visit was arranged and the vision articulated. Several weeks later the expert came back with a design and planting plan. It was impressive and they couldn't wait to get into execution. The designer then pointed out that the conditions were not right to proceed. First, the soil was of such poor quality that something needed to be done to enrich it, or the new plants wouldn't flourish and many would die. Second, it wasn't the right time of the year to launch such a major replanting exercise; early spring would be best. As it was then September, there was plenty of time to dig in the 25 cubic metres of mushroom compost needed to improve the soil. In early spring, the designer returned and laid out all the plants, which were then planted over the coming days. When the job was done the empty pots were counted and to everyone's astonishment there were nearly a thousand! Needless to say all were delighted with the outcome, and grateful to the gardening expert for the knowledge, experience and discipline that she brought to the project. She also understood what resources were needed (25 cubic metres of compost and nearly a thousand plants and shrubs) to turn intent into reality.

The moral of this story is that most of the conditions for success were known at the outset, but, in the gardeners' enthusiasm to get on with it, these conditions were in danger of being ignored. The expert not only brought her design and planting expertise, she brought discipline to the project. Her experience told her that the conditions for success were not in place and that it would be folly – and a tremendous waste of money – to proceed until they were. The question is: how many of us act in the same way, but in a different context? How many of us receive approval for a project, have a clear vision of what it should achieve and choose to proceed while knowing that the necessary conditions for success are not in place – and that the resulting risk of failure is high?

CONDITIONS FOR SUCCESSFULLY OPERATIONALIZING STRATEGY

If operationalizing strategy is about pulling the organization onto its target trajectory, then the obvious question becomes: who does the pulling, and how? The simple answer is: everyone, to varying degrees. The objective is to establish a set of conditions that enable everyone to do so. The precise conditions for success (CfS) are dependent upon the specific strategy and the context within which they are being operationalized. However, the following eight are almost always the most critical.

1. Clarity of strategic intent.
2. Operating and design principles to guide the transition.
3. Pulling organizational capabilities are in place.
4. Anchoring organizational capabilities mitigated.
5. Clarity of decision rights.
6. Opportunity to experience the target future.
7. Forward-focused navigation.
8. Collective leadership.

Note that the conditions are described as if they are an achieved state – that is, they are in place – rather than as actions required to put them in place. The purpose of articulating them in this way is to encourage people to first imagine a future state where the conditions are in place, and then to stand back and ask what needs to be done to actually put them in place. This is a technique Richard Pascale[137] describes as "managing the present as a past condition of the future". It's when you imagine you're in a future state, look back at the present and ask yourself, "What do I need to do to get to where, hypothetically, I am now?"

CONDITION 1: CLARITY OF STRATEGIC INTENT

We covered this condition in some detail in chapter 6, where we discussed how the trajectory of strategic intent needs to be based on an assessment of an organization's trajectory of current reality – one that's taking it to its default future – and its trajectory of strategic opportunity. We also discussed how strategic intent could be expressed as a strategic signature.

When this condition is in place, not only does the leadership team have an aligned view of the target trajectory, but colleagues across the organization also clearly understand it. It's also important that everyone understands the consequences of *not* changing the current trajectory, in terms of the undesirable default future it will bring. It's about people having sufficient understanding of the trajectory the organization needs to be on (and why) so that they can individually and collectively contribute to putting it on that trajectory.

For example, when Jeff Immelt chose a different trajectory for GE, one focused on digitizing in the industrial space, he made the strategic intent crystal clear. As he put it,[13] "We've made the decision that we're going to try to be both a platform company and an application company. So, we have a platform called Predix, and we're building applications on top of that. We're probably the only industrial company that's actually trying to do its own. And we're opening up our platform to our customers. We're saying to our customers, 'Look, if you want to write apps on Predix, you're free to do it.'"

CONDITION 2: OPERATING AND DESIGN PRINCIPLES TO GUIDE THE TRANSITION

As we discussed in chapter 7, it's one thing to know what trajectory the organization intends to take, but it's another thing knowing how the organization needs to operate in order to get onto the target trajectory. Operating principles are a powerful way of achieving this, as they give guidance and insight into how the organization would be operating if it were already on the target trajectory. The thinking is that if colleagues work to the new operating principles, they will begin to pull the organization onto the target trajectory. As these principles are conscious choices between two equally valid alternatives, they also define how the organization should *not* operate going forward. Just as importantly, they define the implications of operating in the new way – which will need to be carefully managed during the transition.

You know when this condition is in place: it's when people begin referring to the target operating and design principles, and it becomes apparent that their actions and behaviours are guided by them. Many years ago we were reviewing a major change programme for a UK financial services company and part of our work involved observing the behaviour and effectiveness of the steering group. About a third of the way through one meeting, the group got stuck in a debate on a particularly difficult issue facing the programme. Just as it looked like a decision was never going to be made, the chairperson reminded the group of the recently agreed operating principles and suggested that they might provide guidance. This intervention brought immediate clarity to the discussion and enabled the group to make a rapid choice on what needed to be done, a decision on which they all agreed. From then on the operating principles provided guidance in all meetings and helped make the steering group a more effective governance body.

Operating principles are a powerful way of guiding new behaviour. At one level, they are constraining as they define how the organization should, and should not, operate. But on another level, they are principles and not practices, and how operating principles are operationalized depends on the context within which they're being applied. This translation of a principle into one or more practices lets employees become more engaged in translating the strategy into action. It allows them to contribute by drawing upon their own knowledge and applying their experience. It gives them an opportunity to become intellectually engaged and encourages them to mentally model how the organization needs to operate at a detailed, practical level. This process of turning operating principles into operating practices is an important aspect of keeping everyone engaged in implementing the strategy.

CONDITION 3: PULLING ORGANIZATIONAL CAPABILITIES ARE IN PLACE

In chapter 3 we discussed how an organization's trajectory is ultimately defined by its organizational capabilities. We described organizational capabilities as the muscles it has developed over time. We looked at how they're formed from a combination of shared mental models and frameworks, common language, beliefs and mindset, processes and practices, conventions and norms, shared experiences and individual skills. We also talked about how some organizational capabilities can anchor an organization to its current trajectory, and that new and different organizational capabilities are invariably required when an organization intends to change its trajectory to one that's aligned with its strategic intent.

Understanding the organizational capabilities needed to pull the organization onto its target trajectory is a critical condition for success – as without them the organization will continue on its current trajectory. Again, we refer to GE to illustrate the importance of knowing and putting these pulling organizational capabilities in place. We earlier quoted Jeff Immelt on his – subsequently mistaken – belief that all he'd have to do was hire thousands of IT people to transform the company into one capable of digitizing the industrial space. While the strategic intent was clear, it took GE some time before it realized the true nature of the pulling organizational capabilities that it needed to put in place.

You will know this condition is in place when things are done differently, colleagues use different language, new concepts are applied and it just feels different. During the transition, some people will feel out of their comfort zone and question why the new ways of doing things are necessary. It's important that they realize nothing will change unless the ways that things are done change – and this requires a different portfolio of organizational capabilities.

CONDITION 4: ANCHORING ORGANIZATIONAL CAPABILITIES MITIGATED

If condition 3 above is about ensuring that the pulling organizational capabilities are in place, then this condition is about addressing those that are anchoring the organization to its current, to-be-changed, trajectory. It's important to remember that these organizational capabilities existed for a reason, which was to enable and support the past trajectory. As the context within which the organization operated changed, so did the need to change its trajectory. As a result, many of the organizational capabilities that enabled and supported the old trajectory became legacy anchors that prevented change.

For example, one of the capabilities that many organizations have developed in recent years is process management. We looked earlier at how these originated in the early years of business reengineering,[132] and they gained prominence with the introduction of the Sarbanes-Oxley Act in 2002.[138] Process mapping, process measurement and process improvement were seen by many as the only way to continually improve performance. Many went as far as appointing process owners and becoming certified with the International Organization for Standardization.[139] Without question, taking an end-to-end perspective of a business process – and redesigning it to deliver target outcomes – brought significant benefits to many organizations. However, over time, as organizations sought greater agility, they found that this has also become an anchoring organizational capability.

Even GE – which had become famous for its lean manufacturing and process improvement 'black belts' under Jack Welch – found that it needed to challenge its focus on process when it began to digitize in the industrial space. As Immelt put it,[13] "We found our culture was too complicated to get the work done the way we needed to get work done, in terms of how we were trying to digitize and how we were trying to survive in a more highly regulated world. We've adapted the lean tools in what I would call a Silicon Valley approach, what we call 'Fast Works'. We've embraced some of the Silicon Valley tools in terms of putting everything on the clock, bringing commercial intensity into the company."

When this condition is in place, you'll notice that the old ways of doing things are respected, and employees recognize that they contributed to making the organization successful in the past, but there's an understanding that they won't necessarily make it successful in the future. You will also notice that people are keen to learn new competencies, either by attending training or being assigned to parts of the organization that are developing and applying the new pulling organizational capabilities.

CONDITION 5: CLARITY OF DECISION RIGHTS

When organizations talk about executing their strategy, they often refer to it as a journey taking them from where they are now to a future state. At one level it's an analogy that's not helpful, as it suggests a single transition from 'A' to 'B'. It also implies that when the target state is reached the job is done and everything can go back to normal. But, executing strategy – either by implementing or operationalizing – is about changing the organization's trajectory, and once on its target trajectory the cycle repeats itself. It repeats in the sense that the target trajectory then becomes the *trajectory of strategic reality* taking the organization to its default future – which, if considered unacceptable, once again triggers the process of defining a new strategic intent. And so the process of assessment, development and execution begins anew. In many respects this cycle is a periodic process, one that you should fully expect to repeat, where each cycle is triggered by a change in context.

As with any journey, it's also important to understand that it is impossible – and definitely impractical – to foresee every eventuality and plan every detail. Some planning is obviously needed, but more important is having people who clearly understand the direction the organization is taking, and who are able to provide guidance and deal with issues as they arise. What's essential is having clarity on who has the decision rights to make the necessary mid-course corrections, reallocate funding, ensure that resources are in the right place and deal with the inevitable 'that wasn't supposed to happen' twists and turns. We are talking about governance – who makes the tough decisions and who has the resulting accountabilities.

All too often, governance is confused with roles and structure, rather than decision-making rights and process. As a result, the governing bodies – whether they are an executive committee, programme steering group or operating model design authority – receive progress reports, risk assessments and benefits-tracking updates in ways that give them the illusion of control. Furthermore, when a critical decision needs to be taken, the preference is for this to be done outside the meeting so that 'important colleagues can be consulted'. Typically, such governing bodies are too large, since everyone wants to be involved and have their say, and they don't meet frequently enough. But if changing the trajectory of the organization is so critical, how can *attending to other business* be more important? And how can executives participating in these governing meetings be expected to make informed decisions if they aren't close to the details and able to sense whether the organization is actually changing its trajectory?

Good governance therefore not only provides clarity on which individuals and groups have decision rights over what, it also devolves decision-making down to the lowest possible level. When asked what good governance looks like, we often say it starts with deciding on the smallest group of individuals who have the organizational power and influence to establish the conditions for success we've been discussing. The rest follows from there.

It's clear that this condition is in place when people know to whom a decision needs to be referred, and that decision gets made quickly. What's more, those taking the decision accept their accountabilities. Nothing kills operationalizing a strategy quicker than a lack of clear decision-making during its execution. Decisive decision-making drives pace and momentum.

CONDITION 6: OPPORTUNITY TO EXPERIENCE THE TARGET FUTURE

Executing strategy is actually a journey in two parts. The first part is about transitioning to the *trajectory of strategic intent*. The second is about continuing to travel along this trajectory until the context changes again and the strategy cycle is repeated. During each stage of the journey the organization needs to operate differently than it did in the past. We've talked about how operating principles can help colleagues understand how the organization should operate, but this is a cerebral process. It requires people to use their intelligence and experience to process data, understand the logic and weigh the arguments for doing things in a particular way. While this is necessary, it is not sufficient, and for some it's a process they simply won't want to engage in. If the essence of operationalizing a strategy is for as many people as possible to pull it onto its target trajectory, then how can we get them to understand that target future and become emotionally engaged in making it happen?

It's often said that 'if you live your life as if it were different, it actually becomes different'. Richard Pascale[137] said that people are "much more likely to act their way into a new way of thinking, than think their way into a new way of acting". The way we like to put it is that people are "more likely to create the future once they've experienced it".

We always encourage organizations to create the future as soon as possible and let employees experience it before it's actually built. More than a quarter-century ago, with the advent of business reengineering, we would establish reengineering 'laboratories' early in the design phase, where the reengineered business operating model was simulated and evaluated from across the organization – all in a 'safe' environment. Not only did this improve the design, it also gave employees insight into what the future might be like. Most importantly it gave them an opportunity to feel involved and participate in shaping their future.

On one occasion, a UK fashion retailer decided to redesign its supply chain. To make it as real as possible, the project team took over a floor in one of its warehouses and created a simulation of the redesigned supply chain. In one part of the building were the 'suppliers based in Asia', in another part were imagined warehouses, in another mock-ups of small and large stores, and in another the imagined buyers. Through a series of scenarios, they not only assessed the current supply chain, but also designed a new one. The beauty of using these scenarios was that they helped people understand how the new supply chain would operate. When participants moved through the exercise, they weren't given a PowerPoint presentation but a role to play in the simulations. This approach not only resulted in a better supply chain design, it also helped the team understand the navigating forces that were defining the organization's current trajectory and what new organizational capabilities were needed to pull it onto its chosen trajectory of strategic intent.

Unfortunately, in recent years we've seen a reluctance by organizations to make this level of investment, which we believe is a false economy. The trend has certainly been to focus more on implementation, where employees are trained in the new ways of working rather than engaged in the process of operationalizing strategic intent. This is a major contributing factor in the poor track record in strategy execution and change delivery.

We recognize that it may not always be possible to create a physical space where employees can experience the future, but there are other options. One of these is the use of Learning Maps,[140] pioneered by Root Inc. These schematics use icons, infographics, drawings, conceptual illustrations and metaphors to tell a story in a visual way and facilitate conversations to create common understanding. This use of pictorial imagery is very powerful in helping people at all levels to better understand how their organization needs to work in the future.

When this condition is in place there is greater confidence in the trajectory the organization wants to take – its trajectory of strategic intent. There is also a deeper understanding of what the future will look like, and less confusion and fear about how the organization will operate in the future. In many respects, the many – as opposed to the few – have the confidence to pull the organization onto its trajectory of strategic intent.

CONDITION 7: FORWARD-FOCUSED NAVIGATION

Changing the trajectory of an organization is a bit like changing the direction of an ocean liner – it takes time to get it onto the target trajectory, and time before it's apparent that the trajectory has actually changed at all. It's therefore important that we have a navigation system that tells us in what direction we're headed and at what speed.

All too often the management of change programmes focuses on the wrong things. For example, there's a tendency to focus on reporting what has been delivered against the plan rather than the direction the programme is actually taking and its momentum. Obviously, retrospective indicators such as milestones achieved against the plan, spend against the budget and increased revenue by channel are important, but they only tell you where you've travelled so far, not where you're going. That's not to say that reporting on progress is not important; it's necessary but not sufficient, particularly when operationalizing – as opposed to implementing – strategy. What's needed is a satellite navigation system that not only tracks the trajectory but also predicts its likely position over time. As this type of tracking system doesn't yet exist for operationalizing strategy, we need to find a suitable alternative, preferably one that is forward-looking, as opposed to retrospectively focused.

The most obvious things to monitor are the eight conditions for success we're discussing here – after all, they are predicated on the assumption that the more solidly they're in place, the greater is the likelihood that the organization will change its current trajectory to one aligned with its strategic intent. Later in this chapter we will discuss how to assess the extent to which these conditions are in place.

The second way to gauge trajectory change is to monitor the extent to which the strategic signature has altered over time, across each of the strategic axes being changed. The importance of this measure is that it's based on outcomes, not project deliverables, which should be seen as a means to an end, not an end in itself.

A third way of assessing whether the trajectory is changing is to listen to what employees are saying. If the language used is forward-focused, then it's highly likely that the trajectory is changing. Even if the programme is reporting that it's on track in terms of deliverables, the language can tell a different story. The problem is that negative comments are often dismissed, attributed to laggards in the organization who will never accept change. What's missed is that language is one important manifestation of the operating state of the organization, and that even if the operating model is being changed successfully, it's likely that the change won't be sustained. It's therefore also likely that the organization will continue to travel on its current trajectory.

You will know this condition is in place when employees can confidently predict where the organization will be, in relation to its transition to the target trajectory, over time. That's not to say that the organization will be on track – that's for the other conditions to determine – but rather that the direction of travel for the transition is understood, enabling any necessary mid-course corrections.

CONDITION 8: COLLECTIVE LEADERSHIP

Operationalizing strategy is about changing the trajectory of an organization, and changing trajectory requires people to change what they do and how they do it. It's unreasonable to expect them to commit to these changes unless they're confident they will succeed, and that the benefits of the future state are worth the pain of transition. And the principal source of this confidence comes – or doesn't – from the organization's leadership.

But if the leadership team is not aligned, either on the strategic intent or the trajectory by which it will be realized, that confidence will be lacking. And it's not just what leaders say that instils confidence; it's what they do and how they behave. If they collectively act as one, use the same language and exercise judgement based upon the same criteria, then it will be evident they are aligned, and exercising collective leadership as opposed to individual leadership. When operationalizing strategy, individual leadership is important, but it is not enough. Changing trajectory requires everyone – starting with the leadership group – to pull in the same direction.

ASSESSING THE EXTENT TO WHICH THE CONDITIONS FOR SUCCESS ARE IN PLACE

The eight conditions for success discussed above – along with additional conditions that are context-specific – should be periodically assessed in order to determine the extent to which they're sufficiently in place. The value of such an assessment is two-fold. First, it can act as a powerful leading indicator of whether operationalizing the strategy is on track. Second, it provides a framework for creating the constructive dialogue with colleagues.

As we discussed in chapter 3, the purpose of these types of assessment is to create dialogue rather than find the 'scientific truth'. That's why we call them dialogic assessments rather than audits. The results can be presented in many ways; the format we've found to be particularly helpful is a spider diagram, which we introduced in chapter 6. Another example appears, in figure 8i, using the following assessment criteria:

0. Importance of the condition for success is not recognized and therefore no action is being taken to put it in place.
1. Importance of the condition for success is recognized, but little progress has been made to put it in place.
2. Condition for success is being put in place, but has yet to reach a level where it is having a positive impact.
3. Condition for success has reached a level where it is having a positive impact.
4. Condition for success is being put in place, but is not yet sufficiently robust.
5. Condition for success is in place and has achieved the necessary level of robustness.

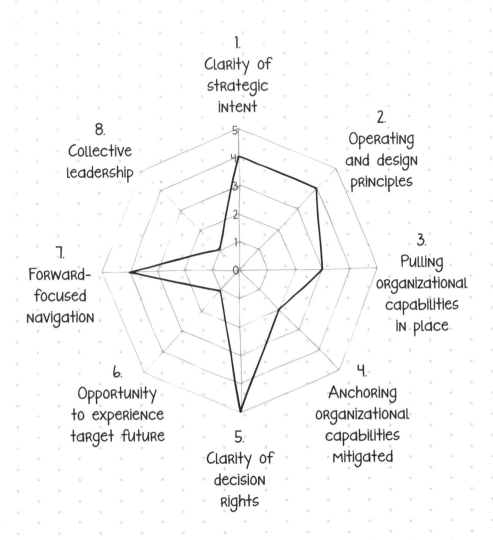

FIGURE 8i:

Results of assessment on the extent to which the conditions for operationalizing strategy are in place

As you will see in the assessment shown in figure 8i, conditions 1, 2, 5 and 7 are largely in place, but more work needs to be done on conditions 3 and 4. Conditions 6 and 8 are of concern, as much more needs to be done to put them in place.

Ideally these assessments would be performed by both an independent reviewer and those involved in operationalizing the strategy, via a process of self-assessment. The benefit of a self-assessment is that it reveals how aligned colleagues are in their views on the extent to which each condition is in place.

Figure 8ii illustrates the results of a self-assessment conducted by a number of people. Each line represents an individual's results, and, as you can see, the majority feel that conditions 6 and 8 are not in place. There are also varying perceptions as to how sufficiently conditions 2, 3 and 7 are in place. And, you'll see that there is relatively good alignment on the extent to which conditions 4 and 5 are in place. There is general agreement that condition 1 is largely in place.

Note that this self-assessment is for the most part aligned with the conclusions of an independent reviewer in figure 8i.

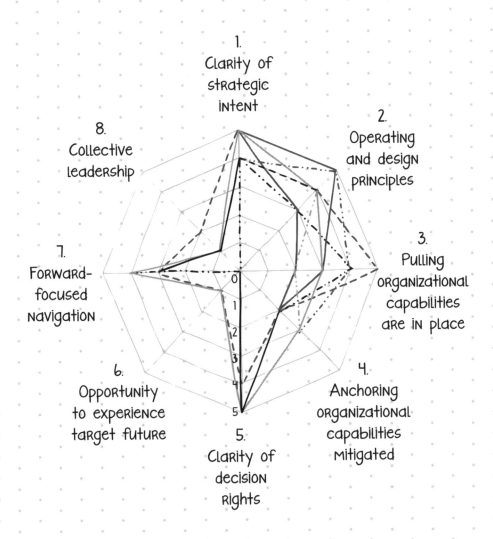

1.
Clarity of
strategic
intent

2.
Operating
and design
principles

3.
Pulling
organizational
capabilities
are in place

4.
Anchoring
organizational
capabilities
mitigated

5.
Clarity of
decision
rights

6.
Opportunity
to experience
target future

7.
Forward-
focused
navigation

8.
Collective
leadership

FIGURE 8ii:

Results of a self-assessment on the
extent to which the conditions for
operationalizing strategy are in place

ASSESSING THE PERCEIVED LEVEL OF IMPORTANCE

By definition, all the conditions for success are important, but not everybody accountable for operationalizing the strategy might think so. If a condition for success is not perceived to be important, it's unlikely to get much attention, and if it doesn't get attention it won't be put in place or maintained. It's therefore essential to assess how important colleagues consider the conditions for success to be, particularly those who have an influential role. If specific conditions are seen as unimportant, the reasons can be investigated and appropriate action taken. If such a self-assessment was performed by a leadership team, for example, it would also indicate how aligned, or unaligned, they are.

In figure 8iii we've given an example of the results of such an assessment, again presented in a spider diagram, where each line represents an individual's perspective. In this example the assessment criteria are as follows:

0. Not perceived as having any relevance or importance.
1. Perceived as relevant, but of no importance.
2. Perceived as having some importance.
3. Perceived as important.
4. Perceived as very important.
5. Perceived as critically important.

In this example, it is clear that conditions 6, 8 and to a degree 4 are not considered important by those who completed the assessment. Unsurprisingly then, in the assessments to determine the extent to which the conditions for success are in place in figures 8i and 8ii, the ratings are low. The example also shows clear alignment on the importance of conditions 1, 3 and 5. There are differing views on the importance of conditions 2 and 7, which could reflect a lack of understanding of these conditions for success.

While assessing the extent to which the individual conditions for success are in place is a powerful leading indicator of success or failure, assessing what people perceive to be important is even more forward-focused as it provides insight into how they will spend their time. What we do know is that the conditions for successfully operationalizing strategy don't fall into place by themselves. Unless time and effort are spent putting them in place, the initial enthusiasm that is often experienced at the beginning of a change programme will quickly dissipate, interest and momentum will be lost, the strategy will be deemed a failure and the organization will move on to the next (likely to fail) strategic initiative.

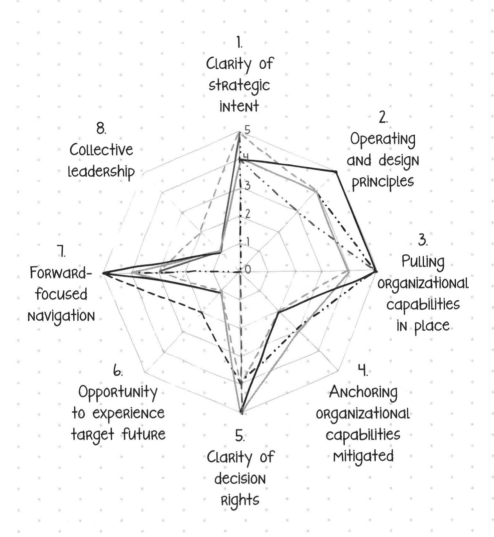

FIGURE 8iii:

Results of a self-assessment on the perceived importance of the conditions for operationalizing strategy

THE CHAPTER IN SUMMARY

Executing strategy is actually a journey in two parts. The first part is about transitioning from the current trajectory of strategic reality to the trajectory of strategic intent. The second part is continuing to travel on the trajectory of strategic intent, until the whole strategy cycle needs to begin again. The question becomes how best to commence with this transition. Should an organization be pushed onto its target trajectory, or should it be pulled? The former we call strategy implementation and the latter strategy operationalization.

If the required transition in trajectory is deterministic – in that the decisions and actions needed can be easily planned, executed and monitored – then the push approach is probably the better option. If, however, the strategic intent requires a significant shift in trajectory, and as a consequence the outcomes of actions are less predictable, then the pull approach is more appropriate. Operationalizing strategy is different from developing and implementing a plan; it's about getting the organization to behave and operate in a way that pulls it onto its target trajectory.

Regardless of which approach is chosen, there are some 'always true' conditions for success that need to be in place. These include sponsorship, funding, communication, commitment and resources. However, if the pull approach is chosen, there are eight additional conditions that are critical. Failure to give sufficient attention to putting these eight conditions in place significantly increases the risk that the strategy will not be successfully operationalized; prioritizing them can significantly increase the likelihood of success.

Furthermore, it's important not to leave thinking about operationalizing strategy until the strategy has been developed. Remember, throughout the strategy development process that it needs to take into account the endogenous navigating forces that are keeping the organization on its current trajectory – the trajectory that needs to change as the strategy is operationalized. In doing so, the strategic intent is more likely to become operational reality.

FIVE QUESTIONS FOR REFLECTION

1. What approach does your organization usually take when executing strategy?

2. To what extent does the approach focus on *pulling* the present into the future as opposed to *pushing* the present into the future?

3. To what extent does your organization recognize the need to establish the conditions for success necessary for operationalizing strategy?

4. To what extent are these conditions for success explicitly defined and their status periodically assessed?

5. To what extent do your organization's leaders recognize that their principal accountability in operationalizing strategy is to ensure that the requisite conditions for success are in place?

CHAPTER 9

IT ALL STARTS WITH COLLECTIVE LEADERSHIP

"*The achievements of an organization
are the results of the combined
effort of each individual.*"

Vincent Thomas Lombardi (1913–1970)
American football player, coach and executive

This final chapter is called 'It all starts with collective leadership' for a reason. Without collective leadership there will be no collective strategy, and without a collective strategy an organization has very little chance of successfully changing its trajectory. Why? Because changing an organization's trajectory requires everyone – particularly its leaders – to pull in the same direction. We touched on this in chapter 8, where we included collective leadership as one of the eight conditions for successfully operationalizing strategy. In this chapter we'll explore what we mean by collective leadership and propose ways in which this form of leadership can be put in place.

First, let's look at what we mean by collective leadership in the context of developing and operationalizing strategy. In our view, it's when the leaders of an organization:

- Acknowledge that it's their individual role and collective accountability to confront the default future that their organization faces
- Have a shared understanding of the exogenous and endogenous navigating forces that are defining their organization's *trajectory of strategic reality* – the one taking it to its default future
- Have a shared perspective on the opportunities that their organization's *trajectory of strategic opportunity* provides
- Make informed choices on their organization's strategic intent and the trajectory it needs to travel – the *trajectory of strategic intent*
- Establish and maintain the conditions for success needed to operationalize the strategy
- Acknowledge that developing and operationalizing strategy is a process that will need to be repeated when the context within which their organization operates changes.

In fact, we are talking about an organization's leaders having collective ownership of, and accountability for, the outcomes and activities we've covered so far in this book. An organization is more likely to have a collective strategy – as opposed to multiple, possibly conflicting, strategies – if collective leadership, as opposed to individual leadership, is in place. But what does collective leadership really mean in this context?

Collective leadership is where multiple individuals exercise their leadership roles within a group – and then the entire group provides leadership to the wider organization. What's more, it's a fluid and flexible approach to leadership, where roles and responsibilities evolve in response to changing circumstances. As a result, the power of collective leadership is greater than the sum of the powers of the individual leaders. Collective leadership is not the same as a 'high-performance team', where the focus is on maximizing the contribution of each individual team member. Collective leadership is where the given roles and functions are, intentionally, broadly defined and the contribution that individual leaders make evolves over time in pursuit of a common purpose.

A key aspect of collective leadership is collective accountability, where the outcomes of decisions and actions are felt by every leader in equal measure. Individuals who exercise collective leadership tend to have similar values and beliefs, but that's not to say they need to come from the same social backgrounds, to have received the same education or to have had similar life experiences. While the makeup of the leadership group can be quite diverse, each individual must believe in the power of collective thought, action and accountability. Executive groups that exercise collective leadership are neither myopic in their outlook nor parochial in their perspective; they collaborate extensively while providing constructive feedback and challenging one another. They are often described as being aligned in their decisions and actions; they act as one and are linked up in their thinking and behaviour.

Furthermore, collective leadership should not be confused with consensus leadership, where group members agree to support a decision in the best interests of the whole, even if it is not each individual's preferred choice.

In the majority of organizations, individual leadership is the default model, and in many it is actively encouraged and the resulting behaviours rewarded. There is nothing fundamentally wrong with the individual leadership model if applied in the right context, such as when the organization is trying to maximize its current performance rather than change its trajectory. This of course is predicated on the organization – in terms of its operating model and operating state – being designed to optimize performance. In our experience, that's rarely the case. That's not to say that collective leadership is not an appropriate organizational leadership model for optimizing current performance. It is, under the right circumstances, but it's an even more effective leadership model when it comes to changing an organization's trajectory.

FACTORS THAT DETERMINE YOUR STYLE OF LEADERSHIP

If you accept that an organization is more likely to be successful in changing its trajectory through collective leadership, as opposed to individual leadership, then it's important to understand the factors that determine leadership style. In our view there are five key factors:

1. Legacy of traditional leadership thinking.
2. Organizational complexity.
3. Incentives and rewards.
4. Fragmented IT landscape.
5. Organization of talent.

Let's take a closer look at each of these factors.

1: LEGACY OF TRADITIONAL LEADERSHIP THINKING

Traditional thinking about leadership is based on the characteristics of the individual leader, rather than those of a group of individuals exercising shared accountability. Often-cited examples of successful leaders include Steve Jobs of Apple, Bill Gates of Microsoft, Jeff Bezos of Amazon, John Chambers of Cisco Systems and Jack Welch of GE. While these individuals have undoubtedly been successful, there are many others – some of whom we cited in chapter 1 – who have been much less successful. This model of leadership, where a larger-than-life individual leads the organization and others follow, is very 'heroic' in style and one that is still the default in many organizations today. It's a traditional leadership style that is emulated by many aspiring junior executives. But is this model still relevant today? And, does this prevailing style of leadership contribute to the poor success rate in strategy execution and organizational change discussed in chapter 1? We believe it does. The model is not only outdated, but also fosters the erroneous belief that organizational leadership is about the individual, not the contribution that a group of individuals can collectively achieve.

This default thinking is predicated on the notion that there can be only one leader, who must take all the tough decisions and live with the consequences – for which that individual is handsomely rewarded. For many, the model is so strong that it drives the behaviour of the rest of the organization, particularly the aspiring leaders who believe that what they observe is how successful leaders should behave. Unfortunately, this behaviour all too frequently leads to divisional and functional strategies that are developed with little or no consultation between, or regard for, their colleagues in other parts of the business. These strategies are often myopic, focused on maximizing short-term results with little regard for the default future they'll bring for the organization as a whole. As a result, the organization ends up with not one strategy, but multiple strategies, each focused on achieving different outcomes. At best, they might have some degree of alignment; at worst, they are in conflict as they end up pulling the organization in different directions. In our view, the best strategy for an organization is very rarely the sum of a diverse set of individual strategies.

The challenge for today's leaders – regardless of the industry or the region in which they operate – is achieving alignment across their executive team, such that the group thinks and acts as one.

2: ORGANIZATIONAL COMPLEXITY

Over the past 40 years organizations have not only become larger, they've also become increasingly complex. Complexity is a result of the number of components in a system and their degree of interaction. The greater the number of components – divisions, business units, departments, distribution channels, territories, customer segments, regulators, suppliers and partners – the greater the organizational complexity. If a company becomes overly complex, it is difficult for employees to understand what's going on in other parts of the organization, and they find it hard to collaborate. Other hallmarks of overly complex organizations include slow, inconsistent decision-making, myopic planning, an evident lack of synced-up thinking, organizational silos and executive behaviour that is often wildly dysfunctional. In this chaotic environment, employees don't know where the organization is headed, feel frustrated, become disillusioned and are unable to contribute to their full potential.

Organizational complexity is not a new phenomenon and since the growth of the industrial age there have been many approaches to simplifying how work is done. For example, the purpose of business reengineering was to remove complexity through the end-to-end redesign of core operational processes, the simplification of work tasks and the introduction of outcome-based performance measures, all enabled by integrated IT systems. Similarly, the goal of other approaches, like total quality management, lean and Six Sigma, was to eliminate waste, which in turn reduced organizational complexity.

The natural entropy of an organization is towards greater complexity – often as a result of incremental changes to meet evolving customer needs and optimize local performance. But it can also be as a result of poor organizational design that places too much emphasis on the hierarchical decomposition of the organization into 'manageable' units. The logic here is that, if the organization is broken down into 'manageable units', each led by a manager who is accountable for the performance of their unit, the performance of the organization will be greater as a whole. This is true to a degree when the goal is to optimize 'the system' (operating model) as it is currently designed, but not so when the organization needs to change its current trajectory to one aligned with its strategic intent. The unintended consequence of an organization that is overly complex – either by design or by default – is an over-emphasis on individual accountability and, as a result, individual leadership. Even if a leader wanted to act collectively, the time and effort required is often seen as prohibitive; as a result it's not unusual in these situations for leaders to 'hunker down' and pursue their own agenda. It could be argued that individual leadership drives organizational complexity and organizational complexity encourages individual leadership.

3: INCENTIVES AND REWARDS

There are many challenges of managing large, complex organizations and one of them is maximizing the contribution of everyone, especially the leaders. The traditional way of achieving this is to give each of the leaders individual targets, on which their rewards and incentives are based. The problem with this approach is that not only does it perpetuate silo behaviour, it actively encourages individual leadership and thereby discourages collective leadership.

Without question, organizations need leaders, but they also need managers – and sometimes their roles get confused. To quote Peter Drucker,[141] who is seen by many as the father of modern management: "Management is doing things right; leadership is doing the right things."

For simplicity, let's define the role of a manager as someone who ensures that things get done the way they should be done and that employees reporting to them are able to do what is asked of them and are motivated and engaged in their work. They are also there to ensure problems are resolved when they arise and deal with matters relating to poor performance. We see the role of a leader as something different: the person – or persons – whose accountability it is to take the organization to a different place than it's currently headed. To put it another way, the role of a manager is to optimize current performance and the role of a leader is to change the trajectory of the organization. Another perspective is that management focuses on short-term performance and leaders focus on longer-term performance.

The problem with this simple model is that leaders also act as managers, as they also have responsibility for the performance of that part of the organization for which they are accountable. Furthermore, the challenge for any organization when it's trying to change its trajectory is to maintain performance during the transition. The question therefore is: how should leaders and managers be incentivized and rewarded? If the emphasis is on rewarding current performance, then the likelihood is that the organization will continue on its current trajectory. However, if the emphasis is on the transition, there's a danger that current performance will slip to the extent that the new strategy is questioned and possibly abandoned.

Problems with conflicting incentives can also arise during the early stages of strategy development, when different trajectories are being explored, some of which may be attractive to some leaders based upon their current incentives and less attractive to others.

Simply put, bonus programmes that incentivize the individual, as opposed to the collective, encourage individual leadership; those that motivate collective performance encourage collective leadership.

4: FRAGMENTED IT LANDSCAPE

In a majority of organizations, the IT landscape is fragmented – it comprises multiple applications, databases and layers of technical infrastructure that have been developed over a number of years to support different functional areas and processes. In many cases, the same key customer data, product definitions and business rules are replicated across the landscape, making enhancements to functionality both complex and expensive.

Yet this fragmented landscape drives unanticipated behaviour among the organization's leaders. While many complain about the functionality of the applications, the cost of ownership and the difficulty of getting their functionality enhanced, they become very protective when it comes to the applications landscape being rationalized or 'their' IT applications being replaced. At one level, this reluctance to change what they know, even with all its deficiencies, is understandable because, as we covered in chapter 1, IT projects have a poor track record of delivering on time, to cost and with sufficiently high quality. But if the strategic intent is for the organization to become more horizontally integrated[130] – resulting in a greater degree of common and shared processes, resources and IT applications – the IT landscape needs to be rationalized, with the resulting applications, data and rules being shared across multiple functions, customer segments and territories.

One of the main challenges of achieving horizontal integration is the reluctance of functional leaders to give up what they own, simply because they believe they'll lose control of an important resource that enables them to exercise individual leadership.

It could be argued that fragmented IT landscapes enable and encourage individual leadership, and that individual leadership perpetuates the fragmentation of the IT landscape.

5: ORGANIZATION OF TALENT

Some years ago, The Concours Group conducted research into various models of talent management.[142] One strand of the study looked at the challenges of aligning business and talent management strategies. It found that how business strategies were developed had an impact on strategies for talent. Likewise, how talent was managed had implications for how business strategy was developed.

How talent is organized, developed and managed not only impacts an organization's capabilities; it also influences the prevailing model of leadership.

The Concours Group research identified a spectrum of talent management models ranging from an 'Organization of Stars' to a 'Star Organization', each of which is described below.

Organization of Stars

An Organization of Stars is individual-centred. It focuses on recruiting and motivating the best and brightest talent in the domains and disciplines most central to organizational success. The main goal is to get the best performance out of the brightest people, with the rest of the organization in a supporting role.

Organizations of Stars seek to create environments where these individuals can grow, perform to their fullest potential and be handsomely rewarded. This talent model is orientated towards specialists performing work that requires high degrees of skill, knowledge and expertise. It is predominant in professional fields like investment banking, academia, consulting, law and medicine, and is also well established in the arts. A prevalent misconception about this model is that teamwork is not highly valued because of its bias towards individual talent. This is wrong. Organizations of Stars in fact often work through teams, but decision-making authority and leadership reside disproportionately with the best and brightest. Among the defining characteristics of Organizations of Stars are:

- **Individual brilliance and initiative predominate.** Organizations of Stars bet their success on optimizing the performance of their best and brightest people. Winning in the marketplace depends disproportionately on this talent
- **'Up or out' ethos is prevalent.** Individual performance and accountability are the primary determinants of success. Those who do not measure up are moved out
- **Constructive contention is preferred over consensus.** Organizations of Stars believe that contention among employees, when directed appropriately, is healthy, and that internal competition leads to the best ideas and the most outstanding performance. Stars collaborate with each other, but in a sometimes bruising manner
- **Stars focus on activities that drive market differentiation.** While everyone plays a role in delivering market value, the stars are acknowledged as the critical differentiators in the market. Their performance makes the most difference to customers and to how the company performs overall
- **Organizational bonds with individual top talent are critical.** Stars tend to be keenly aware of their market value and are willing to move to leverage it. They understand their capabilities and contribution to business success. Other companies frequently try to recruit them. A key challenge therefore is to find ways to bind them to your organization. Stars are often strongly motivated by wealth-creation opportunities, power and control over their own destinies. They will stay connected to those organizations that offer them lucrative contracts, performance-driven bonuses, networking opportunities and top-quality resources in return for their continued affiliation

- **Stars want to affiliate with other stars.** Stars are driven by a strong need to succeed – to be on the winning team. They can be status conscious on behalf of both themselves and their organizations. They thrive on being surrounded by other stars
- **Individual accountability and peer competition are the main forms of control.** Organizations of Stars closely monitor individual performance and often direct performance through competition among individuals or teams
- **Good leaders are role models – often the stars of stars.** Not always but, in industries where specialization and expertise are key, leaders tend to be the smartest or have a strong track record of success in the core disciplines of the organization.

Success in executing an Organization of Stars model demands more than just selecting the best employees or developing good ones. It also requires organizing the company so that these key people are motivated and able to use their ideas and abilities to deliver results. One challenge is getting gifted and ambitious people, often with diverse skills and expertise, to work productively together. Another is to continuously align the interests of individual top performers with the overall interests of the organization. It is also important to make sure that the rest of the organization, which supports the stars, feels included and appreciated for its contributions.

Star Organization

A Star Organization is group-centred, recruiting and retaining more of a cross-section of 'ordinary' people and managing them in ways that produce extraordinary group performance. In Star Organizations, the collective value of the talent pool is greater than that of individual players.

Companies adopting this model feel it is of paramount importance to create an environment, culture and practices that maximize the performance of the organization as a whole, rather than relying disproportionately on the contributions of key individual talent. Instead of chasing the same scarce talent as everyone else, they instead make it possible for ordinary people to perform at elite levels.

This talent model is predominant in organizations that pursue organizational excellence or place particular importance on health and safety, for example logistics and distribution, airlines, power distribution, healthcare and mining. One organization that prides itself on being a Star Organization is the Mayo Clinic,[83] which we looked at in chapter 4. It chose this model for no other reason than it enables everyone in the organization to provide the best patient experience. As Leonard L. Berry and Neeli Bendapudi found when they studied the organization,[84] "Doctors who are focused on maximising their incomes or who want to be a star don't work for Mayo Clinic." As one of the surgeons interviewed during their research put it, "The kind of people who are attracted to work for the Mayo Clinic have a value system that places the care of those in need over personal issues such as salary, prestige and power."

These organizations typically embrace an egalitarian perspective about people and heavily emphasize team-based organization structures and leadership mechanisms. Indeed, in many successful Star Organizations, leadership is broadly shared among the workforce. The following are key characteristics of Star Organizations:

- **Group brilliance and initiative predominate.** The sum is greater than the parts. Winning in the marketplace depends on how the organization performs as a whole
- **'In or out' ethos is prevalent.** Cultural fit – shared values and behaviours – is the primary determinant of whether you succeed and stay in a Star Organization. Those who do not fit culturally are moved out, regardless of their talent
- **Consensus is preferred over contention.** Collaboration often takes place in a consensual way. Star Organizations believe that top performance occurs when everyone gets along and has input into decisions
- **All talent focuses on activities that drive market differentiation.** It is a total team effort; everyone has 'line of sight' to their relative role in serving customers
- **Organizational bonds with all talent are critical.** Management must take a total view of relationships, affiliation and bonding across the organization. Employees feel a strong link to the purpose, values and culture of the organization
- **Everyone's group affiliation is important.** Team players are in most demand, and team players attract other team players. People want to feel tightly connected to their peers
- **Group accountability and peer reviews are the main forms of control.** Responsibility and accountability are shared among

groups – typically work teams. The team monitors and reviews the performance of its individual members

- **Good leaders are role models – often the servants of others.** Successful Star Organizations are often run not by superstar leaders but rather by people who are adept at helping others succeed and realize their potential.

The main challenge of Star Organizations is effectively differentiating between employees and maintaining adequate levels of individual incentives, rewards, recognition and accountability.

On the face of it, it would appear that collective leadership is easier in Star Organizations than in Organizations of Stars. But we shouldn't confuse how talent is managed with the way the organization is led. Organizations of Stars can exercise collective leadership if the stars believe in the power of collective action and accountability, and if they use their considerable individual talent for the good of the organization as a whole.

However, we have seen that organizations that are serious about changing their current trajectory do place greater emphasis on collective leadership. The strategic intent of the mid-sized UK hospital mentioned earlier was to be more patient-centric. One of the challenges it faced during this transition was a lack of collective leadership where individuals – both medical and administrative – acted as one. For some senior clinicians, this transition was beyond their comprehension, especially as the NHS was initially established on the basis of a consultant-centric model where the hospital and all its support staff were there to serve consultants' needs – and, many would say, their egos. The transition to a collective leadership style involved some tough calls by the hospital's senior leaders, who had no option but to invite some of the senior medical consultants to pursue their careers in other hospitals.

FIVE FACTORS CREATE A CONTEXT FOR LEADERSHIP

The five factors described above – and there are possibly more – individually and collectively determine the dominant style of leadership in organizations today. Acting together, they create a context that many would describe as the leadership culture of an organization. If the senior leader wanted to change the management team's leadership style, these five factors would need to be considered and their individual influence assessed.

LEADERSHIP STYLE IS AN ENDOGENOUS NAVIGATING FORCE

In chapter 2 we introduced the notion of endogenous and exogenous navigating forces, which together determine an organization's trajectory of strategic reality. Leadership is one of the most powerful endogenous navigating forces, and our simple argument is that excessive individual leadership can either anchor an organization to its current trajectory of strategic reality or pull it in multiple, often conflicting, directions. Alternatively, an organization that exercises collective leadership is more likely to be successful in pulling itself onto its trajectory of strategic intent.

OPERATING PRINCIPLES OF COLLECTIVE LEADERSHIP

While there is considerable literature on leadership development, much of it is focused on the development of the individual as a leader. The body of knowledge on developing collective leadership is still a work in progress, and it's often confused with the development of high-performing teams. The most recent work in this area comes from the UK NHS, following a series of leadership stumbles in a number of its health service delivery units, which are known as Trusts. Research by The Kings Fund and the Centre for Creative Leadership[143] found that these failings could have been prevented had the Trusts exercised collective leadership, rather than the heroic leadership model that emerged with the establishment of independent Trusts. Furthermore, the findings supported a move to collective leadership across the NHS. We support this view, but with one caveat. Establishing collective leadership is only one of the conditions for successfully operationalizing strategy, as discussed in chapter 8. If the trajectory of individual NHS Trusts is to be changed – and with them the whole National Health Service – equal attention needs to be given to the other seven conditions for success.

So, how can an organization change its leadership model to one that puts greater focus on collective, as opposed to individual, leadership? While this is a huge topic that we cannot cover sufficiently in this book, we do offer the following operating principles. You will recall that in chapter 7 we defined an operating principle as a 'conscious choice between two equally valid alternatives'. Or, in other words, we choose to exercise organizational leadership in this way, as opposed to an alternative way. The conclusions we've drawn from observing organizations that excel in collective leadership is that they operate in accordance with a set of seven principles:

1. Selection.
2. Collaboration.
3. Assignment, not position.
4. Using the strong to strengthen the weak.
5. Learning from shared experiences.
6. Aligned rewards.
7. Improving the collective.

Each of these is described below.

1: SELECTION

We all know that it's difficult, if not impossible, to change people's beliefs so it's far better to select individuals based on their beliefs and focus on developing their competencies and experience.

Furthermore, as employees across the organization see the types of people who get elevated to leadership roles, there will follow a process of natural selection. Those aspiring leaders who believe in collective leadership will be motivated, while those who aren't collectively inclined will not necessarily seek a career path within the company. The guiding operating principle is to:

> *'Select individuals for leadership positions based on their belief in collective action and accountability, and their individual talents and achievements.'*
>
> **as opposed to…**
>
> *'Select individuals for leadership positions based upon their talents and achievements alone.'*

2: COLLABORATION

We all know that groups that collaborate are more successful than individuals who act independently. Collaboration is not in conflict with competition, provided the competition is seen as coming from outside the organization. Collaboration is not only about sharing, it's also about constructively challenging, and having those difficult conversations with colleagues. This is particularly important when considering the best interests of the organization as a whole. Collaboration differs from basic teamwork, where the focus is on maximising the contribution of each individual team member. Groups that collaborate are more fluid and boundaries are more blurred as individual contributions change as required by circumstances.

Working with colleagues who collaborate imparts a strong feeling of confidence. This confidence allows employees to ask their colleagues for advice and help, and there's a sense of reassurance in knowing they're looking out for you. This confidence and sense of assurance will in turn permeate the group. The guiding operating principle is to:

> *'Collaborate with colleagues.'*
>   **as opposed to...**
> *'Act alone.'*

3: ASSIGNMENT, NOT POSITION

During his time at GE, Jack Welch repeatedly reminded his top 750 executives that they were not owned by the line of business where they worked but by him – and that they were just 'on loan'. This was part of Welch's strategy of creating the boundary-less enterprise,[144] which enabled the free flow of ideas, capital and talent. By essentially placing leaders on assignment, he removed the permanency of the position and encouraged a more collegial, collaborative style of leadership. The guiding operating principle here is to:

> *'Place leaders on assignment.'*
>   **as opposed to...**
> *'Place leaders in permanent positions.'*

4: USING THE STRONG TO STRENGTHEN THE WEAK

In his book, *The Wisdom of Doing Things Wrong*, Ron Donovan states that a team "can only go as fast as its slowest necessary member".[145] Therefore, if the group wants to go faster, the performance of the slowest necessary member needs to be improved – or they need to be replaced. We'll come to replacement later, but how can improvement be best achieved? Again, Welch felt that you get the highest-performing members of the group to mentor the weakest members, and align the mentor's bonus to the performance improvement of the protégé. Or, to put it another way, get the more able and experienced to support and accelerate the development of the less able and inexperienced.

The beauty of this simple technique is that it builds the capabilities of the whole, not just the individuals perceived to be most in need of development. It does this simply because it's impossible to mentor some-one without learning from the mentoring process. Whether this learning is about a different part of the organization or the process of mentoring itself, both individuals can benefit from the experience. It's also a way to reduce the risk associated with bringing high-potential, but less expe-rienced, individuals onto the leadership track. The guiding operating principle here is:

> 'For the more experienced to be encouraged (and incentivized) to pull the less experienced to their full potential.'
> **as opposed to...**
> 'Let the less experienced sink or swim on their own.'

5: LEARNING FROM SHARED EXPERIENCES

We know that intelligent, successful people rarely learn from what they are told; they learn from their experiences, particularly when they're tak-en out of their comfort zone and stretched both intellectually and emo-tionally. We refer to this in chapter 4 as *experiential learning*. Individual experiential learning is important, but collectively, across a leadership group, it is a powerful way of establishing shared insight, understanding and commitment. Over time the body of collective experiences goes be-yond learning about specific, individual business situations; it promotes shared understanding and appreciation of one another at the human level.

A case in point is the German insurance company we looked at in chapter 4, whose top 35 leaders needed to learn more about opera-tionalizing strategy. They did this through a learning journey that gave them greater insight not only into the topic but also about each other. As one executive put it, "The collective experience has created a level of trust and confidence where we can challenge the strategy and ask one another for help." Before the learning journey they addressed one another as 'Herr Doctor' and used the formal 'sie' for 'you'. After their shared experiences they now address one another by their first names and use the informal 'du'.

The power of collective experiential learning is that it creates a context within which the learning can be applied. As Steve Kerr, the past Chief Learning Officer at GE's Crotonville Leadership Institute,[80] repeatedly said, "Never put a changed person back into an unchanged organization; the investment will be wasted."

The guiding principle here is to:

'Learn through collective experiences.'
    as opposed to...
'Learn through individual, classroom-based teaching.'

6: ALIGNED REWARDS

The old adage, 'people do what is inspected, not what is expected', is as true today as it's always been. It was well illustrated in Steve Kerr's seminal paper, "On the folly of rewarding A, while hoping for B".[146] Kerr argued that all organisms – be they monkeys, rats or human beings – seek information concerning what activities are rewarded, and then do (or at least pretend to do) these things, often to the exclusion of activities that promise no reward. The extent to which this occurs depends on the attractiveness of the rewards being offered. He gives a number of examples from politics, medicine, sport, education and business of reward systems that are 'fouled up', as the behaviours that are rewarded are those the rewarder is trying to discourage, while desirable behaviour is not being rewarded at all.

In one example, Kerr cites the expectation that university professors will not neglect their teaching responsibilities, yet they are rewarded almost entirely for their research and publishing. While the mantra 'good research and good teaching go together' is often quoted, the reality is that professors often find that they must choose between teaching and research-orientated activities when allocating their time. Kerr also gives examples of other common management-reward follies, including hoping for total quality but rewarding for shipping on schedule, even with defects.

While it's important to hold individuals accountable and reward them accordingly, it's more important to align their accountability with the overarching goal and reward them accordingly. If an achievement is the collective team's, then the reward should be so aligned, recognizing each individual's contribution. We're not suggesting that alignment be extended to the extreme of everyone receiving the same rewards, but if collective action and accountability (collective leadership) is the goal, then personal reward needs to be aligned with the collective achievement. The guiding principle here is to:

'Base individual reward on collective achievement.'
    as opposed to…
'Base reward solely on individual achievement.'

7: IMPROVING THE COLLECTIVE

Collective leadership only works if everyone in the group feels that each individual is both committed and pulling their weight. If this is not the case – through shortfalls either in commitment or ability – then the group's membership needs to be changed. If it is felt that an individual's performance and contribution cannot be improved, then they need to be invited to go elsewhere. Being a member of a group that exercises collective leadership is by no means an easy option. In many respects, there are fewer places to hide than in organizations that advocate individual leadership. Continual improvement of the group's collective leadership qualities is paramount, and one way of achieving this is through the objective selection, retention and removal of its members. As GE's Welch said, "My main job was developing talent. I was a gardener providing water and other nourishment to our top 750 people. Of course, I had to pull out some weeds, too."[144] The guiding principle here is to:

'Improve collective performance of the leadership group.'
    as opposed to…
'Improve the performance of individual leaders.'

THE CHAPTER IN SUMMARY

The success rate of organizations changing their future for the better is not good, and certainly not where CEOs, non-executive directors and shareholders would like it to be. Taking an organization beyond its default future is one of the most difficult challenges facing any leadership team. It is an effort that requires a different model of leadership – one based on collective leadership as opposed to individual leadership.

It's not that individual leadership is wrong. It is of course necessary in many respects, but it's insufficient when faced with the challenge of changing an organization's trajectory. Collective leadership is where multiple individuals exercise their leadership roles within a group, and then the entire group provides leadership to the wider organization. A key aspect of collective leadership is collective accountability, where the outcomes and implications of decisions and actions are felt by every leader in equal measure. They are often described as being aligned in their decisions and actions, acting as one and are 'joined up' in their thinking and behaviour.

The extent to which an organization exercises collective leadership is a choice, and it's a capability that can be developed and guided by a set of operating principles, seven of which we described in this chapter.

Finally, why is collective leadership important? Because without it there will be no collective strategy, and without a collective strategy an organization will pull itself in multiple directions. When that happens it will have very little chance of successfully changing its trajectory and going beyond its default future.

FIVE QUESTIONS FOR REFLECTION

1. Does your organization have a collective, 'joined-up' strategy, or a collection of individual strategies?

2. To what extent does your organization practise collective leadership as opposed to individual leadership?

3. To what extent do the five factors we've covered in this chapter (legacy of traditional leadership thinking, organizational complexity, incentives and rewards, fragmented IT landscape and organization of talent) drive your leadership model?

4. Would you describe your organization as an Organization of Stars or a Star Organization?

5. Are the principles by which leaders are selected, managed and rewarded explicitly defined?

AFTERWORD

IS IT POSSIBLE FOR LEADERS TO CONFRONT THE DEFAULT FUTURE OF THEIR ORGANIZATION WITHOUT CONFRONTING THEIR OWN DEFAULT FUTURE?

The focus of this book has been on understanding and confronting the *default future* of organizations, and making informed choices on the actions needed to change the trajectory to one that leads to a better future. We've talked about how an organization's *trajectory of strategic reality* is determined by its exogenous and endogenous navigating forces, and only by understanding the nature and influence of these forces can informed choices be made on the best trajectory to take – the *trajectory of strategic intent*. We also talked about how exogenous navigating forces shape an organization's *trajectory of strategic opportunity* and how the chosen trajectory of strategic intent can be defined and communicated through the use of *strategic signatures*. We argued that the purpose of strategy was simply to change an organization's trajectory and that strategies should be operationalized – rather than implemented – by 'pulling from the future' rather than 'pushing from the present'. Finally, we made the case that changing an organization's trajectory begins with exercising collective, as opposed to individual, leadership.

But default future thinking is not restricted to organizations; it's just as observable in individuals. Each of us has a default future, the place we'll end up if we take no action other than what we currently have planned. For some people this is perfectly acceptable, particularly if they are prepared to accept whatever life offers. Others will inevitably want to take more control and do everything they can to map out a trajectory to a better future. As with organizations, our personal trajectory of strategic reality is determined by the exogenous and endogenous navigating forces that influence our lives. Whether it is the environment in which we live; our state of physical and mental health; our age, sex, family or community; or, of course, the organization within which we work, they all collectively determine the trajectory upon which we're currently travelling – and the default future it will bring.

We could go further and say that the endogenous navigating forces at play include our individual competencies and experience, our outlook and attitude, our propensity for work, our willingness to learn and our ability to collaborate with others. As they all come from within us they are to a large degree under our own control.

We could also argue that we operate on a set of personal strategic axes – where each axis represents the value we bring to our family, community, employer and society at large – and that changing our personal trajectory involves repositioning ourselves across each of these axes.

But this is not a book about how to define your own trajectory of strategic intent; it's about leaders confronting the default future for which they are accountable, and defining a trajectory that takes their organizations beyond their default future. It's about understanding the context within which organizations operate and making informed choices about what trajectory to take, based upon an understanding of the strategic opportunities and a realistic assessment of what's possible.

So, if the focus of this book is on organizations, why do we introduce the notion that default future thinking is also relevant to individuals? Simply because we believe it's impossible for a leader to confront, and change, the default future of their organization without confronting, and changing, their own personal default future.

One characteristic we've observed in leaders who are passionate about the future of their organizations is that they are never content with the status quo. They are always thinking about what could be done to put their organization on a trajectory to a better future. And they do this knowing that their own future is dependent upon the future of their organization. In many respects, it's one trajectory leading to two futures, one for the organization and one for its leaders. Along the way, this same trajectory determines the future of many other people, within and outside the organization.

We have seen leaders who were passionate about their organization and did everything in their power to improve its future, but for whatever reason their CEO or Board felt that new leadership was required. In these cases their personal default future was dramatically impacted by a change of context.

We've also seen situations where a leader's understanding of their personal default future was totally out of alignment with that of the organization they led. In an attempt to maintain their own attractive default future they weren't prepared to confront the undesirable default future of the organization. As a consequence they made no attempt to change their organization's trajectory and, to their surprise, their personal default future deteriorated accordingly.

In some cases we've seen leaders conclude that their personal default future – should they stay with the organization – was not acceptable, and they chose to go elsewhere. They no doubt arrived at this decision after concluding that they couldn't change their organization's trajectory and put it on a path to a better future. In the majority of cases the decision to leave resulted from a lack of alignment with colleagues on how the trajectory of the organization should be changed.

Why is this important? Organizations are led by people, and people who lead think about the future. It's therefore axiomatic that, when leaders confront the default future for which they are accountable, they also confront their own personal default future. If they choose to take the organization in a particular direction it's natural for them to think about the implications for them personally and for their family. Equally, if a person strives to go beyond their default future – and, as we've seen with many leaders, wants to leave a personal legacy – the choices they make could significantly change the default future of the organizations they lead.

Finally, if corporate strategy is about taking an organization beyond its default future by changing its trajectory for the better, and personal strategy (though we rarely call it this) is about changing your personal trajectory to a better future, then is it possible to achieve the former without the latter? We think not.

What do you think?

REFERENCES AND FURTHER READING

1. *Good Strategy/Bad Strategy – The Difference and Why It Matters*, by Richard Rumelt, Profile Books, 2012.

2. "Fortune 500 firms in 1955 vs. 2014; 88% are gone, and we're all better off because of that dynamic 'creative destruction'," by Mark J. Perry, American Enterprise Institute, 18 August, 2014, http://www.aei.org/publication/fortune-500-firms-in-1955-vs-2014-89-are-gone-and-were-all-better-off-because-of-that-dynamic-creative-destruction/ [Accessed 25 April, 2016].

3. "What does Fortune 500 turnover mean?" by Dane Stangler and Sam Arbesman, Ewing Marion Kauffman Foundation, June 2012, http://www.kauffman.org/~/media/kauffman_org/research%20reports%20and%20covers/2012/06/fortune_500_turnover.pdf [Accessed 15 February, 2016].

4. "Business Transformation," Raconteur, April 2015, http://raconteur.net/business-transformation-2015 [Accessed 15 June, 2016].

5. "Thirty years of the FTSE 100," by Greg Mahon, Rathbones, 4 February, 2014, https://www.rathbones.com/knowledge-and-insight/thirty-years-ftse-100 [Accessed 7 June, 2016].

6. "WilmerHale 2015 M&A report," Wilmer Cutler Pickering Hale and Dorr LLP, 2015, https://www.wilmerhale.com/uploadedFiles/Shared_Content/Editorial/Publications/Documents/2015-WilmerHale-MA-Report.pdf [Accessed 9 May, 2016].

7. "The Deloitte M&A Index 2016: Opportunities amidst Divergence," Deloitte, Q4 2015, http://www2.deloitte.com/uk/en/pages/financial-advisory/articles/deloitte-m-and-a-index.html [Accessed 19 May, 2016].

8. "The new M&A playbook," by Clayton M. Christensen, Richard Alton, Curtis Rising and Andrew Waldeck, *Harvard Business Review*, March 2011.

9. "A new generation of M&A: A McKinsey perspective on the opportunities and challenges," by Clay Deutsch and Andy West, McKinsey & Company, June 2010, http://www.mckinsey.com/business-functions/organization/our-insights/a-mckinsey-perspective-on-the-opportunities-and-challenges [Accessed 9 May, 2016].

10. *A Comprehensive Guide to Mergers & Acquisitions: Managing the Critical Success Factors across Every Stage of the M&A Process*, by Yaakov Weber, Shlomo Y. Tarba and Christina Öberg, Financial Times/Prentice Hall, 2013.

11. "PayPal makes big splash on first day of trading after eBay spinoff," Fortune, 20 July, 2015, http://fortune.com/2015/07/20/paypal-ebay-split-valuation/ [Accessed 21 June, 2016]

12. "EBay and PayPal better off alone," *The Economist*, 18 July, 2015, http://www.lse.ac.uk/fmg/researchProgrammes/corporateFinance/corporateGovernance/pdf/Better-off-alone---The-Economist.pdf [Accessed 16 July, 2016].

13. "The CEO interview: GE's Jeff Immelt on digitizing in the industrial space," McKinsey & Co., 12 October, 2015, http://www.mckinsey.com/business-functions/organization/our-insights/ges-jeff-immelt-on-digitizing-in-the-industrial-space [Accessed 21 June, 2016]. http://www.mckinsey.com/business-functions/organization/our-insights/ges-jeff-immelt-on-evolving-a-corporate-giant [Accessed 18 August, 2016].

14. "M&A Trends Report 2014 – A Comprehensive Look at the M&A Market," Deloitte, 2014 https://www2.deloitte.com/content/dam/Deloitte/us/Documents/mergers-acqisitions/us-ma-trends-survey-060114.pdf [Accessed 27 April, 2016].

15. "The 2011–2012 Change and Communication ROI Study Report," Willis Towers Watson, January 2012, https://www.towerswatson.com/Insights/IC-Types/Survey-Research-Results/2012/01/2011-2012-Change-and-Communication-ROI-Study-Report [Accessed 10 May, 2016].

16. "IBM Global Making Change Work Study," IBM, October 2008, http://www-935.ibm.com/services/us/gbs/bus/pdf/gbe03100-usen-03-making-change-work.pdf [Accessed 10 May, 2016].

17. "Leading change: Why transformation efforts fail," by John P. Kotter, *Harvard Business Review*, May–June 1995 issue.

18. "Factors in Project Success," The Association for Project Management (APM), November 2014, https://www.apm.org.uk/sites/default/files/APM%20Success%20report_NOV%2014.pdf [Accessed 27 April, 2016].

19. "Delivering Major Projects in Government: A Briefing for the Committee of Public Accounts," UK National Audit Office, 6 January, 2016, https://www.nao.org.uk/report/delivering-major-projects-in-government-a-briefing-for-the-committee-of-public-accounts/ [Accessed 18 May, 2016].

20. "Delivering large-scale IT projects on time, on budget, and on value," by Michael Bloch, Sven Blumberg, and Jürgen Laartz, McKinsey & Company, October 2012, http://www.mckinsey.com/business-functions/business-technology/our-insights/delivering-large-scale-it-projects-on-time-on-budget-and-on-value [Accessed 21 June, 2016].

21. The Standish Group, www.standishgroup.com

22. "Doomed from the start? Why a majority of business and IT teams anticipate their software development projects will fail," Geneca, Winter 2010/2011, http://www.geneca.com/75-business-executives-anticipate-software-projects-fail/ [Accessed 21 June, 2016].

23. "Culture's role in enabling organizational change," Strategy& (formally Booz & Company), 14 November, 2013, http://www.strategyand.pwc.com/reports/cultures-role-organizational-change [Accessed 31 May, 2016].

24. "Departing CEO tenure (2000–2013)," The Conference Board, https://www.conference-board.org/retrievefile.cfm?filename=TCB_CW-0561.pdf&type=subsite [Accessed 27 April, 2016].

25. "Strategy& 2015 CEO Success Study," Strategy&, http://www.strategyand.pwc.com/ceosuccess#VisualTabs2 [Accessed 27 April, 2016].

26. "Crist|Kolder Volatility Report, 2015," http://www.cristkolder.com/volatility-report/ [Accessed 18 May, 2016].

27. *CIO Survey*, Harvey Nash in association with KPMG, 2015, http://www.harveynash.com/group/mediacentre/Harvey_Nash_CIO_Survey_2015.pdf [Accessed 27 April, 2016].

28. "Guide to Directors' Remuneration 2014," KPMG, https://home.kpmg.com/uk/en/home/insights/2014/11/kpmg-guide-directors-remuneration-2014.html [Accessed 20 June, 2016].

29. *Onward – How Starbucks Fought for Its life without Losing Its Soul*, by Howard Schultz with Joanne Gordon, John Wiley, 2011.

30. "A scary Swiss meltdown – How a dud strategy brought a solid company to the brink of bankruptcy," *The Economist*, 19 July, 2001, http://www.economist.com/node/705265 [Accessed 2 June, 2016].

31. "So, you think you have a strategy?" by Freek Vermeulen, 1 October, 2011, https://www.london.edu/faculty-and-research/lbsr/so-you-think-you-have-a-strategy#.VzWUh-RBHgU [Accessed 13 May, 2016].

32. "The big lie of strategic planning," by Roger L. Martin, *Harvard Business Review*, January-February 2014.

33. *The Trouble with Strategy*, by Kim Warren, Strategy Dynamics Limited, 2012

34. "The Queen finally finds out why no one saw the financial crisis coming," *The Guardian*, 13 December, 2012, https://www.theguardian.com/uk/2012/dec/13/queen-financial-crisis-question [Accessed 1 April, 2014].

35. "Citigroup chief stays bullish on buy-outs," *Financial Times*, 9 July, 2007, https://next.ft.com/content/80e2987a-2e50-11dc-821c-0000779fd2ac [Accessed 1 April, 2014].

36. "On the money," *The Guardian*, 31 October, 2008, https://www.theguardian.com/business/2008/oct/31/creditcrunch-gillian-tett-financial-times [Accessed 1 April, 2014].

37. "June 4, 1977: VHS comes to America," by Priya Ganapati, *Wired*, 4 June 2010, http://www.wired.com/2010/06/0604vhs-ces/ [Accessed 12 March, 2014].

38. "World Broadband Statistics," Point Topic Ltd, June 2013, http://point-topic.com/wp-content/uploads/2013/02/Point-Topic-Global-Broadband-Statistics-Q1-2013.pdf [Accessed 22 June, 2016].

39. "Xerox: The downfall – The inside story of the management fiasco," *Business Week*, 5 March, 2001, http://www.bloomberg.com/news/articles/2001-03-04/xerox-the-downfall [Accessed 1 April, 2014].

40. "For GE, breaking up is hard to do," *Fortune Online*, 21 August, 2015, http://fortune.com/2015/08/21/general-electric-end-of-conglomerates/ [Accessed 4 July, 2016].

41. Personal notes taken during interviews with the Chairman, Chief Executive and Chief Medical Officer, January 2014.

42. *The Age of Unreason*, by Charles Handy, Arrow Books, 2002.

43. *Fool's Gold*, by Gillian Tett, Little, Brown, 2009.

44. "Wesfarmers agrees £340m Homebase purchase," *Financial Times*, 18 January, 2016, https://next.ft.com/content/69b18908-bd9f-11e5-9fdb-87b8d15baec2 [Accessed 27 June, 2016].

45. "Home Retail accepts Sainsbury's £1.4bn takeover bid," *Financial Times*, 1 April, 2016, https://next.ft.com/content/7cbc7c74-f7dd-11e5-96db-fc683b5e52db [Accessed 17 August, 2016].

46. *The Unwritten Rules of the Game*, by Peter Scott-Morgan, McGraw-Hill, 1994.

47. *The Hidden Logic of Business Performance*, The Concours Group Boardroom Imperative, 2007.

48. *The Last Word On Power*, by Tracy Goss, Doubleday, 1996.

49. "The core competence of the corporation," by C.K. Prahalad and Gary Hamel, *Harvard Business Review*, May–June 1990.

50. *Competing for the Future*, by Gary Hamel and C.K. Prahalad, Harvard Business School Press, 1994.

51. "Capitalising on capabilities," by Dave Ulrich and Norm Smallwood, *Harvard Business Review*, June 2004.

52. *The Essential Advantage – How to Win with a Capabilities-Driven Strategy*, by Paul Leinwand and Cesare Mainardi, Harvard Business Review Press, 2010.

53. *The Power of Habit*, by Charles Duhigg, Random House Books, 2013.

54. "On the hot seat: A.G. Lafley and Jeffrey Immelt," *Fortune Magazine*, 26 November, 2006, http://archive.fortune.com/magazines/fortune/fortune_archive/2006/12/11/8395440/index.htm?postversion=2006112711 [Accessed 8 July, 2016].

55. "Connect and develop – Inside Procter & Gamble's new model for innovation," by Larry Huston and Nabil Sakkab, *Harvard Business Review*, March 2006.

56. "How P&G tripled its innovation success rate," by Bruce Brown and Scott D. Anthony, *Harvard Business Review*, June 2011.

57. "Building a software start-up inside GE," by Brad Power, *Harvard Business Review*, 29 January, 2015, https://hbr.org/2015/01/building-a-software-start-up-inside-ge [Accessed 8 July, 2016].

58. "Number of apps available in leading app stores as of June 2016," Statista, 2017, http://www.statista.com/statistics/276623/number-of-apps-available-in-leading-app-stores/ [Accessed 13 July, 2016].

59. "Regional trade agreements," World Trade Organization, https://www.wto.org/english/tratop_e/region_e/region_e.htm [Accessed 13 July, 2016].

60. "Global Economic Prospects," World Bank Group, June 2016, https://openknowledge.worldbank.org/bitstream/handle/10986/24319/9781464807770.pdf?sequence=5 [Accessed 19 July, 2016].

61. "The China Shipping Prosperity Index Q1 2016," Shanghai International Shipping Institute, 2016, http://en.sisi-smu.org/index.php?c=article&id=14742 [Accessed 19 July, 2016].

62. "China's shipping bankruptcies likely to surge as dry-bulk rates plunge," *Reuters*, 6 January, 2016, http://www.reuters.com/article/china-shipping-bankruptcy-idUSL8N14Q07220160106 [Accessed 19 July, 2016].

63. "Statistics and facts about the IT industry in India," Statista, http://www.statista.com/topics/2256/it-industry-in-india/ [Accessed 21 July, 2016].

64. "The science in science fiction," interview with William Gibson, American-Canadian writer on National Public Radio: *NPR: Talk of the Nation*, 30 November, 1999, http://www.npr.org/templates/story/story.php?storyId=1067220 [Accessed 28 June, 2016].

65. "Automation or interaction: What's best for big data?" panel discussion at IEEE conference on Visualization, October 1999, http://ieeexplore.ieee.org/xpl/login.jsp?tp=&arnumber=809940&url=http%3A%2F%2Fieeexplore.ieee.org%2Fstamp%2Fstamp.jsp%3Ftp%3D%26arnumber%3D809940 [Accessed 28 June, 2016].

66. "That "internet of things" thing," by Kevin Ashton, *RFID Journal*, 22 June, 2009, http://www.rfidjournal.com/articles/view?4986 [Accessed 28 June, 2016].

67. "Computing machinery and intelligence," by Alan Turing, *Mind* 59 (1950), pages 433–460, http://mind.oxfordjournals.org/content/LIX/236/433.full.pdf+html [Accessed 28 June, 2016].

68. "Accenture Technology Vision 2016," Accenture, 2016, https://www.accenture.com/us-en/insight-technology-trends-2016 [Accessed 29 June, 2016].

69. "Five Technology Trends to Watch – 2016 Edition," Consumer Technology Association, 2016, http://content.ce.org/PDF/2K16_5tech_web.pdf [Accessed 29 June, 2016].

70. "8 tech trends to watch in 2016," *Harvard Business Review*, 8 December, 2015, https://hbr.org/2015/12/8-tech-trends-to-watch-in-2016 [Accessed 29 June, 2016].

71. "Top Strategic Predictions for 2016 and Beyond: The Future Is a Digital Thing," Gartner Research, 2 October, 2015, https://www.gartner.com/doc/3142020?refval=&pcp=mpe [Accessed 29 June, 2016].

72. "Megatrends 2015 – Making Sense of a World in Motion," EY, 2015, http://www.ey.com/Publication/vwLUAssets/ey-megatrends-report-2015/$FILE/ey-megatrends-report-2015.pdf [Accessed 29 June, 2016].

73. "2016 Tech Trends to Watch," Goldman Sachs, 2016, http://www.goldmansachs.com/our-thinking/pages/2016-tech-trends-to-watch.html [Accessed 29 June, 2016].

74. Leading Edge Forum, https://leadingedgeforum.com.

75. Ray Hammond, futurist, http://www.rayhammond.com.

76. Patrick Dixon, futurist, http://www.globalchange.com.

77. From: *Vivian Grey*, by Benjamin Disraeli, British Prime Minister from 1874 to 1880, Henry Colburn, 1826.

78. From: *Nicomachean Ethics*, by Aristotle, first published in 350 BC. Later translation available as *The Nicomachean Ethics*, Penguin Classics, 2004.

79. Confucius, Chinese teacher, editor, politician, and philosopher of the spring and autumn period of Chinese history, 551–479 BC.

80. Presented by Steve Kerr during a Concours Group Executive Summit, circa late 1990s.

81. *Experiential Learning: Experience as the Source of Learning and Development*, by David A. Kolb, first published by Pearson Education, 1983; second edition in 2014.

82. Ritz-Carlton Leadership Center, http://ritzcarltonleadershipcenter.com.

83. Mayo Clinic, http://www.mayoclinic.org/about-mayo-clinic.

84. "Cluing in customers," by Leonard L. Berry and Neeli Bendapudi, *Harvard Business Review*, February 2003.

85. "World Population Prospectus 2015," United Nations, 2015, https://esa.un.org/unpd/wpp/Publications/Files/Key_Findings_WPP_2015.pdf [Accessed 8 June, 2016].

86. "World Population Ageing 2015," United Nations, 2015, http://www.un.org/en/development/desa/population/publications/pdf/ageing/WPA2015_Highlights.pdf [Accessed 8 June, 2016].

87. "World Urbanization Prospects 2014," United Nations, 2014, https://esa.un.org/unpd/wup/Publications/Files/WUP2014-Highlights.pdf [Accessed 8 June, 2016].

88. "International Migration Report 2015," United Nations, 2015, http://www.un.org/en/development/desa/population/migration/publications/migrationreport/docs/MigrationReport2015_Highlights.pdf [Accessed 8 June, 2016].

89. "World Water Development Report 2015," United Nations, 2015, http://unesdoc.unesco.org/images/0023/002318/231823E.pdf [Accessed 14 June, 2016].

90. "The State of Food Insecurity in the World," Food and Agriculture Organization of the United Nations, 2015, http://www.fao.org/3/a4ef2d16-70a7-460a-a9ac-2a65a533269a/i4646e.pdf [Accessed 14 June, 2016].

91. "Poverty Overview," World Bank Group, 13 April, 2016, http://www.worldbank.org/en/topic/poverty/overview [Accessed 15 June, 2016].

92. "Globalization: A brief overview," International Monetary Fund, 2008, http://www.imf.org/external/np/exr/ib/2008/053008.htm [Accessed 14 June, 2016].

93. *Why Globalisation Works*, by Martin Wolf, Yale University Press, 2004, pages 107 and 157.

94. "OECD Economic Globalisation Indicators – 2010," Organisation for Economic Co-operation and Development, September 2010, http://www.oecd.org/sti/sci-tech/measuringglobalisationoecdeconomicglobalisationindicators2010.htm [Accessed 30 June, 2016].

95. "International Trade Statistics 2015, World Trade Organization," 2015, https://www.wto.org/english/res_e/statis_e/its2015_e/its2015_e.pdf [Accessed 8 June, 2016].

96. "World Energy Resources – 2013 Survey, World Energy Council," 2013, https://www.worldenergy.org/publications/2013/world-energy-resources-2013-survey/ [Accessed 8 June, 2016].

97. "Global Wind Report – Annual Market Update 2015," Global Wind Energy Council, 2015, http://www.gwec.net/wp-content/uploads/vip/GWEC-Global-Wind-2015-Report_April-2016_19_04.pdf [Accessed 2 December, 2016].

98. "Let there be light," *The Economist*, 2015, http://www.economist.com/news/special-report/21639014-thanks-better-technology-and-improved-efficiency-energy-becoming-cleaner-and-more [Accessed 13 June, 2016].

99. NASA Global Climate Change, NASA, http://climate.nasa.gov/ [Accessed 3 December, 2016].

100. "GRACE: Gravity Recovery and Climate Experiment," NASA, 2014, http://www.nasa.gov/mission_pages/Grace/#.V3UcbKJBFMU [Accessed 30 June, 2016].

101. "Global mean CO2 mixing ratios (ppm)," NASA, http://data.giss.nasa.gov/modelforce/ghgases/Fig1A.ext.txt [Accessed 30 June, 2016].

102. "Statistics and facts about motor vehicle production," Statista, http://www.statista.com/topics/975/motor-vehicle-production/d [Accessed 2 July, 2016].

103. "World vehicles in use – All vehicles," Organisation Internationale des Constructeurs d'Automobiles (OICA), http://www.oica.net/wp-content/uploads//total-inuse-2014.pdf [Accessed 28 July, 2016].

104. "Brief history of the internet," The Internet Society, 15 October, 2012, http://www.internetsociety.org/sites/default/files/Brief_History_of_the_Internet.pdf [Accessed 1 July, 2016].

105. "Internet growth statistics," Internet World Stats, http://www.internetworldstats.com/emarketing.htm [Accessed 1 July, 2016].

106. "Cisco Visual Networking Index: Forecast and Methodology," *2015–2020*, Cisco Systems Inc., 6 June, 2016, http://www.cisco.com/c/en/us/solutions/collateral/service-provider/visual-networking-index-vni/complete-white-paper-c11-481360.pdf [Accessed 8 June, 2016].

107. "Global Internet Report 2015," Internet Society, 2015, http://www.internetsociety.org/globalinternetreport/2015/assets/download/IS_web.pdf [Accessed 8 June, 2016].

108. "AgTech Investing Report 2015," AgFunder, 2015, https://research01.agfunder.com/2015/AgFunder-AgTech-Investing-Report-2015.pdf [Accessed 15 July, 2016].

109. *Blockchain Revolution – How the Technology behind Bitcoin Is Changing Money, Business and the World*, by Don Tapscott and Alex Tapscott, Portfolio/Penguin, 2016.

110. "40 Years of Shell Scenarios," Royal Dutch Shell, 2012, http://www.shell.com/promos/forty-years-of-shell-scenarios/_jcr_content.stream/1448557479375/703c8a8b176922ae312712b355706ce08 7652a860980d5ffecac769817903d88/shell-scenarios-40yearsbook080213.pdf [Accessed 16 June, 2016]

111. "Living in the future – How scenario planning changed corporate strategy," by Angela Wilkinson and Roland Kupers, *Harvard Business Review*, May 2013.

112. "My £2bn bet on sports TV isn't for the faint-hearted," an interview with Gavin Patterson, CEO BT Group, *The Sunday Times*, 15 December, 2013.

113. Hailo, https://www.hailoapp.com/about/ [Accessed 18 July, 2016].

114. Airbnb, https://www.airbnb.com/about/about-us [Accessed 18 July, 2016].

115. "The techie trying to steal the world from travel agents," *The Sunday Times*, 12 June, 2016, http://www.thetimes.co.uk/article/the-techie-trying-to-steal-the-world-from-travel-agents-xcsqwrbb6 [Accessed 27 July, 2016].

116. Uber, https://www.uber.com/ [Accessed 18 July, 2016].

117. "BT's £12.5bn takeover of EE cleared by UK competition watchdog," *Financial Times*, 15 January, 2016, https://next.ft.com/content/51dab668-bb58-11e5-a7cc-280dfe875e28 [Accessed 21 July, 2016].

118. "EDS's merger with AT Kearney – A promising union that fell apart," *Financial Times*, 1 July, 2013, https://next.ft.com/content/962f4fe2-d517-11e2-9302-00144feab7de [Accessed 21 July, 2016].

119. "LinkedUp," *The Economist*, 18 June, 2016, http://www.economist.com/news/business-and-finance/21700605-it-one-most-expensive-tech-deals-history-it-may-not-be-smartest-making-sense [Accessed 28 July, 2016].

120. "Ocado tie-up to help Morrisons start selling groceries online," *The Guardian*, 17 May, 2013, https://www.theguardian.com/business/2013/may/17/ocado-deal-morrisons-online-waitrose [Accessed 21 July, 2016].

121. "Amazon to start selling fresh and frozen Morrisons food," *The Guardian*, 29 February, 2016, https://www.theguardian.com/business/2016/feb/29/amazon-is-to-start-selling-fresh-and-frozen-morrisons-food [Accessed 21 July, 2016].

122. "Bank of Ireland extends exclusive partnership with The Post Office," 3 August, 2012, https://www.bank-of-ireland.co.uk/fs/docs/BOI%20Extends%20Partnership%20with%20Post%20Office.pdf [Accessed 22 July, 2016].

123. "Apple and Nike, running mates," *Bloomberg*, 24 May, 2006, http://www.bloomberg.com/news/articles/2006-05-23/apple-and-nike-running-mates [Accessed 21 July, 2016].

124. "BBVA Digital addition: A big Spanish bank's tech drive prompts some scepticism," *The Economist*, 27 February, 2016, http://www.economist.com/news/finance-and-economics/21693617-big-spanish-banks-tech-drive-prompts-some-scepticism-digital-addition [Accessed 31 July, 2016].

125. "Co-operative Group timeline: return to profit as rebuild starts," *The Guardian*, 9 April, 2015, https://www.theguardian.com/business/2015/apr/09/co-operative-group-timeline [Accessed 22 July, 2016].

126. "The rise and fall of MySpace," *Financial Times*, 4 December, 2009, https://www.ft.com/content/fd9ffd9c-dee5-11de-adff-00144feab49a [Accessed 22 December, 2016].

127. "Amazon stops selling Fire phone after struggling to boost sales," *Bloomberg*, 9 September, 2016. https://www.bloomberg.com/news/articles/2015-09-09/amazon-stops-selling-fire-phone-after-struggling-to-boost-sales [Accessed 23 July, 2016].

128. "Microsoft buys Nokia handset business for €5.4bn," *The Guardian*, 3 September, 2013, https://www.theguardian.com/technology/2013/sep/03/microsoft-buys-nokia-handset-business [Accessed 21 July, 2016].

129. "Can we agree that the Nokia buy was a total disaster for Microsoft?" *Fortune*, 8 July, 2015, http://fortune.com/2015/07/08/was-microsoft-nokia-deal-a-disaster/ [Accessed 24 July, 2016].

130. *Managing across Borders – The Transnational Solution*, by Christopher A. Bartlett and Sumantra Ghoshal, Harvard Business School Press, 1998.

131. "The new industrial engineering: Information technology and business process redesign," by Thomas Davenport and James Short, *MIT Sloan Management Review*, 15 July, 1990, http://sloanreview.mit.edu/article/the-new-industrial-engineering-information-technology-and-business-process-redesign/ [Accessed 25 July, 2016].

132. *Reengineering the Corporation: A Manifesto for Business Revolution*, by Michael Hammer and James Champy, Nicholas Brealey Publishing, 1993.

133. "Changing the way we change," by Richard Pascale, Mark Millemann and Linda Gioja, *Harvard Business Review*, November–December, 1997.

134. PMI Project Management Methodology, http://www.pmi.org/about [Accessed 1 August, 2016].

135. Prince2 Project Management Methodology, https://www.prince2.com/uk/what-is-prince2 [Accessed 23 August, 2016].

136. *The Power of Pull – How Small Moves, Smartly Made, Can Set Big Things in Motion*, by John Hagel III, John Seely Brown and Lang Davison, Basic Books, 2010.

137. *Managing on the Edge: How the Smartest Companies Use Conflict to Stay Ahead*, by Richard Pascale, Viking, 1990, and *Surfing The Edge of Chaos*, with Mark Millemann and Linda Gioja, Texere, 2000.

138. The Sarbanes-Oxley Act of 2002, http://www.soxlaw.com/ [Accessed 1 August, 2016].

139. International Organization for Standardization, http://www.iso.org/iso/home/about.htm [Accessed 1 August, 2016].

140. Root Learning Maps, by Root Inc, https://www.rootinc.com/ [Accessed 2 August, 2016].

141. "About Peter F. Drucker", Drucker Institute, http://www.druckerinstitute.com/peter-druckers-life-and-legacy/ [Accessed 3 August, 2016].

142. *Talent Management in the New Economy*, The Concours Group, 2001.

143. "Delivering a Collective Leadership Strategy for Health Care," by Regina Eckert, Michael West, David Altman, Katy Steward, and Bill Pasmore, White Paper published by The Kings Fund and Centre for Creative Leadership, 2014, http://www.kingsfund.org.uk/sites/files/kf/media/delivering-collective-leadership-ccl-may.pdf [Accessed 14 April, 2016].

144. "Jack Welch: A Role Model for Today's CEO?" by Jeffrey E. Garten, *Bloomberg Business Week*, 10 December, 2001, https://www.bloomberg.com/news/articles/2001-09-09/jack-welch-a-role-model-for-todays-ceo [Accessed 29 June, 2017].

145. *The Wisdom of Doing Things Wrong: Doing Big Things by Starting Small and Strange*, by Ron Donovan, Pencairn Publishing, 2016.

146. "On the folly of rewarding A, while hoping for B," by Steve Kerr, *The Academy of Management Executive*, 9 no. 1 (1995), pages 7–14, available from http://www.ou.edu/russell/UGcomp/Kerr.pdf [Accessed 20 April, 2016].

ABOUT THE AUTHORS

David and Peter have worked together for many years. Their first assignment was way back in April 1992 when they delivered a seminar on business reengineering for an investment bank in London. At that time they both worked for CSC Index, the management consulting division of Computer Sciences Corporation, led by Jim Champy, who pioneered the work that became known as business reengineering. For the next six years they helped clients improve the performance of their organizations by taking a holistic view of how their organizations operated and reengineering those parts most critical to future success.

In 1998 they, along with three colleagues, founded the European operation of The Concours Group. Formed two years earlier in the US, The Concours Group was a highly innovative firm that focused on understanding and applying future – not past – best practices in business and technology management. Executives from the most ambitious corporations across the globe considered working with The Concours Group to be an indispensable source of insight and pragmatic action.

In 2010 they founded Formicio Limited, an advisory business that provides thought leadership and thought partnership on all aspects of assessing, developing and operationalizing strategy. Formicio is passionate about working with people who want to change their organization's trajectory, to one that takes it beyond its default future. The name Formicio comes from two Latin words, *formo* (to form or shape) and *proficio* (to advance, make progress, benefit, contribute) – an accurate reflection of the value it intends to bring.

During the past 25 years David and Peter have worked with some interesting – and often demanding – clients across a range of industries, all of whom had one thing in common: a desire to improve the default future of the organization for which they were accountable. Their experience of working with clients across Europe, Australia, China, Asia, North America and South Africa has shaped their thinking and understanding about how organizations operate and plan their futures. The resultant insights gained from these learning experiences are the foundation for this book.

MORE ABOUT DAVID

After starting his career as a craft apprentice with the English Electric Company, David was awarded a first class honours degree in electrical engineering. He then moved to Cranfield University as the Royal Commission for the Exhibition of 1851 Research Fellow, where he undertook research into computer-aided design. It was during this period that his focus shifted to the broader application of information technology in organizations, specifically how its use could provide sustained competitive advantage.

In 1987, following a meeting with Kenneth Baker (the then Government Minister for Information Technology) and Lord Chilver, the Vice Chancellor of Cranfield University, he was invited to become a founding director of the Cranfield IT Institute, an independent institute that combined the disciplines of computer science and management to bring competitive advantage to organizations through the application of emerging information technologies.

In 1992 he moved into mainstream consulting, where he advised and supported numerous organizations in developing strategies and delivering change, particularly technology-enabled change. David works with people on both sides of IT, namely business executives who want to improve their business through the application of the technology, and IT executives who are expected to deliver new IT applications while maintaining the legacy IT landscape.

Most recently he has advised and provided independent oversight to executive teams and boards on major transformation programmes, particularly from the point of view of assessing whether the conditions for success are in place. Increasingly his focus has been on organizations that hope either to create a truly digital business, or to make their existing business more digitally enabled.

David has a PhD in the design of complex IT systems and is a Fellow of the Institution of Engineering and Technology.

MORE ABOUT PETER

Peter began his working career training and qualifying as a Chartered Accountant with PwC, working on audits of many medium- to large-sized companies across a wide range of industries. This broad experience of business operating models caused him to shift into mainstream management consulting in 1980, initially with Deloitte in Kenya and then Ernst & Young in South Africa.

In 1989 Peter relocated back to Europe and joined the then nascent but fast-growing firm of CSC Index, pioneering the principles and practices of business reengineering. Over the next nine years Peter led a series of major business reengineering programmes across a range of industries including financial services, manufacturing, mining, steel, chemicals and food, and other consumer goods. Central to his work was helping companies realize synergies across multiple divisions and geographies by rethinking their enterprise operating models.

In 1992 he pioneered the application of the principles of business reengineering to the work of IT organizations, which led to an innovative approach of transforming the performance of the IT function and thereby the value it was able to deliver to the business.

More recently Peter has focused on applying the principles of experiential learning to helping business executives gain the insights and capabilities needed to develop and operationalize strategy, including conducting a number of study tours to leading-practice companies in the US and Europe.

Peter holds an MA from Cambridge in Modern Languages and has always been passionate about the power and role of language in helping organizations envisage a future beyond that of their default.

Peter has held a non-executive role for a major UK charity in the retirement care sector, and actively supports educational and medical charity work in Africa.